Robert Shirk's People

Theresa L. Smith

Theresa L. Smith

ISBN: 978-1-62420-744-0

Credits
Cover Artist: Designs by Ms G

Printed in the United States of America

In loving memory of my granddaughter,
Chelsea Rayne Smith, who left us too soon.
You are forever in our hearts.

I'm grateful for God, to whom I prayed for guidance.
For my husband, who went with me to Libraries and graveyards.
For my mother, who encourgaed me to find out more about her family.
For Elane Chapman, a distant cousin who shared information with me.
For Kathie Giorgio and fellow writers at her AllWriters' Workplace and
Workshop, thank you.

Introduction

Let us transport ourselves back in time. Back to the days of my early ancestors. So long ago, it seems like a fairy tale, to compare those days to today. Our ancestors lived in a time when furniture, food and clothing were simple and few. There were no modern conveniences we consider necessary. I hope you enjoy these stories as much as I enjoyed writing them. Storytelling is a way to attach the people of our past with the present.

Knowing your family history gives you a better understanding and appreciation of who you are and how you got here. Family history is entangled in the social, political, and economic conditions of the world at any given time. This book was written after fifty years of research.

Each chapter is the story of a different relative, starting from when they came to America. The people and places are true but put in a story form. In many areas of research, I created a story around the facts I knew of the people. It would be impossible to completely be accurate in all details and descriptions. Instead of writing the story in the character's speech, such as old English with the use of 'ye' for you or the quaint, plain speech of the Quakers, using 'thine' and 'thee', or the Irish accent of the Kirks, I decided to use modern English for the ease of the reader.

It has been estimated 23,000 people left England between 1681 and 1711 for the American Colony. The majority were Quakers. By 1750 Quakers were the third largest religion in the British colonies.[1] Another large group were the Puritans. Followed by Mennonites leaving Switzerland.

The repetitions of names really gave me a hard time. The naming

---

[1] David Hackett Fischer, *Albion's Seed* (Oxford University Press: Oxford, New York 1989) 421-422.

patterns of the 1700s and 1800s for English-speaking families lent to this problem. The first son was named after the father's father. The second son was named after the mother's father; the third son was named after the father and fourth son after the father's eldest brother. The first daughter was named after the mother's mother, second after father's mother, third after mother and fourth after the mother's eldest sister. This was prevalent, but not always the case. Also, in going back to the 1600s and 1700s, the last names have variations of spellings. Documents going back to those days are frequently found with three or four different ways of spelling the last name. In this book, I spelled the name of the person the way he or she spelled their name.

I found different birth and death dates on a few individuals, but I went by the most accurate source I could find.

I never knew anything about my grandfather, Robert Shirk, until I was married and started working on the family tree. Robert died when my mother, Betty, was three. We visited his brothers Le Roy and Dana and his sister Della, about once a year. Only in the last thirty years have I seen a picture of him. So, Robert was a mystery to be solved.

Unable to find Robert and his father James's death certificate in Union County, I finally found them in Logan County, Ohio after much research. Then after locating these elusive documents, they revealed less than I hoped to find and still left me wondering. I received information from the older generation before they died, but they added to my questions. Dana and Ruth Shirk provided information and the old pictures of Robert and his family.

Since the research started, I traveled many miles and spent hours over old documents and history books, not to mention information from family reunions I have attended. Summer vacations were planned around genealogical research. Some of my favorites were the National archives and Library of Congress in Washington D.C., Lancaster County, Pennsylvania, Philadelphia, Washington County, Pennsylvania, Burlington, New Jersey, and Hardy County, West Virginia. Kenneth Poling, a genealogist and cousin, helped me a great deal with the Poling side of the family. Elaine Chapman, a cousin, helped me with the Shirk family. Elaine and I became members of first families of Ohio in Ohio

Genealogical Society with Benjamin Elliott. When I found John Supler, one more generation back, I joined the DAR, Daughters of the American Revolution. How exciting it was the day I was accepted. What a great and patriotic group! To join, you must prove through first-and second-degree information that you are a direct descendant of a Revolutionary Patriot. The wills of Benjamin Elliott and John Supler were first degree information. Bible records, birth and death certificates I found were also first degree.

You never have an end, there is always another generation to find. I hope these challenges you to search and study your forefathers.

Chapter One
Robert James Shirk (1900-1929)

Tin Type of Robert 1917

The stairs were steep and creaky. Robert thought how he was twelve years old and never remembered anyone coming up to the attic. What was up here? The steps of the farmhouse went past the second floor and dead-ended to a large old wooden door. The door was warped and stuck. After several attempts, he opened the attic door, which groaned loudly. He then was hit with the heavy scent of dust mixed with stale air as he looked inside, seeing memorabilia scattered around the dusty floor, along with decades of spider webs. He moved cautiously with his candle, then tilting it slightly over a loosened brick, he formed a puddle of wax to hold the candle secure. He opened the attic window to let in fresh air. Freed to search the attic, he found an old cedar chest. Where did this come from? Was it his grandmother Amanda Shirk's? He lifted the lid and saw a picture album. It was about an eight by eleven-inch leather album with fancy gold and red decorations on it. A metal lock secured it. The key was hanging out of the lock. Each page in the album was like its own picture frame. Who were these people?

Interested, Robert started looking through the book. Some of pictures he recognized, like the one of his grandmother Shirk, but most he didn't remember. Putting the book aside, he then turned to his left and saw a large, framed picture of what appeared to be a mean-looking lady. On the bottom corner was the name Susannah Rossell. Alongside the picture was a wooden box of old letters and some antique clothes.

Then he saw, on the other side of the attic, a picture of his grandfather, Job Shirk, with his old black top hat on his head. He found it leaning against the wall, along with an old rocking chair. Robert remembered his father telling him about Job. He was skinny and had a long beard. The picture reminded him of pictures of Abe Lincoln.

In another box was an Indian arrowhead collection that his father found while walking the farm field after the land was plowed. He also found old church books in an old trunk at the other end of the attic, which were musty. Leaving them, shutting the window and putting the candle out, Robert took the album and box of letters downstairs. He found his mother in the large country kitchen.

Cora was a large buxom lady with a round face. She wore her long light brown hair in a bun at the back of her head. She loved her family and loved to cook. Robert found her making homemade noodles on the wooden table.

"Mother, I found these letters and pictures in the attic. Can you tell me about the people in the pictures?" asked Robert, with his arms full.

"What were you doing in the attic? Be careful, that was my mother's," said Cora, looking at the picture in the album as she rolled out the dough on the kitchen table.

"I was bored. I remember Grandma Amanda, I believe I was seven when she died," said Robert.

"Your grandparents, Amanda and Orsamus, lived next door," said Cora.

"Grandma always seemed happy until she got sick at the end."

"Yes," said Cora, as she held her head down. "She was sick with cancer of the stomach and died shortly after."

"Grandpa was a sad man."

"Well, he had been through a lot, Robert."

"Oh, look, here is my baby picture," Robert said, as he showed his mother the picture.

"Yes, you're in your baptismal gown."

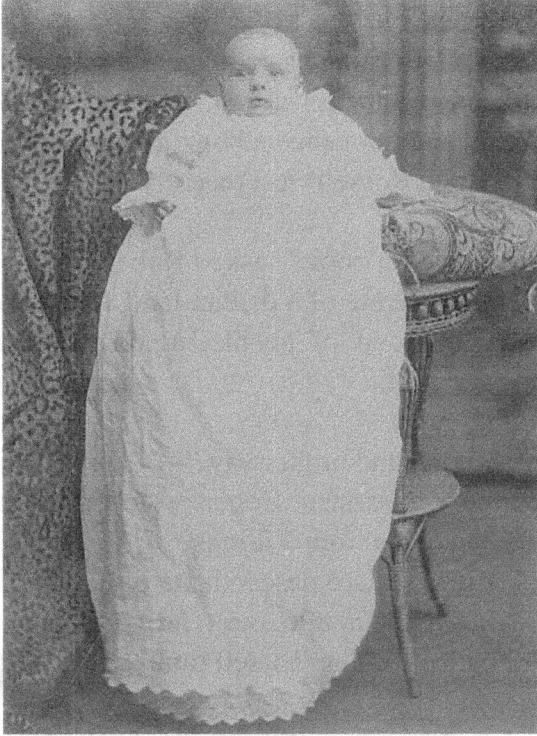

Robert 1900

"Go ahead and set the table and I will tell you more about your family," said Cora as her eyes twinkled with delight.

Robert found the blue plates with the design of a fisherman on a bridge and began setting the table.

"Well, long ago, our people came over on big ships from England," said Cora.

"How long ago?" asked Robert while he finished setting the table with the silverware.

"In the late 1600s and early 1700s. Maybe we should wait until after supper when I can tell the story better."

Later that chilly September night, Robert, curious about his family, sitting by the fireplace in their house, asked his mother, "Can you tell me about the history of our family now?"

"Let me get your brothers and sister to bed and I will come back and tell you. LeRoy, take Emerson upstairs with you. Lura, and I will get baby Dana ready for bed."

A while later, Cora came back down and sat by Robert. "Maybe I should start way back in time. A distant relative, who was a historian, researched the family and published a book called *Stemmata Rossellana*. Your fourth cousin Hugh Rossell[2] just recently updated the story that was written in 1855," said Cora.

"My relative wrote a book?" asked Robert.

"Yes, he did. He wrote of a distant land across the great Atlantic Ocean. There lived a group of people, a long time ago, called the Vikings."

"Where did they live?"

"They lived in Upland or Norway."

Now even more interested, Robert watched his mother and said, "Who would guess we came from Vikings?"

"The book states we are descendants of Sveide. He lived in 760 and was a Norse King. Then in 896, our relative, Drogo, was the brother of the famous Viking Rollo. The Rossell family goes all the way back to these Vikings."

"That is a long time ago." Robert, with his hands on his head, was thinking, *A hundred years is a long time ago and Mother is talking about over a thousand years ago.*

"Yes, it is. I have heard most families from the British Isles go back to the Vikings. When the Vikings took Paris, after many battles, Charles the simple, the king at the time, gave the Vikings the land to the north, Normandy, which means North Man's Land."[3]

"Why did they call King Charles the simple?"

"He was simple-minded or a little slow mentally."

"Oh, why was he king then?" Robert asked scratching his head.

"Because his father was King Louis II." Cora smiled at Robert and continued. "In the 911 treaty, the Vikings had to give up their pagan

---

[2] Hugh B. Rossell, *Stemmata Rossellana*; (Washington, D.C.: J.H. Polkinhorn , Printer, 1912)pp 6-12.

[3] George Holmes, *The Oxford History of Medieval Europe*; (Oxford, New York: Oxford University Press, 1988) 103.

ways and pagan gods for Christianity, the Roman Catholic Church at the time, and defend the Seine River from other Vikings in exchange for the land. Then King Charles III, King of France at the time, made Rollo a Duke. He had to kiss the king's great toe as a way to show homage. Duke Rollo, not relishing this, picked the king's right foot up and threw the king backwards out of his chair."

"That is funny," said Robert, laughing. "Did the king get mad?"

"I'm sure he did." Cora looked down at the book and continued to read. "The first Vikings found it hard to give up their pagan gods at first, but with each generation, they became more Christian. Drogo married Ermina in 896 and his brother, Duke Rollo, gave him the Northern District. Their son Hrolf, or the Christian name, Robert Turstain, in 920, married Gerlotte De Blois, the daughter of Theobald, Count of Blois and Chartres. Then in 1021, his great-grandson Hugh Bertand was of Le Rosel in Jersey, France."

"They had funny names." Robert watched his mother, leaning towards her.

"Yes, they did. Le Rosel was a small village in Normandy. Hugh owned a castle-like home there called Chateau du Rosel and Hugh was called Lord of De Rosel."

Robert looked at the picture of the home in the book. "It looks like a small castle."

"King Edward of England left the Duke of France, William, his successor in his will, but Harold Godwinson crowned himself king after Edward's death. Hugh and his four sons, Roger, Richard, Hugh Jr. and Theobald, accompanied Duke William to England in 1066. By then, they were devoted Catholics and wealthy farmers who owed their allegiance to Duke William of Normandy. They all fought in the battle of Hastings."

Raising his hands, excited, Robert asked, "Was it a big battle?"

"It was quite a battle with at least 7,000 men in 776 ships invading England. On October 14, 1066, William conquered King Harold. Now King William gave his men plots of land for their loyalty. Hugh and his sons built a new Rosel Village six miles from the city of Carn."

"Did King Harold die in the battle?" asked Robert.

"Yes, he did, along with a lot of his men. Hugh de Rosel's name was eventually changed to Rossell. In 1090, the pope pleaded for a crusading movement with bishops, knights and Charlemagne to liberate the holy city, Jerusalem. Hugh de Rossell Jr. was made a knight and made a pilgrimage to the holy land with the crusaders. The first crusade took back Jerusalem from the Muslims. Hugh Jr. had a picture of three shells added to his family's shield of armor for being in the crusade. This was a great honor and continued through the generations. His heirs were knights; all the way to William De Rossell who was Knight of Shire for Derby in 1325."

Robert looked at the picture in the book of the shield. "Knights with armor and swords?" asked Robert, as he jumped up, swinging his right arm around like he held a sword.

"Yes, they were. William De Rossell lived during the Black Plague from 1348 to1349, a terrible disease, which killed almost half of England, mainly the poor. This left whole villages and hamlets wiped out and deserted. It was one of the most terrible times in history. Everyone lost loved ones. There was looting and chaos in the towns."

"That sounds so terrible, I can't imagine it." Robert tried to picture half of everyone he knew dying.

"William was Knight of Shire for Derby, a formal prestige title for members of the Parliament. At the time, you had to be a knight and a gentleman with an estate to be elected to Parliament. With the plague, most of William's workers died and he, like most of the owners of estates, had few if any workers and the crops went to rot. What workers he could find asked for high wages, and some left for other places who offered more money. William tried raising sheep for a while, but the king raised the taxes so high, he couldn't afford to keep the estate. By 1405, the family sold the manor and moved to the village of Salop."

Robert looked at the picture in the book his mother held in her hands. "My ancestor lived in the large house?"[4]

"Yes, he did," said Cora, smiling, as she continued to read from the *Rossell Family History* book. "In the 1650's, England was coming out

---

[4] www.ushistory.org/penn/fox.htm

of a civil war and a preacher named George Fox preached to large crowds of people of the great love of Christ. He started the Quaker religion and our ancestor, Major John Rossell, an officer in Cromwell's army, converted. The family were now Quakers and King Charles II persecuted Quakers and any religion not Anglican, the Church of England. Major John Rossell's son, John Rossell Jr., was born in 1633 in London, England. As a young man, he witnessed the horrors of the Bubonic plague that hit London in 1665 when around one hundred thousand people died. The following year, a great fire destroyed thirteen thousand buildings in London, leaving the center of the city in rubble. John Rossell Jr. married Mary Johnson in 1668, just before they fled from London, England, to America with a large group of Quakers."

Sitting up straighter, Robert asked, "How did they get to America?"

"John and Mary came over to the American colonies in a large ship. They settled in Newtown, Long Island when their son Thomas was born in 1669."

"Where is Long Island?" Robert asked, as he fought back a yawn.

"It is in the state of New York, which is about 500 miles east of here. These colonists were skilled workmen, carpenters, blacksmiths, masons and men trained in other trades. John and Mary were among these colonists."

"How did they get to Ohio?" Robert said as he rubbed his eyes.

"Thomas and his children moved to Burlington County, New Jersey. Their children moved to western Pennsylvania and their children moved to Ohio. That is enough for tonight. You need to get to bed."

Robert 1920

Ten years later, Robert, now twenty-two, went to school in Columbus to study to become an auto mechanic then moved to Toledo, Ohio, where he got a job. There, he met Millie McGill on the Put-In-Bay Moonlight Cruise. A group of twenty passengers were playing musical chairs on the ship soon after they left the port.

"This is my chair," said Millie when the music stopped.

"Beg your pardon, miss," said Robert, smiling, after trying to sit on the same chair.

"I believe you are out of the game," Millie said with a stern look.

Bowing, Robert went to find a chair in the audience. He watched her play, not being able to keep his eyes off her. Later, Robert found Millie and her sister, Minnie, sitting on deck.

"It's a beautiful evening," said Robert, looking at the two young ladies with a smile on his face.

"Yes, the view across Lake Erie as the sun sets is beautiful and the stars are so bright tonight. It truly is wonderful tonight, with warm night breeze," said Millie.

"Miss, can I ask for your name?"

"Millie Mc Gill, and this is my sister, Minnie, in the chair next to me."

"How nice to meet you and your sister. My name is Robert Shirk."

"Come sit and join us," said Millie.

"Where are you lovely ladies from?" asked Robert as he pulled up a chair.

"We live in Toledo now, but grew up around Bowling Green, Ohio."

"I am living in Toledo too. I wonder if I can see you again Millie?" asked Robert.

"Now why would you want to do that?" Millie asked, as she played with her purse, a little round brown velvet sack with a pull cord on top and tassels on the end.

"You are very pretty. Are you seeing anyone?"

Shaking her head, Millie said, "I don't have much time since I work full time at the Overland in Toledo."

"I heard an Overland auto costs five hundred and fifty dollars nowadays," said Robert, scratching his head.

"Yes, you would have to be rich to buy one," said Millie.

Looking into her brown eyes, Robert said. "We could just go out for ice cream. Do you like ice cream?"

Nodding, Millie said, "Who doesn't like ice cream!"

"Well then, let's go next weekend."

Millie, biting her lower lip, asked, "Would it be forward of me to ask where you work?"

Smiling, Robert said, "No. I am an auto mechanic at a garage I own on Bancroft Street."

"I believe the boat is docking. Minnie and I must leave now. Let me give you, my address. Maybe you can write to me?"

Robert wrote little love letters to Millie, telling her how he missed her. Millie lived at apartment at 3234 ½ Monroe Street in Toledo and Robert lived at 1829 Maplewood off Monroe Street which was seven blocks away. It took him fifteen minutes to walk to her place. Then on weekends, they double dated with her sister Minnie and her husband,

Albert Oberly, who were just married the previous December.

Minnie and Albert Oberly

One of their favorite places was Pearson Park just outside the city. Minnie bought a box camera and loved to take pictures as they walked through the park and picked flowers. Then they stopped at a bench.

"Millie, I see you and Minnie are really close," said Robert, thinking of his family.

"Yes, we are only two years apart and shared a bedroom growing up," said Millie as she watched her sister take pictures.

"It must be nice to be that close," said Robert.

"There is so much we share, sometimes I feel we are twins." Millie turned and looked into his eyes.

"I have been thinking of you constantly, Millie," Robert said, as he put his hands on her hands.

Millie smiled. "I think of you often too."

"I love you so much, Millie. You are so special."

"Oh, Robert, I have been waiting to hear you say those words," said Millie. "I love you too."

Cupping her face with his hands, Robert kissed Millie for the first time on her lips.

"I want to always remember this moment." Millie stood and turned, shouting, "Minnie, take my picture with Robert, I want to send one to our father and his wife in Breckenridge, Michigan."

"That would be nice, we haven't heard from the family in a while," said Minnie.

Robert and Millie

Just then Robert picked up Millie, with flowers still in her arms. "Make me the happiest man and marry me, Millie?"

"Yes, I will be your wife," said Millie, smiling with her head on his shoulder.

Albert, standing by Minnie, overheard the conversation and said jokingly, "You better be good to Millie or I'll knock your block off."

Robert put Millie down on the ground and said, "What? You think you can do that?"

Albert playfully said, "Robert, put up your dukes."

"Take that dumb cigarette out of your mouth then," said Robert, laughing, then coughing.

Albert looked alarmed. "You should get that cough checked out."

"It's just your cigarette smoke."

Robert and Albert 1923

Minnie continued taking more pictures. Millie smiled into the camera and said, "I better be getting home, I have to work tomorrow."

Albert walked over to Millie and said, "Wait here, I will get the automobile."

Robert felt relieved, since he had been getting short of breath lately with long walks.

Wedding day Robert and Millie 1923

Minnie and Albert stood up for Robert and Millie when they were married on June 20, 1923.

Millie

Robert and Millie enjoyed swimming at Toledo Beach with Albert and Minnie. It was a fine beach and the place to be on hot summer weekends. Walking hand in hand on the beach barefoot in the sand, Robert said, "It is really nice here at the beach."

"Look, Robert, the kids going down the large wooden water slide. Would you like a child someday?" asked Millie.

Nodding, Robert smiled. "Why do you ask?"

"I believe I am pregnant," said Millie.

"That is wonderful!" said Robert, grabbing Millie and kissing her.

Later, lying on the beach, after running in the water, Robert looked into Millie's eyes. "Would you like to go dancing at the pavilion later?"

"Oh, that would be fun." Then looking around, Millie asked Minnie, "Where is your man?"

"Albert went over to smoke his pipe. He knows how it makes Robert cough." He switched from cigarettes to a pipe, thinking it would help, but Robert coughs around that too," said Minnie.

~ * ~

Robert and Millie rented a house on Upton Ave, in Toledo, Ohio when their daughter Betty was born on August 18, 1926. When Betty was thirteen months old, they decided to make the trip to Breckenridge to see Millie's father, A.J. McGill, short for Andrew Jackson, and Millie's stepmother, Alice. They had not met Robert or seen their granddaughter yet. It was a long drive up Route 25 in their old Ford. It took all day, even though it was only 173 miles. Route. 25 was a good road, but the other roads were not so good. Millie wrote they were coming, so they were expecting them. Betty slept most of the trip. Millie packed a picnic lunch for them, and they stopped at a roadside park to eat. Robert was so nervous about meeting her father, he talked continuously. They got there just before supper.

Robert, Millie and Betty at AJ's house

Standing on the front porch, they were met by a large collie dog, barking. AJ came to the porch to silence the dog.

"Father, it is so good to see you again!" said Millie, smiling. "There are a couple people I want you to meet." Turning to her side, she continued, "This is my husband, Robert Shirk, and your granddaughter, Betty."

Robert, dreading the meeting, said, "It is nice to meet you, sir." Holding Betty in one arm and shaking AJ's hand with his free hand, Robert tried to hide being nervous said, "I'm sorry about not asking you for Millie's hand in marriage."

"Yes, well, I finally got to meet you," said AJ, smiling. Then turning, he said, "And hello to you, little one." Picking Betty up, AJ continued, "Come on in, Alice is cooking supper in the kitchen."

"It smells good, what is it?" asked Millie, stepping into the house.

"Fried chicken with mashed potatoes and gravy, along with sweet peas. She also made apple pie. She really wanted to make you feel welcome, Millie."

"I wish she didn't make a fuss. I know we didn't get along the last time I saw her. I only pray we can be friends."

"That would be nice. I know she isn't your mother, but Ann has been dead for nineteen years now."

Walking into the kitchen, Millie says, "How are you doing, Alice? Can I help you with anything?"

"Well, it is about time you made it here," said Alice in an intimidating voice. "I have everything under control, thank you."

Millie backed off. Then changing the subject, Millie asked, "Where is Everett?"

"He is out back, feeding the chickens. Your brother just turned sixteen a couple weeks ago. He will be happy to see you," said A.J.as he walked into the kitchen.

"Has he made any plans for the future?" asked Millie.

"He is going to finish high school. Alice wants him to go to college. He is thinking about it."

Everett walked in through the back-screen door. "Hi, sis, I missed you. It seems like forever since I last saw you."

"I missed you too, said Millie as she hugged him.

Robert walked in, smiling, holding Betty.

"Robert, this is my step-mother Alice and my half-brother, Everett," said Millie.

"It is nice to meet you, Alice and Everett."

Alice half-smiled and shook his hand. "Sit down, supper is ready. Just make yourself at home."

"Now that we are all at the table, let's bow our heads and say grace," said A.J.

Lifting her head after the prayer, Millie turned to Alice and said, "Thank you for supper," as she fed Betty mashed potatoes.

"How long can you stay?" asked A.J. as he passed the chicken.

"We have to leave in the morning, Robert has to be back at the garage Monday morning."

After supper, they sat in the living room and listened to the radio. That night, Millie, Robert and Betty slept in the same bed. Then in the morning, they sat around the table, eating pancakes, when AJ said, "It was good to see you, I wish you didn't have to go home so soon."

Robert could feel the tension between Alice and Millie. The way they looked at each other. After they said their goodbyes, he walked to the automobile, carrying Betty. They got into the Ford and left for home.

On the drive home, Millie cried, "I don't think I can ever be good enough in Alice's eyes."

Robert felt bad for Millie. "All you can do is your best and give the rest to God."

The next year, Robert finally went to the doctor with his persistent cough. It was getting worse and he needed to do something about it. The doctor examined him and ran some tests. Robert was frightened at what the doctor would say and wished Millie was there with him, but Millie was home with their little girl.

The doctor walked over to Robert, standing by the exam table and said, "The X-ray shows you have an advanced stage of consumption (tuberculosis) of the throat and lungs."

Robert felt his knees buckle. "This can't be true; wouldn't I feel worse?"

"Not always. You probably have your good and bad days."

Robert held his head and tried not to cry, "What can be done?"

Shaking his head, the doctor said, "Not much at this stage. Rest is the best treatment now."

Robert left the office in a daze. It was all he could do to drive himself home. He pulled himself together and walked into the house. Finding Millie cleaning the house, he sat her down on the couch to tell her the news.

"Millie, the doctor doesn't give me long to live. He said six months to a year," said Robert.

"Two great tears rolled down Millie's checks, "There must be some hope! How can this be true?" Millie's face was now wet from tears as she looked at Robert.

"There is always hope, but I must be strong and realistic."

"Oh no, you are my life, my husband, what will we do?" cried Millie.

"What do you think of selling the garage and going back to my parents' farm, about hundred miles south of here, by Marysville, Ohio?" Robert thought how his mother would know what to do. She had been through it before with the death of his brother Emerson and his sister Lura. She became strong in her faith through it and Robert knew she would be just what they needed.

Later in October 1928, Robert saw his father working by the barn as he drove his automobile into the driveway. "Let me talk to Father first," said Robert. He got out of the car and crossed the lawn to his father. "Father, it is so good to see you again."

"Robert, how are you?" asked Jim.

"Not well, I am afraid." Robert's face went from a smile to a frown.

"How can that be?"

"Father, I came back home so you can get to know my wife and baby, Betty, before I die," said Robert.

"What do you mean, before you die?" asked Jim, as he leaned back with a look of shock.

"I have been sick for a while now. The doctor tells me I have consumption."

"Not everyone dies when they have consumption."

"I can feel it. I know I don't have much time."

"Oh, no, I don't want to believe this son." Jim held his head with his hands and now looked at the ground. Then after a few minutes, he looked up at Robert and said, "You and your family can stay here as long as you want. Della and Dana are the only ones still here."

"I will get Millie and Betty. We will see you in the house and make plans."

Later, Robert wandered into the kitchen to find his mother straightening things up.

"Robert, my heart breaks for you, what I can do?" asked Cora as her eyes filled with tears.

"I would like to be buried by Lura at Oakdale Cemetery, if that is alright with you and Father."

"We bought a large plot of land there when Lura died of the influenza. It will be okay; don't you worry about anything; we will take care of all the arrangements." Cora hugged Robert, the tears now streaming down her cheeks.

"Mother, years ago, you started to tell me about the family history. I would really like to hear more about our people."

"Well, I could do that. Why don't we go into the parlor and get comfortable?"

"I have been thinking about our people for years now. What it must have been like for them so many years ago."

"It wasn't easy, but their sacrifices, courage and service to this country made the country and our family what we are today."

Genealogy of Robert Shirk

ROBERT SHIRK b. 30 April 1900, North Lewisburg, Ohio, d. 31 January 1929, Middleburg, Ohio, m. Millie Pearl McGill June 20, 1923, Toledo, Ohio. The daughter of Andrew Jackson McGill and Anna Catherine Hock. Millie b. 16 September 1893, Wood County, Ohio, d. 10 February 1967 Oregon, Ohio.

Child of Robert and Millie:
BETTY JEAN SHIRK b. 18 August 1926, Toledo, Ohio; d. 30 December 2000, Ocoee, Florida, m. (1) George Calvin Jones 8 February 1947 Perrysburg, Ohio b.14 Aril 1922 d. 23 May 1995 m. (2) Clarence Snyder 1970, Toledo, Ohio b. 27 October 1912 d. 10 April 1985.

Chapter Two
John Poling (1620-1700)

John felt he would surely die. The blustery March winds were cold and strong. The ship rocked and so did John's stomach, the rage of the ocean was so great and wild. He heard the ocean splashing on the deck and the sound of the passengers crying and praying as the ship was tossed by the waves. The smell of vomit lingered in the air and made him sicker. John, twenty-six, came along with his mother, Mary, and his younger brothers, James, Joseph, and William, from Gloucestershire County, England. His father, Thomas, arrived in the village of Lynn, Massachusetts on the ship *Scorpion* in 1642.[5] He sent for his family to follow a few years later.

Back in England, the Poling family were well-educated, as were most of the English gentry who owned large farms. Their family descended from the Norman Conquest of 1066. Thomas and his Puritan friends spent time in prison for meeting secretly and going against King Charles, who was a tyrant. This group wanted to set up a New England, based on their beliefs. They came to the new world in search of personal freedom, freedom of speech and especially religious freedom.

Their ship left in March so it could return to England before the winter weather. It took eight weeks to cross the Atlantic. Forty passengers were below deck. Only the extremely wealthy had access to the few cabins above.

The storm passed, the ocean turned calm with still, windless days. The ship drifted. John went from sheer terror to complete boredom.

---

[5] Clerissa H. Tatterson, *History and Genealogy of the Poling Family* (Parsons, West Virginia: McClain Printing Company, 1978), 1.

Sitting on deck, watching his mother mending socks, John said, "Mother, I will be so glad when we arrive in the new world. I do not know if I can stand this trip much longer. I saw a woman die last night and watched as the sailors picked up her body took her upstairs and threw her overboard into the sea. I have been so upset and anxious over it. I am unable to sleep."

"Oh, John, they did that to stop the spread of the fever that killed her. You are healthy and should not worry about it. God will watch over us," Mary said.

John pressed his lips together and forced a smile. "The family at the back of the ship are scratching constantly, I think they have lice."

Looking up from her mending, Mary said, "They probably do, it is best to stay away from them. I thought you brought some books to read."

"I brought William Shakespeare's book with me. I also have John Milton's book of poetry. He is one of my favorite authors. A friend gave me his pamphlets. They are about freedom of speech and religion. He argues against the government's demand of approval of all published works and he is against episcopacy. The people should be free to worship as they want."

"John, we will have more freedoms, but there will still be rules and laws to follow."

"I know," said John, tapping his fingers on his knees. "I am so hungry. Is there just smoked fish left in the barrels?"

"We are lucky to have any food left."

John shook his head. "The hardtack yesterday had maggots in it."

Mary reached over and put a hand on his shoulder. "A sailor told me the cook is cooking salmagundi today in the galley."

John took a deep breath and let it out slowly. "What is that?"

"It is a mixture of meat, vegetables, spices and anything else they have left."

John shook his head. "At least there is still rum and wine to drink, which makes the food taste better."

~ * ~

John was standing on deck when daylight broke out over the sea. It was a beautiful sight of pink, yellow and blues with the sun peeking over the horizon. In the distance, he saw land. Thrilled, he ran back down to awaken his mother and brothers. After dressing, they came up and saw John waving excitedly. They saw the settlement come slowly into view. There was an iron foundry in the distance and the tannery could be seen on the other side of the village. Houses and shops lined the streets near the water.

Once the ship docked at Lynn in the Massachusetts Bay Colony, only the passengers with money could leave; others waited until they were purchased as indentured servants. The poor came over by signing a contract with the captain who had a right to sell them in America for enough money to pay for their passage. They were not allowed to leave the ship if sick, and if they didn't die or get well, they would have to return to England.

Thomas was there to get his family. John, laughing and jumping, was exuberant to see his father and get off the ship.

"Father, I have missed you," said John with a big smile on his face.

"I am so glad my family is together again. I have been busy building a nice home for you," said Thomas while he hugged his wife. "Let's gets your trunks and put them in my wagon." It was a short ride in the horse-drawn wagon to the house.

Not far from the village, standing in the front yard, John said, "It reminds me of our home in England." He could see massive trees went into building the one-story house with a steep roof. He walked into the main room where a large fireplace centered in the back of the house and large, hand-hewed beams ran across the ceiling. There, he could see four bedrooms that went off the main room, two on each side.

After a few months, John was pacing outside the house, talking to his brother.

"Joseph and I met a group of men going up to Salem. They say they are looking for men to work and there is very little work here. You should go with us. It is only five miles north of here," said James.

"That is a Puritan settlement. What did dad say?" John asked.

"He wishes us the best."

"No, I know we were raised in the Puritan faith, but I have been having problems with the Puritans. They want you to believe the same way they do or else they lock you in the stocks."

James gave John a stern look. "After arriving in Lynn, you have been preaching on the street corners, making them angry."

Trying to ignore James' eyes, John said, "I am just repeating what John Milton says in his pamphlet. A person has a right to personal freedom. My favorite John Milton quote is "Give me the liberty to know, to utter, and to argue freely according to conscience above all liberties."

"John! The Puritans have already locked you in the stocks for a couple hours. Didn't that change your mind?"

"No, I will always believe in personal freedom. They want me to leave town and threaten to run me out. Dad is really angry too."

John was run out of the village of Lynn after a few months, the same year he arrived. The Puritan leaders told him to leave. From there, he went with forty other families by ship to Gravesend, which was a coastal village, part of the Dutch colony on Long Island.[6] Gravesend was founded earlier in 1640 by Lady Deborah Moody, the widow of Wiltshire baronet, Sir Henry Moody. She organized an association of fifty persons from the village of Lynn for the Dutch colony, which was near New Amsterdam.[7] The land had been purchased earlier from the Canarsie Indians, who were their neighbors.[8]

John found the people of Gravesend very friendly and open to new ideas. He helped build a fence twenty feet tall to keep out the numerous wolves. The men of the village were required to share in repair of the wall and took turns at night watch. John joined the Reformed Protestant Dutch Church of Gravesend. They believed work was a way to glorify God and

---

[6] Newball, *History of Lynn* (Boston, 1865), 214.

[7] Stockwall, A.P., Rev. *Gravesend, L.I., Old and New*, New York Genealogical and Biological Record, XVI, No. 3 (July, 1885), 97-110.

[8] Stockwall, A.P., Rev.,*A History of the Town of Gravesend, New York* (Munsell, Brooklyn, NY: 1884),7.

idleness was a sin. Sunday was devoted to the Lord. The preachers would speak with energy and excitement and would go on for a good hour. They spoke of alcohol as a gift from God to be enjoyed, as long as one did not partake too much.

When John was thirty-four, he met Mary Elizabeth Fry at church and was taken by her beauty. She was fourteen years younger than him. John watched Mary, at the back of the church, as she sat with her feet next to the fireplace, to warm them. Her knit stockings were pulled down to her thick leather shoes. She wore a long frock, with a wide linen collar, short bodice with little sleeves and a long skirt falling in soft folds to the floor. Her hands were crossed on a large white apron in front. Her face was so pretty under her bonnet. She had light brown hair with loose curls that came down past her shoulders.

John wore a tall black hat with a wide brim. His sandy-colored hair was shoulder-length and tied in the back. His dark blue woolen jacket was long with a wide collar and large sleeves that came down to his wrists. His leather breeches came down to his knees where they met his knit stockings. After a brief courtship, John and Mary were married on March 11, 1654, in Gravesend.

Mary Elizabeth planted beautiful purple stockgilly flowers in front of the small house they rented. Her favorite flower, she loved the scent they left. John made her a bed from the large trees around the property. It had four posts that almost reached to the ceiling. He carved designs on the posts and used a rope-corded bedstead which required all his strength to get it good and tight. Then Mary made a linen cover for over the ropes, and on top of this, she placed feather beds. She used homemade linen for the sheets and pillowcases with knitted lace for the ends. The blankets were made from wool sheared from their sheep and dyed. She used the spinning wheel to make the yarn. Other blankets and towels were made from flax grown on the land. She had a huge chest made of Cherrywood, in which she placed her linen and blankets.

~ * ~

In the fall of 1655, John, frightened, raced home. In the house, he saw Mary standing by the fireplace, nervously rubbing her hands together.

"John, what is going on with our neighbors? They all seem angry," said Mary.

"The townspeople let their cows outside the fence during the day to graze on the wild grass and they wandered into the Indians' corn field. This made the Canarsie Indians enraged, and they slaughtered the cows. Now the townspeople are infuriated, and they are going after the Indians," said John. He hurried and grabbed his musket along with his pouch of musket balls and powder. "Mary, stay inside and keep the door barred shut," said John as he ran out the door.

When he got back later that night, John was shaking and pacing. "When we got outside the gates, some of the men were really mad and burned the Indians' lodges and corn fields. We killed some of the Indians who came after us."

Mary, with both hands on her hips, looked at John with a stern disapproving glance. She yelled, "This will cause the Indians to rise up against us. Now what are we going to do?"

John, with his head down, stood by the fire, warming himself, devastated, avoiding Mary. Finally raising his head, John said, "I have to go back out and defend the town."

A large body of Canarsie Indians rose up and killed sixty-seven white settlers, before they fiercely attacked the village. When they saw the Indians, the men of Gravesend sent a man to Fort Amsterdam on their fastest horse. John, along with the men of Gravesend, bravely held the town inside the large fence, shooting and killing several Indians, until a large detachment of soldiers came from Fort Amsterdam. Seeing the soldiers, the Indians took off running, but not before more were killed. [9]

By 1660, John and Mary had two boys, John Jr. and Richard. One day, John came home after he had been down at the docks.

"Mary, one of the sailors on a ship coming from the village of

---

[9] Stockwall, A.P., Rev.,*A History of the Town of Gravesend, New York* (Brooklyn, NY: Munsell, 1884),7.

Lynn brought a letter," John said as he came over to the fireplace where Mary was cooking.

"What does it say?" Mary asked.

"My brother, William, writes our father died last month at his home. Mother is doing well. William is still living there and helping her."

"How old was Thomas?"

"Seventy. Mother is sixty-six now. I will probably never see her again," John said, as he hung his head, deeply distressed.

"John, only God knows."

Then John looked up at Mary. "Wait here." He went outside and came back with a wooden crate. "Mary, I bought a pendulum clock from the merchant at the ship from the Netherlands. It is the latest invention and keeps good time." John wound the black ebony clock and the chimes made a beautiful sound.

Mary looked at the lovely painted flowers on the front of the clock. "It is a lovely thing, John, but where did you get the money?"

"I traded the wolf skins for it. The governor gave me the reward bounty of twenty guilders per wolf."

"I know there are a lot of wolves around here, you can hear them howling at night." Mary smiled at John. "What do you have there?"

"I also got a game of nine pins for the boys. There are nine wooden pins they set on the table or in the yard in rows of three. Then they try to knock the pins down with a ball. Whoever knocks the most pins down wins. According to the merchant, the Dutch children love to play this game."

"We will save it for Sinterklaas, it will be fun to see their faces when they actually get toys instead of just clothes."

John, unpacking the nine pins and setting them up, said, "Christmas is such a happy holiday. We need something to look forward to, not just all work all the time."

"True, but we better hide the nine pins before the children come home from the neighbors." Then Mary looked at the fireplace and said, "When it gets close to Christmas, I will trim the house with evergreens and any colored fabric I have left over. This will be a great Christmas."

John, thinking back to his own childhood, said, "It is a shame the

Puritans banned Saint Nicholas and Christmas, since they couldn't find it in the Bible."

Mary shook her head. "I am glad the Dutch love Christmas with great festivals, drinking, good food and dancing."

A few years later, the British were at war with Holland and protested against the Dutch settlement. The people of Gravesend could only ship goods on English ships with high fees, which made supplies cost more.

In 1664, the British ships anchored off Gravesend and sent a letter to the Dutch Governor, Peter Stuyvesant, in Amsterdam to surrender. One thousand British soldiers marched from the ships, while two ships aimed their guns on Fort Amsterdam. The governor surrendered the Dutch colony without firing a shot. The new governor was British and he wasted no time encouraging the Dutch families of Gravesend to settle in Monmouth County, New Jersey. Several families, along with many of their friends, left Gravesend for Monmouth County. They took a sloop and went across the bay, where land was one-half penny per acre. John and Mary, being English, stayed in Gravesend.

Shortly afterwards, John rushed home from the town hall meeting to find Mary sewing by the fireplace.

"Mary, the new governor redefined the town boundaries. Each family was given a twenty-five-acre lot. I claimed lot thirty-five for us. We must build a habitable house on it in six months or forfeit the land," John said.

"John, what wonderful news, now we can have a farm of our own, instead of renting," Mary said as she stood to hug him.

"After I build the house, I want to build a large barn for the animals and plows."

"The governor is really generous."

"Well, one-tenth of the winter wheat crop, up to six bushels, has to be paid to the Governor yearly."

Once a month, there was a town hall meeting and John was on jury duty frequently. John and his son Samuel always signed their name "Poling," but some officials spelled their name Poland on the town records.[10] The town hall sat at the center of the town at the intersection of the only two roads; Gravesend Road and Gravesend Neck Road. Gravesend Road ran north and south while Gravesend Neck Road ran east and west. They opened the meeting with everyone standing while the officer of the court said, "Court held the seventeenth day of March by his Royal Highness' authority, twenty-fifth year of the reign of our sovereign Lord Charles, the second year by the grace of God of Great Britain, France and Ireland. King defender of the faith in the year of our Lord 1668."

Tonight, they were discussing what to do about neighbor, Jack, on lot thirty-seven who killed the other neighbor's pig on lot thirty-eight. They finally decided that he would pay for the pig or work for the neighbor until the pig was paid off.

John and Mary's family grew. A daughter, Mary, was born in 1671. Then Elizabeth, in 1679, followed by Samuel in 1680. The children slept in trundle beds. They had a large wooden cupboard for dishes, and iron pots hung on cast iron hooks by the large fireplace. On the mantel lay John's long pipe for smoking. Next to the fireplace was a broad-seated armchair made by one of the neighbors, where John sat evenings, smoking his pipe and reading. He still liked John Milton and just purchased *Paradise Lost*.

They rose in the morning with the cock crowing and fixed breakfast, then ate lunch when the sun was overhead and supper at six p.m. They went to bed when the sun set.

Nine years later, John bought forty-four more acres of land. He already had three cows, chickens, four sheep and two horses. John, Richard and Samuel were now old enough to help.

Later that year, in 1689, a smallpox epidemic cut through New England. Their children developed headaches and a fever. Two weeks later, red spots spread over their bodies, followed with sores and pustules.

---

[10] Tennis G. Bergen, *Register in Alphabetical Order of the Early Settlers of King's County, Long Island* (New York: S. W. Green's Sons, Printer, Electrotyper and Binder, 1881) 228.

By the fourth week, the sores scabbed over and left scars. Three out of ten people died that year, including John and Richard. The dead were picked up in carts and buried together in a pit in Gravesend cemetery. Families were grieving everywhere.

"I miss John Jr. and Richard so much. Why did they have to die?" Mary said, as the tears filled her eyes and ran down her face.

"Everyone lost someone. It was the scourge, smallpox," said John, with his head down and eyes closed. Then he held Mary tight and they cried together.

"Thank God Mary, Elizabeth and Samuel made it through," said Mary, as she turned to wipe her eyes with her handkerchief.

"I noticed when I rode to the town of Flatland yesterday, the Canarsie Indians abandoned their village. Smallpox wiped out most all of the Indians."

"Oh, how terrible," Mary said, shaking her head. "There is always someone who has it worse."

Two years later, in 1691, John and Mary were all excited about the engagement of their daughter, Mary, now twenty years old, to Fernandus Van Sicklen Jr. The Van Sicklens were the pillars of the Reformed Protestant Dutch Church of Gravesend. Mary's dress was made in London and shipped to Gravesend. It was a beautiful gold silk floor-length dress, low cut in front with lace around the neckline. The sleeves were wide and puffy and came just past her elbows. On her hips, she wore large pads, making the dress come out at the hip. Her hair was layered on top of her head with jewelry placed in the middle. Fernandus wore a large colorful dress coat with long sleeves that came to his wrists. He wore dark breeches, with long stockings. The wedding was held at the bride's parents' house. The ceremony was performed in the evening with the immediate family present. On the table was a great spread of food and the bridal cake. The next day, the party went to the husband's parents' house where there was another celebration. It was custom for the bride to wear her dress to church on the following Sunday.

John died at his home in Gravesend, on June 5, 1700. Before his death, the women in the neighborhood made the shroud for John. Mary wore black crepe to John's funeral. Any glass windows in the house were covered with black material. No services were performed. The minister, close family and friends received commemorative funeral rings made by the goldsmith, who kept a supply on hand. John was buried at Gravesend Cemetery. After the burial, everyone went back to the house for wine (the choicest wines were saved for funerals), cider, choice baked meats, cakes and pies.

Estate Inventory of John Poling

Genealogy of John Poling

THOMAS POLING b.1590 Gloucester County, England d. Lynn, Mass 1660 m. Mary Thomas 1619 Gloucester County, England b. abt. 1594.

Children of Thomas and Mary:
1. John Poling b. 1620 Gloucester County, England
2. James Poling b. 1614 Gloucester County, England
3. Joseph Poling b. 1616 Gloucester County, England
4. William Poling b. 1618 Gloucester County, England

JOHN POLING b. 1620 Gloucester County, England d. 05 June 1700 Gravesend, New York m. Mary Elizabeth Fry 11 March 1655 Gravesend, New York b. abt.1640 Gloucester County, England d. 1707 Gravesend, New York.

Children of John and Mary:
1. Richard Poling b. abt. 1665 Gravesend d. abt. 1689 Gravesend
2. John Poling b. abt. 1657 Gravesend d. abt. 1689 Gravesend
3. Mary Poling b. 10 December 1671 Gravesend m. Fernandez Van Sickle Jr.
4. Elizabeth Poling b. 25 October 1679 Gravesend m. Joseph Dorset 23 July 1702 Middletown, New Jersey d. 1759
5. Samuel Daniel Poling b. 1680 Gravesend m. Grietje Margaret Wyckoff 1702 Gravesend d. after 1734

Chapter Three
Samuel Daniel Poling (1680-1732)

Wyckoff house built 1652 Flatlands, New York

Four-year old Samuel squirmed as he felt the water poured over his head. He agreed to be baptized, but now he wasn't too sure. This Sunday, in 1684, the Dutch Reformed Church of Gravesend was full of people he knew. His father, John, was holding him, while his mother, Mary, was praying along with the pastor. His godparents, Martin Peterse and Hannah Willemse Wyckoff were also there, praying and holding candles. His parents and Martin and Hannah were old close friends. They brought their two-month-old baby girl, Grietje Margaret, with them. She was a happy baby and so sweet.

Afterwards, there was a party at their home. Samuel's mother made his favorite foods; chicken, dumplings and apple pie. The family and friends brought food and presents. It was a joyful time, except his older sister, Mary, who was thirteen, always gave him a hard time. She was always telling him what to do. Today was no different, although her friend, Fernandus Jr, seemed to want her attention. His sister, Elizabeth, who was five, wanted to play games. His favorite game was hide and seek. He got into trouble when he hid in the chest with his mother's clothes. His mother, upset, found him playing in her bedroom and took Samuel back to his party. "This is your special day, Samuel. You are now a member of the church. You need to come out and thank your family and friends for coming and the gifts."

Four years later, Samuel, now eight, was old enough to go to school and today was his first day. He walked with his mother, Mary, to the center of the town. The school was across the street from the town hall. Catty-corner was the Dutch Reformed Church and across from there was Gravesend Cemetery.[11] The school was a small one room building, for boys only.

Standing in front of the school, Samuel looked towards his mother with concern. "Mother, why can't my sisters come to school?"

Mary turned to Samuel with a frown on her face and said, "It is not allowed. I taught them to read the Bible and write their names. Your sisters need to learn to cook and sew. They can already spin wool better than me. They also need to know how to make things for the home, like candles and soap."

Shaking his head, Samuel looked across the street. "Look, Mother, in front of the town hall is our neighbor Goulder in the stocks with a paper on his shirt. What does it say?"

Mary looked and tears filled her eyes. "The paper has a large S on it for slander. I heard he told the townsmen the mayor took money from the tax money for himself. Sometimes you say things in anger you would not otherwise."

Samuel continued to watch Goulder. "Oh no, some of the boys are yelling names at him."

---

[11] Rev. A.P. Stockwell, *A History Of the Town of Gravesend N. Y.* (Brooklyn N. Y.: Munsell and Co., 1884), 7.

Mary turned to Samuel with a stern look on her face. "I better not catch you doing that, Samuel."

Looking up at his mother with wide eyes, he said, "I wouldn't, it is mean. How long will Goulder be there?"

"Depends on the crime, usually a couple hours. It makes you think twice before saying mean things. We need to get to school."

In school, Samuel learned to read, write and cast up accounts. His reading was mainly the Bible and catechism. The teacher just got a new book for the boys, which was called *The New England Primer* which was shared by all. School lasted only a few hours and only when they were not needed on the farm. Reading and the ability to count was considered required by all the boys in the community. After school, Samuel ran down to the water with the boys to watch the fishermen dry their nets out on the beach. The fishermen caught all kinds of fish, along with clams and lobster which they traded with the villagers and sold to ships docked nearby.

Eleven years later, in 1699, Samuel ran into the house, all excited. "Father, I just got a job as surveyor," said Samuel.

John stood by the fireplace. "Samuel, how did you get the job?"

"One of the town surveyors died and I was appointed by the sheriff to fill his place. The Sheriff said I can learn on the job."

"Wonderful." John said, "With the money, you earn you could buy the land you talked about."

"Not only that, but I also want to raise hogs."

"Hogs?" John said, a little shocked.

"Yes, the neighbor said he would give me a start with a baby hog when I am ready."

"I am glad you have plans for your future." John then walked to the front door. "What is all the noise I hear coming down the street?"

"Father, the governor of New England, Lord Bellomont, has arrested Captain Kidd. The merchants are shouting and marching in the streets in front of town hall."

His father shook his head. "Arrested him, why?"

"What I hear, the governor claims Captain Kidd was a pirate and in mutiny and has him locked in a cabin in Boston."

"I can see why the merchants are upset, they carried on a good business with Captain Kidd. He sold them a lot of goods cheap. I heard he was commissioned by the governor and the King of England. It sounds like it's political. You just stay out of it."

"Father, I know better."

The next year, Samuel's father died at his home and was buried in Gravesend Cemetery. As sad as Samuel was, he worried about his mother who was not in good health.

Two years later, Samuel's older sister, Elizabeth, married James Dorsett Jr., at the Dutch Reformed Church of Gravesend on July 23, 1702. After the ceremony, outside the church, Samuel walked over to Elizabeth and James. "God grant you a long and happy marriage, Elizabeth and James."

"Thank you, Samuel." After a moment of silence, Elizabeth said, "We are moving to Middletown, New Jersey, where James has land. His father owns a large farm there and he is too old to travel, or he would have been here."

Samuel, sad to see his sister leave, said, "I will miss you. I hear the land has good soil there, which is great for farming."

Elizabeth hugged Samuel and said, "I will miss you too. You will have to come and visit; it is just across the bay."

"One day, I will," said Samuel, smiling.

The next year, Samuel and his childhood girlfriend, Grietje Wyckoff, made plans to get married. They always knew they would marry someday. It was planned since they were young. Sitting at the table at Grietje's family house, they discussed their future.

"I am sorry your father, Martin, died before the wedding," said Samuel.

"Thanks. I wish my grandparents were here too, you would have loved them," said Grietje.

"I barely remember your grandfather, Peiter. The only thing I recall was how tall he was, he must have been over six feet tall. I wondered what I had to do to build those kinds of muscles."

"Yes, Grandfather was very muscular. He had the bluest eyes and tawny yellow hair. I remember him telling me of how he came to this country as an emigrant from Friesland, Holland. He told me how he came over on the ship Rensselaerwick in 1637 at the age of twelve as an indentured servant. He was contracted as a farm hand for six years, at a salary of fifty guilders[12] annually. His life was hard when he first came over, but he worked hard and made something of himself."

Samuel shook his head and said, "I wonder why a boy of twelve would leave his homeland and travel so far to a strange land?"

"Peiter said his mother was a single woman and never married. He was bought with thirty-seven other labors to work with various farmers in the new country."

"I guess there weren't very many people in the colonies then. It was a way to get the workers who were needed. I remember your grandmother too, I thought she was a proud lady."

"That is a nice way to say it. She was a stiff neck lady, very stubborn. Her family was also from Holland, a prominent family there. She was wealthy and received a superior education. Grandfather worked for her father. He was a very dashing young man. Grandmother couldn't help herself but to fall in love with him."

"Wasn't Peiter prominent too, eventually?'

"Peiter became a judge. He was well known for his honesty and was appointed by the mayor. He was influential in starting the Dutch Reformed Church in Flatlands. I loved going to their home, it was a fine house. They built it in 1652, when few people were here. My father, Martin, was born there in 1663."

"Yes, I remember my parents were good friends and I was there once for a party. The house was five miles east from here in Flatlands. I remember it was a nice place."

"Samuel, my mother thinks we should set the wedding date for February 26th."

Samuel looked at Grietje, holding her hands. "That's next week, which is good, because I want to get married before my mother dies."

Grietje's eyes widened, "Well, I hope you're wrong."

"Can we plan the wedding that soon?"

---

[12] Guilder is a gold or silver coin used in Holland equal to 100 cents.

"Samuel, Mother planned it already, except for the date. She had my dress made, it will be blue with lace around the neckline with wide hips and ruffles on the ends of the skirt that touches the floor. The hardest part was finding the material. She had to order it from London."

Samuel squeezed Grietje's hand and said, "I would really like the ceremony at the Dutch Reformed Church of Gravesend."

A few years later, in 1706, John was born and named after Samuel's father. On March 8, 1707/1708[13], after the death of his mother, Samuel, the only living son, was the administrator of his parents' estate, which consisted of fifty-one acres of land and eleven garden spots and the total amount of personal property was L11.10.[14]

The second son, Martin Cornelius, was born in 1708 and was named after Grietje's father. Followed by William in 1710, both born in Gravesend.

To keep the land safe from Indian attacks, New York formed a militia. Samuel joined Captain Thomas Stillwell's Co. New York militia, troop IV, in 1715 in Gravesend. They ran drills and stood guard at the wall.

Samuel and Grietje's first daughter, Elizabeth, was born in 1718. Then June 25, 1720, they sold their land in Gravesend and moved to Middletown Township, Monmouth County, New Jersey. Hearing stories of the pirates in the waters between Long Island and New Jersey, the family was frightened as they crossed the bay in a sloop, even though it

---

[13] , (The old Julian calendar was becoming more and more inaccurate. The calendar was changed by Pope Gregory in the late 1583 to the Gregorian calendar to bring the calendar back into alignment with the solstices. The Catholic countries changed right away, but for almost *200* years, Protestant countries refused to change. Holland accepted the new calendar. Great Britain and her colonies changed in 1752. The double date was identified with the slash mark and represented the old and new calendars, apparently, it was still being used in Gravesend in 1704.)

[14] *Abstracts of Wills on File in the Surrogate Office City of New York,* (New York: Vol.1, 1665-1707), p 332. In the *New York, Estate Inventories and accounts, 1666-1822* list his estate.

was daylight. John, now sixteen, helped his father while Martin hid under the blankets with his brother William as they crossed. Grietje held baby Elizabeth in her arms. Every boat they passed made them even more aware of the danger. They landed safely in Keyport where they bought a wagon and horse to take them the seven miles to his sister Elizabeth's house by Middletown, New Jersey.

Samuel and his family stayed with his sister Elizabeth and his brother-in-law James until they bought land and built their own house. Sitting at the table, drinking tea with Elizabeth, Samuel said, "Elizabeth, I want to thank you for telling me about this land. We needed to get out of Gravesend, it was getting too crowded. Would you believe, at last count, there was over two hundred and sixty people in the village and that was just the men."

"It is crowded for just a small village. You will find the land here is rich and the people are friendly. Our old Dutch friends from childhood are here, they moved when the English took over Gravesend," said Elizabeth, passing him the biscuits.

"Yes, I saw an old friend in town," said Samuel as he took a biscuit.

"How was your trip here?" Elizabeth asked.

Samuel let out a huge sigh. "I was worried we would get held up by pirates in the bay."

Elizabeth eyes widened. "Yes, there are a few pirates still in the bay. Captain Kidd's pirates came to live in Middletown after Captain Kidd was hanged in London. One of his men was arrested and tried. His fellow pirates came in with muskets and held the governor and court officer's hostage while they freed the prisoner. The bay isn't as bad as it was six years ago."[15]

"I heard even Black Beard and his pirates were up the bay then."

"Yes, an angry mob of townspeople and farmers got together and stood up to the pirates on Kings Highway. The pirates had been looting

---

[15] Ernest W. Mandeville, *The Story of Middletown* (Middletown, New Jersey: Christ Church, 1927), 54-59.

the stores and farms for food and supplies for their ship."[16]

Samuel, shaking his head, said, "That must have been a rough time."

"Yes, it was. We have a good honest government now, not like the old days, so you don't see the pirates. The merchants bought silk and French lace from the pirates at a low price, turned around and sold it at a great profit. They bought out the officials. Now those merchants are very wealthy."

"Which doesn't seem fair."

"It is what it is. Now that you're here, I would like you and Grietje to come to church with James and me next Sunday," said Elizabeth.

"What kind of church?" Samuel asked, frowning.

"The Baptist Church, it is similar to the Dutch Reformed Church."

"Where is it?"

"In Middletown, just down the road on Kings Highway. The governor sometimes has horse-racing down Kings Highway on Sunday. They race by the church. Someone brings small fried cakes and applejack for the prize."

"I'm sure that makes the minister happy."

The next week, Samuel came home from town to find Grietje had made candles. "Grietje, I bought the two tracts of land just down the road," said Samuel.

"Good. How much land?" asked Grietje, smiling.

"About two hundred and sixty acres, plenty for farming and close to my sister, Elizabeth and James. We can build a house there in no time."

"Good, it is crowded at your sister's house with all the children."

Samuel built a house, twenty-six feet long, sixteen feet wide and ten feet high. There were two doors, two windows and a clapboard roof with two chimneys, one in the middle of each side wall. The kitchen possessed a large stone hearth with a brick oven built in the chimney for baking. Big cast-iron pots and pans suspended on cranes hung over flaming logs. There was a loft for sleeping and a root cellar. Samuel

---

[16] Ernest W. Mandeville, *The Story of Middletown* (Middletown, New Jersey: Christ Church, 1927), 13.

experienced no problem getting supplies to build his house. The town of Middletown was close by with a sawmill, grist mill, tannery, blacksmith shop, and a general store. After the house was finished, they built a barn. In the spring, they planted wheat, flax and a vegetable garden.

Genealogy of Samuel Daniel Poling

SAMUEL DANIEL POLING b. 1680 Gravesend, New York d. aft. 1734 New Jersey m. Grietje Margaret Wyckoff, daughter of Martin Peterson Wyckoff and Hanna Willemse in Gravesend, New York 1702. b. 30 March 1684 Gravesend, d. April 1734 Keyport, New Jersey.

Children of Samuel and Grietje:
1. John Poling b. 1706 Gravesend, New York m. Mary Fry 11 March 1755 Middleton,
   New Jersey.
2. Martin Cornelius Poling b. 1708 Gravesend, New York m. Sarah (Sary) Wells 1725. d. 1770 New Jersey.
3. William Poling b. 1716 Gravesend, New York m. Sarah Wyckoff 1732. d. 1758.
4. Elizabeth Poling b. 5 October 1718 Gravesend, New York.
5. Peter Poling b. 1720 Gravesend, New York.
6. Richard Poling b. 23 June 1723 Freeport, New Jersey.

Chapter Four
Martin Cornelius Poling (1708-1770)

A dramatic change in life came to Martin at the age of twelve, when he left Gravesend and came across the bay with his father, Samuel and his family to Middletown, New Jersey. There no longer was the strict rules and punishments put down by the puritans. The government no longer used the stocks, but punished with fines, which didn't work as well. More crimes were committed. There was no embarrassment, just pay the fine and leave. There was a Baptist church in the area, but a lot of families stopped going to church. The morals of a lot of people were disintegrating. Gangs of young men hung out in the woods and at night, robbed people on the road and looted the farms.

Martin and his family lived with his aunt, uncle and cousins until his parents could build them a house of their own. One morning, awakened from sleep, Martin heard his mother drop a cast iron pot.

"Mother, are you hurt?" said Martin has he pulled the quilt off.

"Martin, get up and come down here," said his mother.

He climbed down from the loft where he slept with his cousins and helped with the heavy cast iron pot. His mother was trying to cook hot porridge over the fireplace for breakfast.

"Mother, I don't want to go to school today," said Martin, as he cast his eyes down.

"Why?" asked his mother as she stirred the porridge. "You used to like school."

"It is farther to walk here than it was in Gravesend and I have to walk by Indian Will," he said as he gave her a sad look.

"Who is this Indian Will?" asked his mother as she moved over and placed her hand on his shoulder.

"My cousins tell me he was an old Indian who stayed behind when his family sold their land and moved west."

"That is probably true. There are still a few Indians that stayed behind in the area."

"He lives in a wigwam by the roadside."

"I have seen the old hut by the road, someone lives there?"

"Indian Will does, and he is really ugly, Mother. He is fat with big shoulders, dark leathery skin, long black dirty hair and bloodshot red eyes. His large ears have a gold ring in each of them, and he has a large-size ring in the middle of his big nose. There are stories going around. Indian Will found pirates' money buried at the beach in an old trunk. Some even say he killed his wife, since she came up missing one day."

"Sounds like your cousins want to scare you."

"I hear Indian Will never shot an animal for food, but would strangle it with his large bare hands, then eat it raw."

"Do you really believe this, Martin?"

"You should hear him talk; he sounds so scary. He drinks from a whiskey jug he keeps nearby and keeps a pack of wild dogs who growl when we pass by his place." [17]

"He probably doesn't speak much English. This is not going to keep you from school, Martin. Just be sure to walk with your cousins."

Martin and his cousins ran all the way past Indian Will's wigwam, not stopping until they were well down the road and they could no longer hear the dogs or smell the bad odor. Years later, Martin loved to tell stories at night about Indian Will to his children around the fireplace.

~ * ~

When Martin was seventeen, he fell in love with Sarah Wells (she was called Sary) who he met at Six Mile Run in Somerset County, New Jersey. Sary was shopping with her parents, Thomas and Mary Elizabeth Wells, at the Mercantile. His father knew her parents and introduced them. For Martin, it was love at first sight. Then, a few days later, Martin decided to go see Sary. He saw Sary sitting in a rocking chair on the front porch, doing needlepoint, as he rode up.

"Martin, how did you get here? It is about thirty miles around the road." asked Sary.

"I rode my black mare, cutting through the land, which is half the

---

[17] Edwin Salter and George C. Beekman *Old Times in Old Monmouth* (Genealogical Publishing Co., Inc.: 1980) 25-27.

miles," said Martin.

Sary stood up and walked over to him. "What a nice surprise. I was wondering if I would see you again."

"I can only get here once a week if the weather is good," said Martin as he got off his horse.

"My parents will be surprised to see you."

Martin smiled. "I hope your parents like me."

Sary returned his smile. "They will."

Martin visited Sary for several months. Then one day in the late fall, he made it through the fields when it started to rain.

"Come in by the fireplace, Martin," said Sary when he came up to the front door.

Martin warmed himself by the fireplace. He then turned to Sary and hugged her. "Sary, visiting you once a week is not enough, I want to be with you always," said Martin.

Sary stepped back. "I love you, but you will have to ask my parents for my hand in marriage."

"I will," promised Martin, thrilled as he tried to kiss her.

Sary moved back. "Stay for dinner, we are having rabbit stew. Mother has it cooking in the large cast iron pot over the hearth."

"If your parents will have me, I would like that," said Martin, smiling.

After dinner, Martin helped Sary clean the pewter dishes while her parents drank their tea by the fireplace. Martin and Sary walked to the fireplace where her parents were sitting.

"It is getting too late and it is too cold for Martin to try to make it back home safely. Father, can Martin spend the night?" Sary asked.

"He can spend the night in your bed, bundling," said Thomas Wells. "We will place a bundling board between you two."

"Keep your clothes on, except for your shoes," her mother said as she shook her head, closing her eyes.

Later that year, the Wells were upset when they found their fifteen-year-old daughter was pregnant, but about half of the girls in the area were pregnant by the time they were married. There was no shame as long as they married. Martin and Sary were married in 1725 at Sary's parents' church, Six Mile Run Dutch Reform Church. Their baby was born not long after they were married and they named him after Martin's father, Samuel. He was baptized in Sary's parents' church. The little family lived with Sary's parents until they were able to make it on their own. A few years later, they rented a farm nearby with apple trees and grew wheat and corn.

In 1732, Martin's older brother rode over to his farm. John pulled his horse to a stop and jumped down. Martin walked out from the barn, startled to see John. It had been a while.

"Hi, Martin, I have some bad news." John took a breath and continued, "Father has died at home, last night, in his sleep."

"Oh, no," said Martin with his hand over his eyes. After a long period of silence, Martin said, "Father lived a good life, even though he was only fifty-two years old. I will miss him."

"He wanted to be buried at Green Grove Cemetery in Keyport," said John.

"How is Mother doing?"

"She is extremely sad. She won't eat, I am worried about her. I should get back to her," John said, as he got back on his horse.

Martin, concerned, said, "Sary and I will be by later, as soon as I get little Samuel from school."

There was a brief funeral at the farm the next day. The neighbors and friends came with food and good wishes. Then there was the long trip to the cemetery.

Two years later, Martin's mother died in Middletown Township at her home and was buried alongside Samuel in Keyport.

"Mother was never the same after father died," said Martin with tears in his eyes. "She loved him so much she couldn't live without him."

"Yes, she didn't sleep or eat much and became weak," said John, choked up.

"They are together now," Martin, after brief silence said. "I know the farm goes to you since you're the oldest. What are your plans for the farm now?"

"I plan on living here for a while. You have some money coming to you from the will."

"Father was thoughtful. I can use it."

A month later, Martin drove five head of cattle down Kings Highway from Middletown, which was about four miles from his farm, where he lived in 1735. "Sary, I got a good deal on some cattle with my inheritance," said Martin.

"Where are you going to keep them? I don't want them in my vegetable garden," said Sary.

"I thought I would keep them out behind the apple trees. I need to make ear marks on them first."

"You didn't have me helping you in mind?" Sary had a stern look with her hands on her hips.

Smiling, Martin said, "John is coming over to help. Just fix him a good dinner. He loves your cooking and will do anything to get some."

Samuel overheard the conversation and asked, "Father, can I help with the cattle?"

"No, Samuel, you're too young."

"But, Father, I'm almost ten."

"Okay," Martin said, "but you will have to be with me or your uncle John."

Once John arrived, he held the cow while Martin cut marks in her right ear to show his ownership. Ear marks on cattle in 1700s was required.

The next week, Martin went to the courthouse to register the ear marks on the cows and were taxed six shillings. (A shilling is about a quarter).

Martin and Sary waited seventeen years to have their next child, a son, Petrus (Peter). He was baptized on December 4, 1743, at Six Mile Run Church. Then another son, Richard, was born in 1746, the same year their first son, Samuel, now twenty-one, married Madelene Digman. Everyone called her Lena. Martin and Sary's younger children were around the same age as their grandchildren.

Martin became active in the church of his parents, the Baptist Church of Middletown. At a church meeting on December 1, 1753, Martin was asked to talk to his brother, John. The church elders voted to excommunicate John for keeping a woman in his house out of wedlock.

They became a public annoyance after many times being warned of living in sin.

Martin rode over to John's house and found him chopping wood.

John, surprised, asked, "Martin, what are you doing here?"

"John, the church had a meeting last night. They are saying you and the widow, Mary Fry, are living together in your house," said Martin, getting off his horse.

John, putting the ax down, said, "Yes, she is living here, you know that."

Martin, now upset, said, "You need to put her out or marry her!"

"I will put her out," said John, shaking his head.

"You said that before, but you still keep her. Now I see she is pregnant. Is it your child?"

"Guilty. I have met with many trials in life, but none at times more than I was able to bear. This breaks my heart. I asked God and all his brethren to forgive me and to pray unto the Lord for me." John dropped his head in anguish.

"I will pray for you," said Martin, "but until you put her out or marry her, you cannot come back to church."

The next year, Martin's brother Samuel Jr. was courting Mary's sister-in-law Elizabeth Fry at the time. He talked John into having a double wedding. Martin went to his brothers' weddings at the church on March 11, 1755. It was a year after the baby, John Jr. was born.[18]

Martin's brother John was executrix of their father's estate. In 1756, he sold the family farm (a good ten years after his mother died), by auction to the highest bidder which consisted of two tracts of land. One for hundred acres and one for sixty-one and half acres.

One fall evening in 1760, Martin went to a secret town meeting at the tavern on Kings Highway.

"Greetings," said Martin as he walked into the tavern.

"It is about time you got here," said one of townsmen. "We want to get this meeting started."

"Give me some ale," said Martin.

---

[18] *Archives of the State of New Jersey, First series,* XXII, p. 303.

"We are all upset about the British adding more taxes!" shouted the townsman.

"I hear you," Martin said as he lifted his tankard.

"It is their way to make us support the government back in England. We are also upset with the government's policy of not buying goods from the colonies. English goods are sent to the colonies with cheap prices, but very few items are sent back to England."

The High Sheriff barged into the tavern with the king's liegemen. "You're all under arrest!" shouted the sheriff. "Men, take away their swords!"

"What are we under arrest for?" asked Martin.

"For riotous assembly."

Mad, Martin made a fist and struck one of the king's liegemen in the face. A fight ensued. One man had his wig torn from his head; another had his clothes torn off. The men in the tavern were hauled off to prison by the sheriff for riotous behavior and fined L5 (British pound is $1.33).

~ * ~

A group of riders galloped down Kings Highway in the spring of 1764, yelling, "George Whitefield is coming. George Whitefield is coming. He is going to be preaching in the field down the road."

Martin dropped his hoe in his garden and ran into the house. Finding his wife sweeping the floor, he smiled. "Sary, remember the pastor at the church talking about this great Evangelist, who is going around the country with his revival movement?'

She nodded. "Didn't he say he was a missionary from England? Why?"

"Some riders came through just now saying he is going to be preaching in the field down the road, let's go."

When they approached the field, there were many people standing around. Reverend George Whitefield was a good-looking, distinguished man, cross-eyed with a large white wig and dressed in a flowing clerical gown. He was standing on a mound in the middle of the field, talking about how the people turned away from God. His words could be heard and understood from a great distance. He was a powerful orator and Martin could see his fellow neighbors crying. This was no ordinary sermon. Martin watched as George portrayed Saint Peter from the bible with such realism he never saw before. It totally spellbound Martin while he continued to listen to this great man. His words of loving all God's children, whatever denomination they might be, reached the hearts of the people. When he finished his speech, there was a collection and Martin found himself emptying his pockets of the few copper coins into the hat, even though he silently told himself he would not give when he first came there. Reverend George Whitefield changed his life and those of his neighbors. For weeks later, he found himself talking about the sermons with his family and neighbors. When he walked through town, he heard people singing religious songs. Attendance at church on Sunday increased to the point there wasn't room for everyone. The people were more loving and helpful. Neighbors went out of their way to do things for others. It was a dramatic change in the life of the community.

~ * ~

Martin's grandson was born Samuel S. Poling to Samuel and Lena Poling, their sixth and last child, on September 2, 1767. Lena died the next year at the age of forty-three. Martin and Sary went to the funeral at their home where there was an elaborate dinner. Everyone within miles came and brought food. The inside of the house was draped in black with a black bow on the door. Afterwards, sitting at the table with his family, Martin looked at his son.

"Father, the land prices in Virginia plummeted and I heard in town how good land opened up for farming in Loudon County, Virginia, really cheap. I am thinking of taking my children and going to Loudon County, Virginia, now that Lena is gone. I want you and Mother to come with us," said Samuel.

Shaking his head, Martin said, "Son, I'm too ill, I'm sixty years old, I could never make the journey."

Standing, Samuel looked at his father. "I want the family to move away. War is coming and we will soon be in the middle of it here."

Shaking his head again, Martin, with tears in his eyes, said, "I don't feel I have much more time on this earth, son. Take your mother and your family and leave for Virginia."

Samuel placed his hand on his father's shoulder and said, "Father, I will not leave you!"

Martin died in 1770 and was buried in Green Grove Cemetery in Keyport, New Jersey, by his parents' graves. After his father Martin died, Samuel left for Virginia with his mother Sary. She lived with her son Samuel in Virginia until the time of her death in 1771.

Genealogy of Martin C. Poling

MARTIN C. POLING b.1708 Gravesend, New York d. 1770 Monmouth Co., New Jersey m. Sarah (Sary)Wells daughter of Thomas and Mary Elizabeth Wells, 1725. Sary b. 1710 New Jersey d. 1771 Loudoun Co., Virginia.

Children of Martin and Sary:
1. Samuel Poling b. 1725 Monmouth Co., New Jersey d. 1782 Loudoun Co., Virginia
2. Petrus Poling b. 1743 Monmouth Co., New Jersey d. 5 August 1835 Barbour Co., (West) Virginia m. Hannah Barnett
3. Jonathan Poling b. 1749 Monmouth Co., New Jersey d. 1810 m. Ann Watson

Chapter Five
Benjamin Ellot/Elliot 1720-1803

Touching the rustic wooden door of his father's old house, Benjamin recalls his childhood. How primitive everything was then. Life so simple and carefree. So happy. Benjamin's father, John Ellot, and his mother, Sarah, were Quakers who came from England to British Colonial America in the company of many others around the time of William Penn. They were very young then and they came with their parents and in the company of many others. Some of their relatives were already in New England. One was Reverend John Ellot, the Indian Missionary. Benjamin's parents settled near Philadelphia with their three sons, Benjamin, Jacob, Abraham. His father was a virtuous man with a strong moral sense and instilled this in his children. The Quaker community was a holy experiment, a democracy, giving the power to the people and one of a loving caring community.[19] They also felt it was wrong to take an oath or take their problems to a court of law, preferring to work out disagreements at the monthly meeting. For this reason, they kept careful records, especially of marriages.

Benjamin opened the old door and walked through the abandoned house. He came here in his old age to see the homestead one more time before they tore it down to build a new house. As he walked into the main room, he noticed in the middle of the rotten floorboards a tree growing with its branches winding around the room. He walked over the branches and looked into the bedroom he shared with his brothers. Benjamin stayed in Pennsylvania, but his brothers Jacob and Abraham both settled in North

---

[19] Charles P. Morlan, *A Brief History of Ohio Yearly Meeting of The Religious Society of Friends* (Lyle Printing and Publishing Co. Salem, Ohio:1959)161.

Carolina. He wondered whatever became of them.

Benjamin looked at the old stone fireplace, now dirty and musty. It was beautiful in its day. He thought about his marriage to Ann Wall, how it was arranged by his parents and Ann's parents. Ann's parents were John Wall and Mary Harris (Haines) of Goshen, York County, Pennsylvania. There was a need to marry outside the community. Too many first and second cousins were marrying within their community. This was unhealthy.

Benjamin and Ann Ellot's wedding Certificate[20]

---

[20] Copy from Shirley Mitchem 2001

Their wedding certificate stated ...*in the county of Lancaster, Thornburt Township, Pennsylvania. Benjamin and said Ann Wall have fulfilled their marriage with each other by the fifth day of the eleventh month in the year of our Lord one thousand seven hundred fifty*, followed by the signatures of those present. Marriages were performed without a preacher and every guest signed the certificate as witness. It was framed and hung on the wall of their home. They left Lancaster to settle in York County, Pennsylvania after the marriage. Benjamin thought back about Ann, how she was so good to him and how he grew to love her. Their life together was so full.

Benjamin smiled as he thought of his job as supervisor of highways back in 1754. Horseback was the chief mode of traveling and wagons hauled food and supplies with teams of four to six horses. The roads were full of ruts, making it hard for a wagon or coach to get through, not to mention the horse manure. He worked with a team of men, six days a week, to maintain and repair the roads which were mainly dirt and cobblestone. There was so much horse manure and urine in the road in the village streets it was a smelly muck. He would shovel the manure and take it to the farms. Most of the manure was removed for farmers to fertilize their fields. It was hard work. The best part of the year was the birth of their daughter Lydia. How sweet and precious she was then.

Benjamin remembered how in 1755 he was an elected as an unpaid officer of the overseer of the poor. He administered money, food and clothing to the poor. It made him feel good to help the needy, who were mainly orphans and widows. The following year, their first son, Isaac, was born. How proud and exciting it was to have a son. Then Ann's father John Wall died on March 15, 1765. He was only sixty-one years old. Ann was pregnant at the time with their fifth and last child, John.

Benjamin became constable that year. For this, he was paid, and his duties were to capture and arrest lawbreakers. Most frequently, he fined people for bad conduct, cursing in public, working on the Sabbath and for failure to properly pen their animals. Not long after that time, Benjamin bought land in Newberry Township, York County, and was one of the first settlers in the upper end of York County in 1767. He built a house on the hundred acres; thirty acres were cleared. He owned seven sows, three horses and mares, ten sheep and chickens.

Walking through the back door and looking at the old barn caving in and falling apart, Benjamin was saddened as he remembered the War for Independence. How terrible, men killing men, everything he was against. It was a hard time, insulted by fellow neighbors who weren't Quakers and fined for not participating in the War, he was emotionally drained. He owed his first allegiance to God and he would stand up for his beliefs, even if he had to pay stiff fines. The war was all around him then; first the British would march through, pillaging any food they could find, and then the Americans would come through, confiscating anything left that was edible.

Some of his children left for Washington County, Pennsylvania in 1780 with their families. It was a chance to get away from the war and a promise of better-quality land. Before Isaac left, Benjamin gave him his silver-headed cane with his initials and date on it.[21] How he missed Isaac and the grandchildren and wondered how they were doing in the land on the other side of the mountains. His son, John, stayed on and worked the farm. Benjamin willed the farm and land to John for all the work he did. It was such a cold and sad day when Ann died the second month of 1803. They buried her in Dillsburg, Pennsylvania at the Monaghan United Presbyterian Church Cemetery.

Leaving the old, abandoned childhood home on this spring day and all the memories, Benjamin returned home to his son John and the farm.

---

[21] John D. Elliott *Reunion and Sketch of the Elliot Family* (Sumner Folsom and Co., Toledo, Ohio: 1875) 3.

Genealogy of Benjamin Ellot

JOHN ELLOT b. 1690 England d. 1734 Pennsylvania m. Sarah b. 1700 d. 1765

Children of John and Sarah:
1. Jacob Ellot b. Pennsylvania d. North Carolina m. Elizabeth
2. Abraham Ellot b. Pennsylvania d. North Carolina m. Priscilla
3. Samuel Ellot b. Pennsylvania d. 15 September 1746 Pennsylvania
4. Joseph Ellot
5. Benjamin Elliott b. 1730 Chester Co., Pennsylvania d. 15 February 1803 York Co., Pennsylvania m. Ann Wall daughter of John Wall and Mary Haines 5 November 1750 Lancaster Co., Pennsylvania b. 1700 d. 1765 York Co., Pennsylvania.

Children of Benjamin and Ann:
1. Lydia Elliott b. 1754 Pennsylvania m. Enock Vanscoyoc 1780
2. Isaac Elliott b. 24 March 1756 York Co., Pennsylvania d. 18 June 1839 Stark Co., Ohio.
3. Absalom Elliott b. 1757 York Co., Pennsylvania d. 1803 Clark Co., Indiana m. Ruth Ann
4. Mary Elliott b. 1760 d. 1809 m. Samuel Paden
5. John Elliott b. 1765 Pennsylvania d. 1854 Columbiana Co., Ohio m. Prudence Parsons 1814 Pennsylvania

Chapter Six
John Jacob Brake (1730-1809)

Ship Sonnendach

Standing on his property in 1747, Jacob looked out over the beautiful South Branch of the Potomac River in Hampshire County, Virginia. He thought about his father, Johann Jacob von Brake, and the stories he told of the family. All the trials the family went through to get to this new world. Johann was born in Lemgo, Hanover, Germany to Baron Wilhelm Joseph Dietrich Von Brake and Mauri Elizabeth Lady Ailkinoch of Douglas on January 5, 1714. When Johann was only two and half months old, the family fled from Germany in fear for their lives after losing the war. The country was now under the rule of Prussia. They left suddenly in the middle of the night, taking only their silver. They traveled over land by horse-drawn carriage to the port Wilhelmshaven,

Hanover, Germany where they boarded the ship Sonnendach to Edinburgh, Scotland, the home of Mauri's family.

The family settled in the Parrish of Cannomach, Prestonpars, East Lothan, Scotland where Mauri gave birth to Uncle Jacob in 1728.[22] The family struggled in Scotland with the decline in the economy and high rent. Then King George II purchased the North Carolina Colony back from the seven original landowners in 1729. Every person, regardless of their age, who went and settled in the Royal Colony of North Carolina for two years was given fifty acres. It was called the head right system. The family jumped on it to own their own land. They departed Leith, Scotland on the ship Fortune, bound for Newtown (Wilmington now). Not long after Johann arrived in the new land, he married Mary Margaret Butchdor.

John Jacob was born a year later in 1730 and named after his father Johann Jacob Brake, but always went by his middle name, Jacob. Virginia passed a land law in 1730 encouraging people to settle in the western section of Virginia, giving them one thousand acres per family. Lord Fairfax had the land there surveyed by George Washington. After his father, Wilhelm, died in 1731, Johann sold his land which he worked for two years and departed for western Virginia with his wife and baby.

They left grandmother Mauri and Uncle Jacob in Edgecombe County, North Carolina.

Johann settled on land by Cedar Creek, Frederick County, Western Virginia and ended up building a fine home on the one thousand acres there in 1740. They were among the first settlers. Jacob remembered how his father worked as a chain carrier for a land surveyor in those days. The surveyor would have two strong men assisting him with two poles, each attached to a thirty-three-foot chain comprised of fifty links. Axe men would clear the trees and brush, to allow the two chain carriers to stretch the chains tight and get an accurate measurement. They would then make notches in the trees as they went along. They divided the land up into lots for settlers.

---

[22] David D. Edwards, *Brake, a Family, a Tradition, a Contribution and a Legacy (Baltimore: Gateway Press, Inc.) 2-4.*

Jacob brought his thoughts back to the present and continued to look over the river. He dreamed of building a home and settling down on his land. The next day, Jacob went to Moorefield to the blacksmiths to have new shoes placed on his favorite horse. He then saw Bemino Killbuck of the Lenape Indians, who were peaceful Indians of the area. Bemino was a medicine man, well known and liked by the white settlers of the valley of the South Branch River. Jacob saw Bemino in buckskin and moccasins, walking across the street in front of the blacksmith's shop.

"Bemino, what brought you to town?" Jacob asked as he waved him over.

"Oh, I just caught a runaway indentured servant for Peter Casey and now he will not pay me the thirty shillings he offered. He knocked me to the ground with his cane. This Peter is a crooked, mean man. Jacob, you are a good man, I can trust you," said Bemino as he rubbed his head by the headband which held his long black hair back.

Jacob frowned. "That is not right what Peter did! I will talk to him about this."

Shaking his head, Bemino said, "It will not help, Jacob."

"Maybe you're right, I might make matters worse." Taking a deep breath, Jacob continued, "Bemino, I wanted to talk to you about your daughter. I have a fondness for your Naddie ever since I saw her picking berries by my land. Do you think she would want me for a husband?"

"She says good things about you, Jacob. You need to talk to mother Nyeswanan. Women in tribe hold power."

"Tell Nyeswanan I will give her two of my fine horses and white man's metal needles for Naddie," said Jacob, rubbing his chin with his right hand.

Smiling, showing his missing teeth, Bemino said, "Needles will win her over, Jacob, much better than quill for sewing."

Bemino Killbuck and Nyeswanan gave Jacob their daughter to marry. Naddie was a beautiful but strong, rugged girl of fifteen. She wore her long hair in braids with a beaded band around her head. Her long buckskin dress had many colorful beads sewed to the neckline. Her moccasins came up her legs to mid-calf. The Lenape women would trade with the settlers for English clothes, which they wore also. The Lenape were a matriarchal tribe and families ran down through the woman's side.[23] The women decided who would be Chief among them and when to make a change. Naddie was very proud and headstrong, but warm and kind when needed.

In the area, there were a group of German families who only spoke German and belonged to the Evangelical Reformed Church. The main congregation met at a church in Frederick, Maryland, but the minister would make regular stops on horseback to the South Branch River area in Virginia. He married couples and baptized children, then recorded them in the church records. On a beautiful day, later that year, along the South Branch River, the minister married Naddie and Jacob.

Naddie worked hard alongside Jacob as they chopped down the trees and built a log house and farmed their land.

Eight years later, Jacob came home from Moorefield in 1755 and found Naddie working in the garden. Jacob hurried over to her, worried, with a frown on his face, he said, "Naddie, with the British and the French settling the land hereabouts, the Iroquois, the Delaware, and even the Shawnee are starting to raid neighboring settlements in the area."

"But they are only fighting back to keep their land," Naddie replied. "I really do not believe they would hurt us. They are part of my people."

"I hope you're right, but keep a rifle near you, and make certain it's ready to fire," said Jacob.

A year later, Jacob heard from town that war was declared with the French and Indians. Over the year, they had no problems with the Indians, but Jacob became more concerned. He stayed closer to the house as much as possible and taught his young sons to shoot a rifle.

By 1758, their little family had grown to five children. One day, while Jacob was out farming, the Shawnee Indians broke into their house through a window. His wife and her friend, Mrs. Neff, shot and killed a couple of the Indians.[24] The other few Indians ran away. Worried the

---

[23] Don Greene, *Shawnee Heritage IV, (No place: Lulu.com, 2014)*

[24] E.L. Judy, *History of Grant and Hardy Counties, West Virginia* (Charleston, West Virginia: Charleston Print Co., 1951) 98.

Shawnee would return, Jacob stayed home as long as possible. A week later, a large group of Shawnee Indians returned to attack their homestead. Jacob was out in the field with his six-year-old son, John, at the time. His wife, seeing the Indians coming, hid the three smaller children. Eight-year-old Mary Magdalene held little three-year old Isaac and 18-month-old Elizabeth, down in the brush behind the house. Ten-year old Jacob Jr., Naddie and Mrs. Neff kept firing on Indians from the windows, but it was useless. They were taken captive by the Indians and forced to walk at a fast pace toward northwestern Ohio. Hearing the Indians attacking the house, Jacob ran back with John and found his little children crying behind the house. His wife and son, Jacob Jr., were gone. Anxious and angry, Jacob rode into Moorefield, dropped the children off with friends and warned the people. Then he rounded up a group of men to track the Indians.

Terror-stricken, the people of the valley hurried to the fort which was really a stockade two miles away from Moorefield. The stockade was a large log house with enough room for several families. It had a wall of logs surrounding the building. It was considered a primary defense for the colonies at the time by Colonel George Washington.

While tracking the Indians, Jacob was horrified to find his wife scalped and dead on the trail. She couldn't keep up, being large with child, so the Shawnee killed her. The British paid the Shawnee Indians money for the scalps. Grief-stricken and beside himself, Jacob could find no signs of his son Jacob Jr. and the trail grew cold. Mrs. Neff escaped in the middle of the first night, after the Indians went to sleep, and made it to Fort Pleasant. Surprised and glad for her escape, Jacob realized the Shawnee wanted her to escape.

After the attack, Jacob was anxious the Indians would return, and he was too upset to take care of his children. He returned to Frederick County to his parents' home. He needed help with his children and emotional support.

~ * ~

The next year, still living at his parents' home, Jacob, sitting at the kitchen table, watched as his mother fixed supper. "Jacob, you are a young widower with four young children who need attention and motherly care," Mother said. "You cannot continue to live here; you need to get on with your life."

Jacob looked up and smiled. "Mother, I will marry as soon as I can find the right woman."

"You are a good-looking man with money. It shouldn't be hard for you to find a good woman."

Jacob stared at his mother but didn't say anything.

Soon afterwards, Jacob was invited to a social gathering at the neighbors' house. With his mother's push, he decided to go there. He wore his brown hair tied in back with a ribbon and a cocked three-sided hat. His clothing came from London, which was cheaper than clothes made in the colonies. The waistcoat hung over his white cotton shirt and brown breeches which were buttoned down the front. He prided himself with a clean-shaved civilized appearance. Jacob was a good-looking upright man in those days.

At the gathering, he saw a lovely woman across the yard. She was fair with delicate features and wore her blonde hair up in curls on top of her head. Her clothes were a large, long and wide dress with dome-shaped hoop skirts underneath. The front of the dress was revealing, but she wore a lovely scarf to cover the top of her breasts, which was the style of the day. Her name was Elizabeth Cooper. It was love at first sight. He found her to be an attractive good Christian lady who came from a good German family in the area.

Three months later, they were married, and the family moved back to his farm on the South Branch. The Indians were out of the area and living west of the mountains now. Even though he wrote a letter and sent money to his neighbor to fix up the farm, it still needed work. As he looked at the farm, it brought back memories of his first wife and eldest son. How different Elizabeth was to Naddie, like night and day. Elizabeth was more refined and delicate, while Naddie was a tough Indian girl. He wondered if Jacob Jr. was still alive and if he was living with the Indians.

A short time later, his father, Johann, suddenly became very ill and made out his will. Then in 1760, he died. Jacob and his family went back to his parents' house as soon as they received the news.

Jacob hugged his mother at his father's funeral, and with tears in his eyes, he said, "Mother, you need to come back to my house and live with us. This large home is too much for you."

"I know this is true, but let me stay here until the property is sold," said Margaret as tears fell down her cheeks.

Concerned for his mother, Jacob said, "I will build you and Elizabeth a beautiful big house. You will always be comfortable."

Jacob's father's farm in Frederick County, Virginia sold on June 2, 1762. With his inheritance money, Jacob bought six hundred and forty acres on the South Branch River in Hampshire County a few miles from his farm. The land was fifteen miles south of Moorefield, Virginia. It covered a broad valley between two mountain ranges in a breathtakingly beautiful countryside.

Jacob built a house on the land, resembling the castles along the Rhine River in Germany. The stone house was beside a beautiful cascading waterfall. High mountains with rough terrain rose up on both sides of the valley which were lined with heavy forests. Wildlife, which consisted of elk, deer, bear, rabbits, and muskrat, was plentiful. There was a powered grist mill at the foot of the falls, which became known as Brake's Mill. In the midst of all the building, Elizabeth gave birth to their son Abram in 1763.

Jacob then built a blacksmith shop, a distillery, a horse stable and a barn. Eventually, he possessed many cows, chickens, geese, pigs and sheep. He planted a large field of oats in the rich and fertile land behind the buildings. Jacob had quite a business and it was called Brake's Corner. The house became known as Brake's Castle. He even had a post office there for a while. It was a busy place, with people coming and going frequently.

The children went to the South Branch Valley School where they learned to read, write, math and help run the business. Jacob's mother, gravely ill, received communion by the minister of the Evangelical Reformed Church, on August 4, 1767, which he recorded it in the church books. She died a few days afterwards.

Part of the Treaty of Paris signed in 1763, ending the French

Indian War, was the return of the white captives, but it wasn't until 1768 that his son Jacob Jr. was to come home. A fur trader found Jacob Jr. with a band of Indians at White Woman's Creek. His brother John went back with the fur trader and found him at Fort Pitt.[25]

Jacob Jr. told his father how he tried to fight the Indians when they scalped his mother. The Indian then tied her scalp to his belt. Devastated, Jacob Jr. was then forced to walk three hundred miles, which took three months, to a Shawnee camp in Northwestern Ohio. There, he was adopted by a Shawnee family who lost a son in the Romney massacre in Virginia. At the camp, he was forced to run the gauntlet to gain acceptance of the tribe. The gauntlet consisted of two rows of Indians who held tree branches and as Jacob Jr. ran between the rows, the Indians would repeatedly strike him. Bruised and hurt, he crawled to his Shawnee mother who protected him. Once, after the Indians returned from a raiding party, they gave Jacob Jr. a bible, since he was the only one in the camp who could read. This gave him comfort and he became involved in the Baptist Church when he returned. He was accepted and lived with the Shawnee for ten years and ten months. Jacob Jr. acted more like an Indian than a white man. Even though Jacob was overwhelmed with joy to see his son, he was a stranger to him. He wouldn't wear white man's clothes, but wore buckskin and moccasins. He walked Indian style the rest of his life. Jacob Jr. was moody and kept to himself the first year he returned. Jacob was heartbroken for everything his son went through and frustrated over not being able to help him, but Jacob Jr. finally remembered his family and came out of his shell.

Jacob's beloved Elizabeth then died in childbirth in 1770. A great heaviness came over him at the loss. His sorrow was so great; Jacob couldn't eat for days. Across the country road was a small cemetery with a wire fence around it, where Elizabeth was buried with the infant. It became known as Brake Cemetery.

The large house was becoming emptier as Jacob watched his children marry and move away. Mary Magdalene married her childhood

---

[25] Lucullus Virgil McWhorter, *The Border Settlers of Northwestern Virginia from 1768 to 1795*(Baltimore: Genealogical Publishing Co., 1975) 309

friend, John Stump, who lived a short distance from Brake's Run off a tributary of South Branch at Stump Manor in 1771.

There were several German families in the area who were close friends to Jacob and called him Baron, a title his grandfather passed down to him. Jacob catered to his friends, the loyalists, who still pledged alliance to King George, which made a lot of people mad. They felt Jacob was a Tory, a name given to the loyalist, but Jacob really wanted to stay out of the fight and just run his business. Sitting at the table, Jacob had a tumbler of ale with his son, Isaac. Jacob, frowning, said, "I don't know whether you heard what happened to our neighbor?"

"What, Father?" said Isaac, leaning on the table.

Jacob took a deep breath and said, "He was out, complaining about the talk of war, and how we should not fight the British. He was beaten up and now he is afraid to leave the area."

Jumping out of his chair, upset, Isaac asked, "Who beat him up?"

Shaking his head, Jacob said, "The townspeople who are Patriots."

Now angry, Isaac asked, "You mean he isn't allowed to say what he thinks!"

"Not if it is against war with the British. You better be careful what you say and don't take sides," Jacob continued. "This rebellion can never succeed. There is nothing so foolish as to fight the British."

Frowning, Isaac said, "Father, I hate to tell you, John and Jacob Jr. are talking about joining the Patriots."

"I wish they would just stay out of the war, but they have a right to their beliefs." Taking another drink, Jacob said "Isaac, I cannot keep good help at the mill, with the young men leaving to join the militia, so I acquired an indentured servant from England. I paid for his passage to the colonies in exchange for him working for us for three years. The owner from the neighboring manor is renting me two of his slaves."

Scratching his head, Isaac asked, "Father, where are you going to keep them? We are not able to house them."

"They can stay in the room at the mill."

A few weeks later, the indentured servant and the two slaves all ran away, and Jacob never found them. It was a very expensive endeavor, which Jacob would never try again. They stole a rifle, ammunition, a large bag of buckskin and elk skin, linsey frock (overcoat) and a tow sheet and a bag. The servant was an Englishman, John Young, who had a lisp in his speech and stooped when he walked. The two slaves were Joe and Dick. Dick has one foot much longer than the other. Jacob posted an ad in the *Virginia Gazette* on March 25, 1775, offering a reward of forty shillings for their return.

MARCH 25. 775.　　　　　THE　　　　　NUMBER 1473

VIRGINIA GAZETTE

With the Freſheſt ADVICES,　　　　FOREIGN and DOMESTICK.

EI CIVITATE LIBERA UNGUAM MORTEMQUE　　　ALIERAS ESSE DEBERE —— Seen. de Ira. p. 18

Printed by JOHN DIXON　　　　Wm. HUNTER, at the Post Office

ALL Perſons may be ſupplied with this Paper as 12/6 a Year, and have Advertiſements (of a moderate Length) inſerted for 3/. the firſt Week, and 2/. each Week after. —— Printing Work done at this Office in the neateſt Manner, with Care and Expedition.

RUN away from the Subſcriber, on the ſouth Fork of the *South Branch*, In *Hampſhire* County, a Servant Man named JOHN YOUNG, an *Engliſhman*, he took with him a Linſey Frock, liſps in his Speech, ſtoops very much when he walks, and his Hair clipped on his Forehead.——— Alſo two NEGRO MEN, one named *JOE*, with a Linſey Frock, and other Clothes uſual for a labouring Slave. He ran away before, and was taken up at *Port Royal*, to which Place it is probable he intends again. The other Negro is named *DICK*, with the ſame Kind of Apparel that *Joe* had, and one of his Feet is much longer than the other. They took with them a Rifle and Ammunition, a large Buck-ſkin and Elk-ſkin dreſſed, and a Tow Sheet and Bag.——— Whoever brings the ſaid Servant to me, or ſecures him ſo that I may get him, ſhall have 40s. Reward, beſides what the Law allows; and whoever brings me the ſaid Negroes ſhall have what the Law allows.　　(1)　　JACOB BRAKE.

☞ I forewarn all Perſons from harbouring them, and Maſters of Veſſels from carrying them off the Continent.

George Jackson married Jacob's daughter, Elizabeth Brake, on November 13, 1776, in Moorefield, Virginia. Jacob watched his daughter, Elizabeth, now twenty years old. She was just a baby when her mother was killed by the Shawnee. Elizabeth wore a gold silk dress; she looked so pretty, and her husband was so handsome in his military uniform. Jacob looked at the two, so in love. Standing inside the church, Jacob walked over to the couple.

Even though it was a beautiful wedding, they could not avoid discussing the war.

"Down the road there was a group of men straggling along with muskets over their shoulders," said Elizabeth as she looked in George's eyes.

George lovingly placed his hand on her shoulders. "They are men on leave from the continental army. Elizabeth, I have been made Captain. I will probably have to leave soon. General Washington wants me to track the Indians the British have recruited."

"How could you leave me now? That doesn't give us much time together," Elizabeth said with her hands on her hips.

"I will come back to you. This war won't last long. I will get a Captain's pay and then we will have our own house together."

Jacob said, concerned, "Elizabeth can stay on with us while you are gone, George."

"Thank you, Jacob. I hear they are drafting the young men in the war as soon as they turn sixteen," said George.

"Yes, it worries me Abram will be sixteen soon," Jacob said, frowning.

Their son, John George Jackson, was born a year later while George was off, fighting.

Jacob married for a third time to Catherine Stump, the daughter of Michael and Anna Catharina Stump, a German neighbor. Anna, Jacob's mother in-law, didn't like Jacob. She made out her will, leaving Catherine the household goods and money, stating Jacob had no right or claim to them. Catherine was sixteen years younger than Jacob and married him for his money and fame. She never got along with Jacob's children. The following year, Catherine had a son, Michael, who she was devoted to the rest of her life.

Jacob's sons, John and Jacob Jr., were drafted in the Revolutionary War. John served one year under Captain Hohn and Colonel Van Metre. He marched to the mouth of Big Beaver and on to Fort McIntosh. From there, he marched on to Tuscarawas, Ohio and assisted in building a fort. Later, he served under Captain George Jackson (his brother-in-law) at Fort Buckhannon and fought the Indians. Jacob Jr.'s Indian training placed him as a lieutenant under Captain George Jackson's Company of Spies. If that wasn't enough, sixteen-year-old son Abram was drafted. Jacob was furious his sons were off fighting in this war and he was worried sick.

The Continental Congress passed a heavy tax law in 1780 to finance the war. They wanted eighty pounds for every hundred pounds of property. Taxation was just too steep! Jacob was enraged and hung the British flag on his house. Then in 1781, the Tory, John Claypole, and fifty of his men used Jacob's house as headquarters. When Governor Thomas Jefferson heard of this, he sent General Morgan and four hundred mountain men to break up the Tories. The four hundred men surrounded his house. Jacob, scared to death they were all going to get killed, readily surrendered. Some of the Tories were so ashamed they joined the Continental Army and fought as Patriots. Jacob was taken prisoner, along with his son, Isaac, but was released after a formal petition for pardon. Jacob and Isaac signed the petition.

I promised to return my allegiance and become a good citizen convinced by my error and freed from those mistaken prejudices that seduced me from my duty. 'I humbly pray for pardon, that the honorable board will save my innocent wife and children from ruin and misery.[26]

The judge said they were ignorant and misguided. Jacob was so glad the judge was lenient with them, because he heard others were hung for such charges.

When Jacob and Isaac returned home, they were shocked to find their place in ruins. Jacob, looking at his property, fuming with anger,

---

[26] H.U. Maxwell H.L. Swisher, *History of Hampshire County West Virginia* (Morgantown, West Virginia: A. Brown Boughner, Printer, 1897), 63.

cursed. "Isaac, the mill was half torn down, the house and outbuildings were burnt, and the oat fields are gone. Morgan's men confiscated my animals and feasted on my food and beer from the distillery."

Sitting on his horse, Isaac gasped. "Father, why would you have those Tories over against your own good judgment?"

"Those men were friends of mine. I feel horrible now that I let them use my house."

Isaac, beside himself with anger, said, "This will take a lot of work to rebuild. We need to find men and supplies. Since the house was made from stone, it can be fixed, but it will never be the same."

"Catherine's at her parents' house with Michael. They will stay there until I can rebuild," Jacob said, now with tears in his eyes.

"Where are we going to find the men and supplies?" asked Isaac.

"We will go to Fort Buckhannon; they will have men and supplies there."

A few weeks later, Abram, thin and tired, made his way back from the war. Hugging him, overjoyed, Jacob said, "It's so good to have you home. I thought I would never see you again."

"Father, it is so good to be home! It seems like all we did was march; my legs are so sore, I can hardly walk. I marched under Captain Bernina to Catfish on the Ohio River, then to Morgantown, Virginia, then back to Moorefield," said Abram.

When the census taker came by in 1782 to get a census for the heads of families in Hampshire County, Virginia, Jacob listed eight white and zero black. The house was livable, and the mill was back in operation. Jacob now had his sons back home. The next year, he found out in the *Virginia Gazette* that, even though the war ended on November 30, 1782, the final treaty was signed ten months later in Paris on April 11, 1783. That same year, Isaac married Mary Davis and settled nearby on a farm on the South Branch.

Hardy County was formed from Hampshire County in October of 1785, changing the county line, making Jacob's residence in Hardy County now.

Jacob, in 1788, rode home from Isaac's farm to find Catherine by the fireplace, sitting there knitting. "Catherine, Mary died in childbirth, but they were able to save the baby boy. Isaac is extremely upset and depressed. He wants nothing to do with the baby. I have offered to bring the baby here."

Catherine, hearing the news, fell back in her chair, for it was too much for her.

Jacob grabbed her smelling salts, placed them under her nose which brought her around. "Catherine are you, all right?" asked Jacob.

Catherine sighed and rubbed her forehead. She gave Jacob an indignant look. "What now, you want me to raise Isaac's baby?"

"I will find you help, but yes, he needs us now. Besides he will be like a brother to Michael," said Jacob with a stern voice. Michael, who was almost ten years older, loved little James and they grew to be inseparable best friends.

"Well, I guess that will have to be fine," Catherine said in a sarcastic voice.

"Isaac is going to have to move back here with his two-year-old son, Abraham, until he can get his feet on the ground again."

Catherine sighed. "I wonder how long that will be?"

Then a year later, Isaac married Rossana Almond. Nine months later, Sarah was born, and they all lived with Jacob and Catherine.

On the first census of the United States in 1790, Jacob listed the house and four outbuildings along with nine white souls, which would be Jacob, his wife Catherine and his sons Michael, Abram, Isaac, Isaac's wife, and Isaac's three children. Shortly after, Abram married his brother-in-law George's sister, Elizabeth Jackson and moved to Harrison County, Virginia.

Jacob, sitting in the parlor in 1803, smoking a pipe, looked towards Catherine in the rocking chair and said, "Did you know, Elizabeth and George are talking about moving to Zanesville, Ohio?"

"Yes, I heard George received a large parcel of land in Fails Township for being captain in the war," said Catherine.

Jacob frowned. "It might be a long time before I see the grandchildren again."

Catherine, looking up from her book, said, "You know, I can't see George farming, after being in politics for the last eight years.

"Maybe this will be a good break for him."

"Maybe."

"You know Isaac has been talking about moving to Ohio too."

Five years later, in 1808, Jacob, now seventy-eight years old, looked back over his life. It was quite a time in history.

Genealogy of John Jacob Brake

WILHELM JOSEPH DIETRICH VON BRAKE b. 27 April 1689 Hanover, Germany d. 1731 North Carolina m. Mauri Elizabeth Douglas b. 1694 Ayrshire, Scotland d. North Carolina

Children of Wilhelm and Mauri:
1. Johann Jacob Brake b. 5 January 1714 Hanover, Germany d. 1760 Frederick County, (West) Virginia m. Mary Margaret Butchlor 1729 North Carolina b. 1708 Lemgo, Hanover, Germany d. 1767 Hampshire Co., (West) Virginia.
2. Jacob Brake b. 1728 Cannomach, Prestonpars, East Lothan, Scotland d. 1820 North Carolina

Children of Johann Jacob Brake and Mary Margaret:
1. John Jacob Brake b. 1730 North Carolina d. 1809 Moorefield, Hardy Co., (West) Virginia
2. Martin Brake d. Germany
3. Elizabeth Brake House
4. Catherine Brake Gryder
5. Margaret Brake Batchler

John Jacob Brake b. 1730 North Carolina d. 1809 Moorefield, Hardy Co., (West) Virginia. m. (1) Naddie Nyeswanan 1747 Hampshire Co., (West) Virginia b. 1732 d. 1758 Hampshire Co., (West) Virginia. m. (2) Elizabeth Cooper 1759 b. Augusta (West) Virginia d. 1770 (3) Catherine Stump b. 1746 d. 1816.

Children of Jacob and Naddie's:
1. Jacob Brake Jr. b. 1747 Hampshire Co., (West) Virginia d. 1831

    Upshur Co., (West) Virginia m. Mary Slaughter d. 1830 (West) Virginia

2. John Brake b. 1752 Hampshire Co., (West) Virginia d. 1838 Clarksburg, (West) Virginia m. (1) Elizabeth Weatherholt in 1771 (2) Katherine Sears Shook in 1784
3. Isaac Brake b. 1755 Hampshire Co., (West) Virginia d. 1833 Union Co., Ohio m. (1) Mary Stiles Davis (2) Rosanna Alman 1789 Hardy Co., (West) Virginia
4. Mary Magdalene Brake b.1750 Hampshire Co., (West) Virginia m. John Stump 1771
5. Elizabeth Brake b. 1757 Hampshire Co., (West) Virginia d. 1812 Zanesville, Ohio m Col. George Jackson 13 November 1776 Moorefield, Hardy Co., (west) Virginia.

Children of Jacob and Elizabeth:
1. Abram Brake b. 1763 Hampshire Co, (West) Virginia d. 1842 (West) Virginia m. Mary Elizabeth Jackson
2. Infant Brake b.1770 d. 1770

Child of Jacob and Catherine:
Michael Brake b. 1779 Hardy Co., Virginia d. 17 April 1861 West Virginia m. Elizabeth Dasher.

Chapter Seven
Isaac Brake (1755-1833)

It was a simple funeral and Catherine left right after the graveside ceremony. She never said a word and never shed one tear. Even though Isaac knew his father was going to die, he was grief-stricken. When his father, Jacob, became gravely ill, he called his family together to say goodbye. Father believed when it was your time to go, God had the last say. He left everything to his wife, Catherine.

Isaac never got along with his stepmother, Catherine. He was upset with her and felt she married his father for his wealth and reputation, not for love. She came from wealth and there were few men in the area who met her standards. She was never close to any of Jacob's children. Catherine's parents didn't want anything to do with them either. After Catherine gave birth to Michael, she wanted everything for her son. Catherine disinherited all of the family, except her own son Michael, when Jacob died in 1809 at the old age of seventy-nine. He was buried in the Brake cemetery across the road from his homestead, beside his second wife, Elizabeth. This made Catherine mad.

As Isaac's wife, Rossana, stood by her father-in-law's grave and looked at the tombstones, she asked, "Isaac, is this your mother buried next to Jacob here in the cemetery?"

"No, Rosanna. That is Elizabeth, his second wife with her baby. She died in childbirth, along with the baby. My mother is buried a few miles from here. It's still so hard to believe my mother was killed by the Shawnee Indians when I was three. I'm sure you heard the story before, about my mother and my brother Jacob Jr. being captured by the Shawnee. Mother was killed because she couldn't keep up since she was pregnant. Then she was scalped in front of my brother, Jacob Jr. He was scared out of his mind, but was forced to march on to the Shawnee camp. He stayed for over ten years. Mother hid me in the brush when she heard the Indians, with my baby sister, Elizabeth and my older sister, Mary Magdalene, who protected us. It was not easy for us in those days, from what I have been told. Father was out of his mind, worrying and us children crying all the time. We were all scared the Shawnee would come back. A year later, Father went on to marry Elizabeth and we all loved her. He always wanted to be buried next to her."

"It all sounds so sad, now that you explain it more." Rosanna taking all this in, went on walking through the cemetery with Isaac, looking at each tombstone. Some were hard to read and covered with moss. "You never talked about that time in your life, Isaac."

Isaac, frowning, said, "I wanted to put it behind me."

"Isaac, where is your first wife, Mary, buried? Is she here in Brake Cemetery?"

"Yes, she is a few rows over. She died in 1788, in childbirth. It was just a miracle my son, James, didn't die with her. It was a very hard time for me. I lost my house on South Fork, after living there for five years, even after Father paid the taxes. I was so depressed; I didn't eat, work and I could hardly get out of bed. I could hardly take care of myself, let alone three-year-old Abraham and a new baby. My father took custody of Abraham and James. I was depressed, but Catherine held it against me."

Rosanna held Isaac's hand. "That is a lot to lose, Isaac."

Tears falling down Isaac's cheek, he continued, "My father's death has brought back a lot of memories. Abraham left as soon as he was old enough, married and moved to Upshur County. I haven't seen him or his family since then."

"James seems to like living at your father's house. He enjoys being with his Uncle Michael. They seem to be close," Rosanna said.

"True." Looking into Rosanna's eyes, Isaac said, "A powerful good came into my life when I met you, Rosanna. You brought happiness back into my life. Now ten years later and four more children, life is good."

~ * ~

Three years later, war broke out in 1812. Isaac, now fifty-seven, was thin and too old to fight. Several of the young men in the Moorfield, Virginia area were drafted and went off to fight.

After America beat the British in 1815, England flooded the American market with goods, making it easier to buy quality English products cheaper than what could be made in America, making jobs scarce. Everyone was talking about moving west, where there was more opportunity.

Isaac heard of a wagon train getting together to go west to Ohio in 1818. They had five children at that time, Sarah, also called Sallie, was twenty-eight and married to John Shirk. Adam was twenty-five, Margaret was twenty-three, Michael was twenty-one and Elizabeth was sixteen.

One night while eating supper, Isaac looked at his wife with a concerned look. "Rosanna, I want to go west with the children to Ohio. All Sallie talks about is going west with her husband. The government is giving land away there to anyone who fought in the wars. Some of the soldiers are selling their land cheap. The land is fertile with lots of game and it is getting crowded here."

"Isaac, we are getting old for such a trip, but if it means better life for our children and grandchildren, I want to go with them. Sallie and John will have their hands full with seven children. Those twin boys can be quite a handful. I can't believe they are two already," Rosanna said.

"We are going to have to leave in a few months. I know we have lived on the farm since 1799, but we will have to sell it and anything we don't need." Isaac continued. "James does not want to go to Ohio. He is courting Anna Mumford and working at the mill. He likes it here in Virginia, living with his Uncle Michael."

"James is a young man who has lived most of his life at Brake Castle, Isaac, but it will be sad to leave him," said Rosanna.

Isaac smiled and said, "I know the other children are excited about going."

Rosanna nodded. "It will be quite an adventure."

So, they said goodbye to their many friends and relatives and took off to the new land. Worried about what was ahead and wondering if they made a mistake, the Brake and Shirk families went to the Ohio wilderness, with other families around Moorefield. They loaded their wagons with all their belongings, leaving little space for the family. The spinning wheel collapsed and didn't take up much room. The axe, shovel and other tools were kept in a box alongside the wagon. Pewter plates, cast iron pots and pans were kept in another box, along with the silverware, an expensive wedding present from Jacob, that was kept in its own little box. Large trunks held their clothes, linen, the featherbed, and the treasured Bible. They took lots of food, including a smoked ham, squash, potatoes, dried beans, apples, walnuts, and corn. They brought barley, oats and turnips for the horses, along with two cows. As they pulled out with the large group of wagons, Isaac looked back over his shoulder for one last look of what they were leaving behind.

Travel was slow and they could only do a few miles a day. At first, they went through every town on its way west picking up more wagons. Then the road went through rugged dirt trails through the mountains and streams. Every so often, a wooden wheel would break, and they would have to pull up and put on the spare. It was a long and hard six-week journey.

They crossed the Ohio River at Sistersville, (West) Virginia. There, they found a large ferry run by Henry Jolly.[27] They moved one wagon at time on the ferry and slowly went across to the other side into the new state of Ohio. Large, covered wagons were pulled by oxen and the smaller wagons with teams of horses. The ferry toll rate was six cents a person or a horse. It took three days to get all the wagons across. Before the ferry, they would have had to cross in the winter when the river was frozen. How scary that would be, knowing the ice could crack at any moment. They went on through Ohio until at last, they came to Chillicothe in Ross County, where there was a land office. It was nice to see civilization again!

It was a boom town of about fifty family houses, stores, offices

---

[27] Luke N. Peters, *Sistersville and Tyler County* (Charleston, South Carolina: Arcadia Publishing, 2007), 96.

and a distillery. People were putting up buildings at every turn. There was a steady flow of wagon trains coming through the city. They went to the land office to apply for land, and from there, they went to the courthouse and registered the land. They waited here for land in the Virginia Military District of Ohio and stayed until they got the deed for the land, along with enough supplies. Then in 1820, they moved on to Liberty Township, Union County, Ohio, which was another eighty-eight miles.

The census taker came that same year. He wrote down the names of the families where he found them. Isaac and his family were in Union Township at the time on their way to Liberty Township.

Virginia gave her soldiers who served in French and Indian War, Revolutionary War and War of 1812 land bounty in Ohio and Kentucky; one hundred to fifteen thousand acres, depending on rank and length of service. Some of the families on the wagon train received land bounty from the war. Isaac purchased his farm from Joshua Judy, who owned a great deal of land in Liberty Township.

While in Ross County, Isaac met the family of Mordecia Baughan and his wife Eve Baumgartner Baughan from North Carolina, but they were originally from Culpepper, Virginia. They also went on to Liberty Township with the Brakes and Shirks. Isaac's daughter, Elizabeth, fell in love with Mordecia's son, Jeremiah on the trail. Then in 1824, four years later, Elizabeth married Jeremiah Baughan

Isaac Shirk settled in Liberty Township, on the farm by Mill Creek. John and Sallie and the grandkids stayed with them on the farm until they could get their cabin built. Liberty Township was covered by a huge forest, where large walnut trees were in abundance. Walnut trees were sturdy strong wood that could be used to build the cabins. They dug a square trench two feet deep to the size of the cabin. Then set up logs, leaving space for the fireplace and door. They closely placed rows of logs all the same length. The earth was packed in around each log, and over the logs was placed a bark roof. There was a rough puncheon floor, hewed flat with an axe. Leather hinges were attached to the door and windows. They all worked together to build the log cabins, one at a time.

There were very few settlements in the area and no roads, just Indian trails and bridle paths. Wild animals could be seen everywhere;

turkeys running across the paths and deer standing off in the distance at the edge of the woods. People stayed together when walking in the woods, knowing that danger could be lurking only a few feet away. At night, they could hear the howl of the wolf and the scream of the panther in the woods. Isaac slept anxiously, with his rifle at his bedside. A few Indians were in the area still, but they were mostly friendly. The people on the wagon train grew closely connected and lived in a close area in Liberty Township. They were always ready to help one another and became part of a big family.

The last few years of Rosanna's life, she experienced spells where she would become extremely thirsty and felt she would die if she didn't get something to drink. One day in 1826, they went to the neighbor's house, where a shooting match was being held, where you could win prizes. It always was a good time.

Rosanna, not feeling well, walked over to Isaac who was waiting his turn at the shooting match. "Isaac, I am going home now."

"Rosanna, do you want me to go with you?"

"No, you stay and enjoy yourself."

Later that day, Isaac left to go check on her. He became anxious when he did not find her home and rode back to the neighbor's house. Everyone went out looking for her. They went through the woods, blowing horns, covering as much land as we could before dark. The next morning, the neighbors found her body by the main road near a stream. She must have gone for the water and passed out before she got any. It was so sad, looking for his wife and then finding her dead. It was a hard thing to lose Rossana. Isaac missed his wife and thought of her daily, but he had the love and company of his large family around him. Sarah and John Shirk had fourteen children, Adam and Eve Baughan had eight children, Michael and Polly Shirk had twelve children, and Elizabeth and Jeremiah Baughan had six children. Isaac did get letters from James and Anna, who married and had several children, back in Virginia.

When Isaac died, he was buried by his wife at New Mill Creek Cemetery, by his farm.

Genealogy of Isaac Brake

ISAAC BRAKE b.1755 in Hampshire County, Virginia d. 1833 Union Co., Ohio m. (1) Mary Stiles Davis (2) Rosanna Alman in 1789 Hardy Co., Virginia. Rosanna b. 1769 Virginia d. 1826 Liberty Twp., Union County, Ohio.

Children of Isaac and (1) Mary Brake:
1. Abraham Brake b. 21 January 1786 (West) Virginia d. 27 January 1864 Licking Co., Ohio
2. James Brake b. 1788 (West) Virginia m. Anna Mumford d. 1825 (West) Virginia

Children of Isaac and Rosanna:
1. Sarah Brake b. 02 January 1790 (West) Virginia, d. 25 September 1869 Union Co., Ohio m. John Shirk 02 August 1805 (West) Virginia.
2. Adam Brake b. 15 Mar 1794 Moorefield, Hardy Co., (West) Virginia. d. 15 May 1870 Union Co., Ohio m. Eve Faye Baughan 19 January 1826 Union Co., Ohio.
3. Margaret Brake b. 1795 Hardy Co., (West) Virginia d. 1869 Union Co., Ohio.
4. Michael J. Brake b. 1798 (West) Virginia d. 15 Jan 1879 Ohio m. Mary Shirk 15 January 1829 Union Co., Ohio.
5. Elizabeth Brake b. 15 June 1802 Hardy Co., (West) Virginia, d. 27 September 1878 Union Co., Ohio m. Jeremiah Baughan 28 December 1824 Union Co., Ohio

Chapter Eight
Job Rossell (1750-1830)

Angry and sad, Job could not accept his grandfather Zachariah's death. Now eleven years old, Job wondered how God could let his grandfather die. Job had been very close to his grandparents, since they practically raised him. His mother Elizabeth died right after his birth, leaving James, his father, to raise infant Job and his sisters Hope, just five then and Margaret, only two. He was born in Northampton,[28] Burlington County, in the Providence of New Jersey in 1750. Northampton was close to Philadelphia. His father, a farmer, lived close to his grandparents.

At the graveside funeral, there were his aunts, uncles and cousins. It was a quiet funeral. No open mourning or long prayers, only silent prayers. Standing by his uncle, Job heard someone call his uncle "Zachariah Rossell Esquire." To Job, he was just Uncle Zach. Job, looking up into his uncle's eyes with tears running down his cheek, asked, "How can Grandfather die, he wasn't old?"

"He was sixty-nine, Job," said Zach as he placed his hand on Job's shoulder.

Job was impressed with his uncle who held a prestige title; he was very popular and wealthy. Zach owned the Black Horse Tavern. It was a prosperous hotel on Main Street. In fact, he owned most of the property on the west side of Main Street.[29]

---

[28] What is now Mount Holly was originally formed as Northampton on November 6, 1688.

[29] Henry C. Shinn, *The History of Mount Holly* (Mount Holly, New Jersey: The Mount Holly Herald, 1957) p31.

"Sixty-nine, I didn't know he was that old."

"He was young at heart. Always remember him, his good nature and how much he loved you, Job," said Uncle Zach.

"I will. I will miss him and his stories," said Job has he wiped the tears from his eyes.

"Yes, he loved to talk about his own childhood. You can always come to me if you need anything."

After the funeral, Job and his family went to the Black Horse Tavern where a large sign hung outside by the front porch with a picture of King George III, in his red coat, mounted on a large black horse. The sign creaked in the wind and gave Job a chill up his spine. Inside, Uncle Zach had food laid out on the bar along with pitchers of rum and tea. Uncle Zach was Justice of Peace under King George III but talked publicly for liberty. This led to many debates, some heated, even among the relatives.

The next day, the family met back at Grandfather's farm where his will was read by the lawyer. Job stood by his father and listened. Grandfather left his farm to Uncle Zach, but his grandmother, Mary, was to live there while she was his widow. Job's father was given twenty shillings,[30] which was about two weeks' wages for the middle-class man.

---

[30] AncestryLibrary.com-New Jersey, Abstract of Wills, 1670-1817.

Zachariah Rossell

ZACHARIAH ROSSELL, ESQ., AGE 86

Ten years later, Job's father, James, moved to Lancaster County, Pennsylvania in 1771, but Job stayed in Northampton and close to Uncle Zach.

Job married Huldah Kemble, the daughter of Vespasian and Rachel Kemble, an old and prominent Quaker family who came to the colonies in 1693 from England. They were married on May 13, 1775 in Northampton Quaker meeting house.

After coming home from the business trip, in mid-January of

1776, Job found Huldah pounding bread dough in the kitchen.

"Job, you're home late," said Huldah, with a frown on her face.

"Sorry, they were passing out pamphlets downtown by the town hall today. In the pamphlet called *Common Sense,*[31] the author argues for independence from England and how we should create a democratic republic," said Job excited as he held up the pamphlet.

"Who wrote it?" asked Huldah, while she placed the bread dough in the bread pan and placed a cloth over it. She then set it in a warm area to let the dough rise.

"I don't know. It doesn't say," said Job.

"You read it already?"

"Yes, most of it. It does make me want to tell King George to leave us alone. We don't need a King thousands of miles away ruling us. It is not fair that we are not allowed to vote on any decisions made by Parliament that concern us here in the Colonies."

"I would like to read it too."

"I noticed Uncle Zach painted King George III off his sign at the *Black Horse Tavern.*"

"Yes, his wife told me about that at the quilting bee. I also heard your Uncle Zach has donated his money to the revolutionary cause," said Huldah.

On the hot day of July 8th, 1776 Job was meeting some Quaker men in Philadelphia at a meeting house to discuss joining the militia when the large bell in the steeple of the Pennsylvania State House began ringing continuously. Everyone ran out of their buildings and down to the town hall were a man in white shirt, dark breeches, and a white wig with a tricorn hat read the letter to King George. It was called *The Declaration of Independence.* Afterwards, men tore down the flags of England and set them on fire. Men were shouting, "Yes!" with their arms up in the air. Job watched and was caught up in the excitement.

When Job returned home, he told his wife what he saw.

---

[31] Thomas Paine, *Common Sense; Addressed to the inhabitants of America, on the following interesting subjects* (Philadelphia: R. Bell, 1776)

Huldah was working on the spinning wheel with the flax sticks which she worked to make thread to make clothes for her family. She said, "How exciting, what are you thinking of doing?"

"There are men who call themselves Free Quakers since they have been disowned by their Quaker community. In their society, no one is disowned. Everyone is encouraged to do their military duties. Everything else is the same as the old Quaker faith. I met two men who were Free Quakers at the town house.[32] They are starting meetings with others with the same belief. I am joining them."

"I don't know, Job," said Huldah with a worried look on her face.

"Why the worried look?"

"Wondering what my parents will think."

A few months later, after much thought, while Job ate his dinner with his wife he said, "I am enlisting in the New Jersey militia. One of the officers came to town, asking for men to defend New Jersey in the War for Independence.[33] I will only sign up for a few months. They promise to pay me a good wage."

"Holds thee in the light," said Huldah.

Job loved the Quaker expression for keeping someone in their thoughts and in their prayers. "God will keep me and bring me home to you, but I want you to go someplace safe until I can come home."

"I will go and stay with my parents until you come for me," said Huldah.

"That is good, they live further out in the country, away from the main roads," said Job.

"I pray my beloved country will be free," said Huldah. She joined the New Jersey Society of the Relief and Encouragement of the Men of the Continental Army. They were a group of women who made hand-sewn shirts, hose and woolen wraps for the men.

---

[32] Rufus Jones, *The Quakers in the American Colonies* (New York: W. W. Norton and Company, Inc. 1966), p 570.

[33] New Jersey single citations of the NJ DOD materials FHL Roll #571320 paid for services rendered. Private in NJ Militia.

Late in 1776, two thousand British and Hessians stormed into town under Carl von Donop. They forced people out of their houses in order for their officers to have a place to stay. Then they set up camp kitchens in the middle of Main Street. The army turned their horses into the crop fields of the farmers and making total chaos of the town.[34] Fear gripped the town people. There were British spies posted in the town. Uncle Zach was arrested by the British and his home was completely sacked. He was forced to walk to New York with other prisoners where they were placed in the prison ship *Jersey* until the end of the war.

Job served with the New Jersey militia encampment of six hundred men under Colonel Samuel Griffin on the Iron Works Hill outside Northampton on December 23 and 24, 1776. After several skirmishes with the British and Hessians, the New Jersey militia were run off. They prevented the Hessians from being where they were assigned to be in Bordentown, New Jersey to assist the British at Trenton. There, the British and Hessians were defeated by George Washington the night of December 25th when he crossed the Delaware.

On February 29, 1780, Job received certificate number 112 for eight hundred and ninety-one dollars. He received the money with interest on January 1, 1787 from the New Jersey State Treasury.[35] Job was also given land in the Western Reserve of Pennsylvania for fighting in the war. In 1783, Uncle Zach was exchanged for British prisoners and returned home. Later that year, Job walked into the tavern to find Uncle Zach cleaning the walls. He was skin and bones with dark sunken eyes, but he had spirit. "Uncle Zach, it is so good to see you again," said Job.

"Yes, I never thought I would get off that prison ship alive," said Zach.

"Was it as bad as they say," asked Job, grabbing a broom.

"It was hell, over a thousand men were cramped below deck with no light or fresh air. I watched at least a dozen men die every day and thought I would be next."

---

[34] Lloyd E. Griscom, *Burlington County and The American Revolution,* (New Jersey: Burlington County Cultural and Heritage Commission,1976) p. 9- 10.

[35] New Jersey State Archives: Documentation of Payment to Job Rozel.

"I can't even imagine; how horrible."

"So many had dysentery or the fever. We heard moans and crying constantly. Very little to eat or drink. I prayed constantly for strength to live through it."

"We all prayed for you to return to us. It is so good to see you never gave up. You plan to reopen the *Black Horse Tavern?*"

"Yes, and it will be better than ever. Enough of me, how are you and Huldah doing?"

"We are doing well; we have three boys and one daughter."

~ * ~

In 1786, Huldah died shortly after giving birth to their daughter, Mary. Job's sister Hope helped with the children. Even though Quakers don't show grief, it was a sad time for Job. Heartbroken, Job went on living through his depression. Then two years later he met Mary Hughs and started courting her. Life was full of joy again.

On April 30, 1789, everyone in town was in the streets, cheering with the new American flag flying, for it was George Washington's inauguration in New York City. There were parties and celebrations all over the country. Job and his children went to the *Black Horse Tavern* for a grand party put on by Uncle Zach. The big old sign still creaked in the wind as they opened the large red wooden door to the tavern. The tavern was packed with cheerful people. When he saw Mary Hughs placing cherry pies on the bar with the other food, he walked over to her.

"It's so good to see everyone happy again," said Job.

"I really like what your uncle Zach has done to *The Black Horse Tavern*, it is better than ever," said Mary.

Job looked inside the large open room. Next to a large stone fireplace, people congregated around the fire. It was a chilly day for April. The townspeople were cheerful and in high spirits. Their beloved George Washington was their new president of their new independent country. New round tables and chairs were scattered around the room with a candle in the middle of each table. On the tavern wall was posted the *New Jersey Gazette* where people were reading the latest news. The bar was new and had a large spread of food. In the back corner was a leathery-faced man, with a near-toothless grin, playing the fiddle. Zach was all smiles, going around, shaking everyone's hands.

"Uncle Zach looks like his old self again," said Job.

"He is the most industrious man I have ever met," said Mary.

"Yes, he is." Job smiled as he watched as his eldest son, James, now eleven, take care of his two brothers and two sisters, getting them food and finding a table. The two youngest, John, four and Mary, three, were being extra good today. Job and Mary went around, visiting with the neighbors. It was a great day to be alive.

Riding back in the buggy that night as Job took Mary to her home, they watched night lamplighter fill the lamps with whale oil and light the lamps along the streets. It left a beautiful glow down the cobblestone street. Job placed his arm around Mary and asked her to marry him.

~ * ~

In 1790, Job and his family decided to move to Fayette County, Pennsylvania along with his sister, Hope, and her husband, Caleb Gaskill. Job received eighty-one acres of land from the government there. His father, James, already left and moved to Bedford, Bedford County, Pennsylvania in 1787. Job's land was another ninety-six miles west. His family built a log home and farm in Franklin Township. Job died in Franklin Township, Fayette County, Pennsylvania in 1830. Job's will:

In the Name of God, Amen. I John Rosell of the Township of Franklin in the County of Fayette, farmer being very weak in body, but of sound mind memory and understanding (blessed be God for the same) do make and publish this my last will and testament in manner and form following. to wit. Principally, and first of all, I commend my immortal soul unto the hands of God who gave it. and my body to the earth, to be buried in a decent and christian like manner, at the discretion of my Executor hereinafter named, And as to such worldly estate, wherewith it hath pleased God to bless me in this life. I give and dispose of the same in the following manner. to wit. first it is my will, and I do order, that all my just debts and funeral expences, be duly paid and satisfied as soon as conveniently can be after my decease. And as touching all the rest, residue, and remainder of my estate real and personal, of what kind or Nature soever the same may be — Item it is my will and desire that my wife Mary Rosell shall keep and retain all the prop-

1050

...erty that she brought with her at the time of our marriage and also our goods and copper kettle, and likewise I give and bequeath to her a comfortable maintenance, and support from the proceeds of my Estate so long as she shall remain my widow. Item I give and bequeath unto Elizabeth Nagle our grey mare & colt, as a compensation for services rendered to the family it is my wearing apparel to be divided equally between my three sons, James, Job and John Russell. And with respect to the remainder of my Estate both real & personal, I dispose of it in the following manner to wit — to my son Job Russell our equal part, to my son John Russell our equal part, to my daughter Ann Rodgers our equal part, to my daughter Mary Addis our equal part, and to my grand son Job Russell son of James Russell one equal part. All the above mentioned legacies to my said wife. I do hereby declare to be in lieu and stead of her dower at common law. And lastly I nominate constitute and appoint my said wife, and my son James Russell, to be the Executors of this my will, hereby revoking all other wills legacies and bequests by me heretofore made and declaring this and no other to be my last will and testament, in the presence of us who, who in his presence and at his request have subscribed as witnesses — In witness whereof I have hereunto set my hand and seal the twenty first day of March — in the year of Our Lord eighteen hundred and twenty nine. N.B. The words interlined between the 16 and 17 lines from top down before signing

Job Russell (Seal)

Witnesses present
Robert Smith
Robt Smith Junior
John Patterson.

Genealogy of Zachariah Rossell

ZACHARIAH ROSSELL b. 1700 Eayrestown, Burlington, New Jersey d. 26 March 1761 Northampton, New Jersey m Mary Hilliard daughter of John Hilliard and Martha Devonish 4 July 1725.

Children of Zachariah and Mary:
1. Joseph Rossell b 1716 d 1756 m. Anne Alcott 27 December 1737
2. Sarah Rossell b. 1718 d. 1767 m. Martin Scott 12 January1735.
3. Anne Rossell b 1720 d. 1767 m. Samuel Hollingshead 9 July 1736.
4. Zachariah Rossell Jr. b. 1723 Eayrestown, New Jersey d. 21 February 1815 Mt Holly New Jersey m. Margaret Clark 25 January 1748 Mount Holly, New Jersey.
5. Zebulon Rossell b. 1725 d. 1817
6. James Rossell b. 1727 Northampton, New Jersey d. 1817 Somerset, Pennsylvania m. Elizabeth Allcott daughter of William Alcott and Ann Nomaiden 13 May 1745 Northampton, New Jersey b. 1720 Burlington, New Jersey d. 1750 Pennsylvania
7. Brazillai Rossell b 1729 d. 1817

Children of James Rossell and Elizabeth:
1. Hope Rossell b. 1745 Northampton, New Jersey d. 1817 Pancoast burg, Ohio m. Caleb Gaskill 16 July 1765.
2. Margaret Rossell b. 1746 Northampton, New Jersey m. Mathew West
3. Job Rossell b. 1750 Burlington, New Jersey d. 21 April 1830 Fayette, Pennsylvania. (1) m. Huldah Kemble daughter of

Vespasian Kemble and Rachel Haines 13 May 1775 Northampton, New Jersey. Huldah b. 1754 d. 1787 (2) m. Mary Hughs after 1787.

Children of Job and Huldah:
1. James Rossell b. 1778 New Jersey d. 1812 m. Anna Fits
2. Job Rossell Jr. b. 1779 New Jersey d. 5 May 1857 Ohio, m. Elizabeth Rogers 1801.
3. Hope Rossell b. 16 October 1783 New Jersey d. 20 August 1867 Columbiana Co., Ohio m. Thomas Rogers 1801.
4. John Rossell b. 25 October 1785 New Jersey d. 6 Dec 1858 Union Co., Ohio (1) m. Phebe Dooley 1807 Fayette Co., Pennsylvania (2) Susannah Elliott 1845 Marlboro, Ohio.
5. Mary Rossell b. 1787 New Jersey m. John Addis.
6. Thomas Rossell
7. Caleb Rossell

Chapter Nine
Isaac Elliott 1756-1839

It was hard to be a good Quaker in 1776. You wanted to fight for your country's Independence, but your religion says no. "The light of God is in everybody. You must love your enemy and not fight," said his father, Benjamin Elliot. His father was a stern man who always knew right from wrong. Now twenty years old, Isaac wished he knew. Isaac felt torn, but he would stay true to his religion. His friends his were going off to fight and he felt left behind. Was it right to stay and court the love of his life, Alice, while there was a war going on in the area? Alice Wilkinson, the prettiest girl around, was the daughter of Joseph Wilkinson, a Quaker immigrant from Ballina Cree, Antrim, Ireland, and now of London Grove, Pennsylvania.

A military man rode to the farm on March 17, 1777 and announced Pennsylvania had passed a law that all white men between the ages of eighteen and fifty-three were automatically enrolled in the militia and those who sought to avoid the conscription would have a steep fine.

Two months later, Isaac received a statement from the government. Upset, he found his father in the barn feeding the horses.

"Father, now I'm fined 3.10.0 lbs. by this warrant. It states, 'For failure to meet and exercise in order to learn the art of military as required in the Act of Assembly of Feb 14, 1777'," said Isaac.

"I also received a fine. We will pay the fine, Isaac. It is a small price to pay to stay faithful. I also need you here on the farm to help me," said Benjamin.

"This is not right to fine us!"

"Maybe so, but with so many gone, there will not be many crops this year. Someone has to grow the wheat and corn."

"Father, we should double the crop this year. It will be our own way of helping the cause."

"Yes, and God will show us the way to help without fighting."

"The people in town treat me like I was a spy for the British. It makes me feel so uneasy, even though they know my beliefs."

"Show them love and never hate for their beliefs. Tell them, if asked, you are for independence and you are not a Loyalist."

Two years later, Isaac and Alice Wilkinson found the need to marry and were married in York County, Pennsylvania on March 7, 1778. They stayed with his father, and their first son was born five months later. He was named Benjamin, after Isaac's father.

In the parlor of the farm, two years later, Isaac found his father resting, smoking his pipe.

"Father, there is a group of Quakers in the area that are leaving for Washington County," said Isaac.

"Yes, I heard of the group of young families getting ready to leave. It has been hard on you and Alice, living here, and I know you want your own place," said father.

"Yes, and now I was fined another fifteen lbs. for failure to provide one able-bodied recruit for the Continental Army. We are more than ready to move away from this war."

"It will be hard with Alice pregnant and two children. Little Ben is only two and Joseph only a few months old."

"We are healthy and with all our friends going, we will be fine. The land is fertile and cheap there."

"You can take two cows and two horses with you. The children will need milk."

After long goodbyes to the family, Isaac and Alice moved west of the mountains to Washington County, Pennsylvania and settled in East Findley Township in the newly settled Quaker settlement.[36] Then later in 1780, their son, Moses, was born there in their log cabin.

Coming home from a hunting trip the following year, Isaac found

---

[36] Boyd Crumrine, *History of Washington County, Pennsylvania* (Philadelphia: L.H. Everts and Co. 1882) 777.

Alice in the garden. "Alice, I saw a roaming band of Delaware Indians in the area. It looked like a hunting party of young men. I was told their camp was by the Ohio River."

"Did they give you any problems?" Asked Alice.

"No, but it is the first time I saw Indians and didn't know what to expect. It was scary."

Three years later, Isaac bought eighty acres in Monaghan Township and built a two-story house and barn. [37] After the War of Independence, more Quakers moved to the area from Eastern Pennsylvania. Among them were their soon to become close friends, the Kirk and Supler families. (The story of John Supler covers 1780 to 1816 in Washington County).

~ * ~

In the spring of 1816, Isaac and Alice, eight grown children and their families all moved to Stark County, Ohio to a Quaker settlement. There, the government sold them fertile land, cheap.

Isaac, now sixty, with the help of fellow neighbors, erected a small cabin in Lexington Township, Stark County, Ohio. The winter of 1817, there was a great snowstorm. It snowed for four days, leaving four feet of snow that lasted for four months with the temperature staying below freezing. Some of the deer died of starvation. Once they stepped in the snow, they couldn't get out. Isaac made snowshoes from the branches of trees and got out with his neighbors to collect the frozen deer, hauling them with help on sleighs. They sold the deerskins for seventy-five cents apiece. With plenty of meat, the family survived that terrible winter. The game was abundant with not only the deer but large flocks of turkey. What a welcome sight spring was that year, [38]

Isaac and Alice were in the garden, planting seed, when Alice saw a rattlesnake.

---

[37] 1783 tax records for Monaghan Township, Washington County.

[38] William Henry Perrin, *History of Stark County Ohio* (Chicago: Baskin and Battey Historical Publishers, 1881), 424.

Standing stiff as a board, Alice yelled, "Isaac, help."

"Don't move," said Isaac, as he grabbed the water barrel, dumping it and putting it down by the snake and gently moving the snake into the barrel with his hoe. Then turning the barrel up, he trapped the snake inside the barrel. It was four feet long with eight rattles. Isaac ran and got his rifle from over the fireplace and shot the snake. He went to gather the neighbors and they went out shooting all the rattlesnakes they could find.

Not long after that, Isaac and Alice were awaken in the night by wolves howling. Isaac got up and grabbed his rifle not waiting to dress. He ran off shooting at the wolves to drive them off before they injured his animals. He came back into the house to find Alice standing by the door.

"Isaac, what are you doing?" asked Alice.

"I wanted to kill the wolves, but all I did was scared them off," said Isaac.

"The way you ran out, I was afraid they would get you."

"The wolves killed three of our neighbor's sheep last night and they were big sheep."

"Did they get our chickens?"

"No, but it was close. They were near the chicken house. I bet there was over six wolves in the pack."

"Sometimes I wish we were closer to our children."

At the Quaker meeting house, one of the elders talked about slavery and how the Quaker communities in the area worked to help the runaway slaves. They talked about the settlement close by and the need to help them.

One night, Isaac sat at the kitchen table and asked for a second helping of apple pie. "Alice, we need to help the black settlement nearby. It is about a mile east of Williamsport," said Isaac.

Alice cut him a generous piece then folded her hands on the table. "Is that the group called New Guinea they were talking about at the meeting, last first day?"

"Yes, would you like to take some clothing and food to them?"

"That would be nice, let me gather some things together."

Upon entering the settlement in a hilly area by the Mahoning

River, Isaac saw Alice's eyes widen as she looked at the twenty wooden shacks with vegetable gardens behind each place in the small area. There were a large number of skinny children in rags, playing. One of the large black men came out to greet them. The women and children all looked scared at first, but after finding out that Alice and Isaac were Quakers, they became friendly. They had been told the Quakers were friends and were to be trusted.

"Hello, friend, we bring food and clothing," said Isaac.

"Thank you, sir," said the black man.

"How many are there?"

"There are about two hundred freed and runaway slaves here. I am a freed slave from Virginia. I work as an operator in the Underground Railroad. I hope to get them to Canada, a few at a time, where they are welcomed."

"Is that a church over there with a cross on the door?"

"Yes, it is called Christ's Disciples and there is a small cemetery behind it."[39]

"It must be a comfort to the people."

"Yes, a pastor from a local church comes out once a week to give services."

"The other friends in the area are gathering more food and clothing. Is there anything else you need?"

"Any old blankets you have and dishes you can get would help."

"I will get the word out what you need. We will pray for your safety."

As they left in the buggy, Alice said, "I feel so sorry for those people. Isaac, is there more we can do for them?

"Yes, we will tell our family and friends. They will be more than willing to help."

~ * ~

[39] William Henry Perrin, *History of Stark County Ohio* (Chicago: Baskin and Battey Historical Publishers, 1881), 429.

Seven years later, feeling old, Isaac and Alice moved into a small house next to their son, Ben, who lived seven miles by Marlborough. Alice, at seventy-one, became sick and died on June 29, 1827. She was buried nearby in the Deer Creek Quaker Hill Cemetery.

Isaac's father, Benjamin, had a silver-headed cane made with his initials and date on it which he passed down to his oldest son, Isaac.[40] Now Isaac passed it on to his oldest son, Ben.

In 1838, Ben left one dollar to each of his sons, Benjamin and Moses and the heirs of Joseph in his will made in Lexington Township, Stark County.

---

[40] John D. Elliot, *Reunion and Sketch of the Elliot Family* (Toledo, Ohio: Sumner Folsom and Co., 1875), 3.

Genealogy of Isaac Elliott

ISAAC ELLIOTT b. 24 March 1756 York Co., Pennsylvania d. 18 June 1839 Lexington, Stark Co., Ohio m. Alice Wilkinson 7 March 1778 York Co., Pennsylvania b.10 December 1755 Chester Co., Pennsylvania d. 29 June1827 Stark Co., Ohio

Children of Isaac and Alice:
1. Benjamin Elliott b. 21 February 1778 York Co., Pennsylvania d. 4 August 1859 Marlboro, Ohio
2. Joseph Elliott b. 1779 York Co., Pennsylvania d. 1837
3. Lydia Elliott b. 1780 Washington Co., Pennsylvania
4. Alice Elliott b. 1782 Washington Co., Pennsylvania
5. Francis Elliott b. 1784 Washington Co., Pennsylvania d. 1870 m. Mary Burden
6. Elizabeth Elliott b. 1785 Washington Co., Pennsylvania d. 1850 m. William McCall
7. Isaac Elliott Jr. b. 1787 Washington Co., Pennsylvania d. 1859 Logan Co., Ohio m. #1 Rebecca Greer #2 Ruth McCall
8. Mary Elliott b. 1788 Washington Co., Pennsylvania
9. Moses Elliott b. 1793 Washington Co., Pennsylvania d. 1853 m. Rebecca Dooley

Chapter Ten
John Supler 1758-1835

John Supler (stone replaced by the DAR) in West Alexander, Pennsylvania

A chill settled in the air that early spring morning of 1777. John Supler felt it in his bones. It was hard for him to sit quietly at the First Day meeting, as Sunday was called. Everyone was silent, then one of the members spoke. He said he was moved by God to talk against this fight with Britain. "We are taught there is an inner light of God in everyone. We cannot kill anyone." This was followed by a debate with Bible readings. Even though it was customary for people to go to the church services or meetings, as they were called, there were quite a few empty seats. This session lasted three long hours. John felt anxious, sitting there and uncomfortable in his woolen dress clothes with a plain brown jacket over a white shirt and brown breeches. His mind kept drifting to the war.

After leaving the meeting, John headed home in the buggy with the family. The Suplers lived on a farm in Chester County, Pennsylvania not far from Philadelphia, where a large Quaker population existed. John thought about his father, John Supler Sr., who was born in Berwick, Saint Leonard's, Wiltshire, England and came to America in the 1740s with a large group of Quakers. His mother was from Westminster, London, England and came with her parents, John and Susanna Gray, around the same time. Both were from strong Quaker roots, seeking religious freedom.

Now, standing in the backyard by the barn, John and his father talked about the war. The father's apprehension showed on his face as he leaned on the barn, looking at John.

"I know our religion is against fighting in the war," said John. "But the British have taken possession of New York City since last winter. Now, they are marching toward Philadelphia. The governor has asked for four thousand men to protect the city."

"Son, you know what they said at the meeting. It is against our principles to take any part in the war. We cannot be given to violence. We believe we should wait and submit to whatever suffering might be our lot. We have to trust in God," said his father.

John removed his hat and ran his hand over his light brown hair. He loved his father, but he had strong convictions. "Father, I have been drafted and I will go to war. I will fight for independence."

"Son, you are only nineteen. You know you will be disowned by the church."

John considered this. He recognized what he would have to do if and when he returned. How he would have to write a statement acknowledging his mistake and show repentance. "I have seen soldiers disowned before, only to be accepted back later."

Shaking his head, his father said, "Yes, but there is no guarantee, and it takes time, sometimes more than a year."

"I hear those who can leave the city are fleeing further west into the county. There is so much anxiety and confusion among the people. I cannot stay here on the farm and wait my fate. I will fight!" John said with authority and left to say goodbye to his mother, brothers and sisters. John went through the front door and found his mother cooking. He told her he decided to join the war effort.

"I'm unhappy I have to leave, but I feel it is my duty, Mother. We don't need King George, thousands of miles away, ruling us. We need independence from England so we can create a democratic republic, just like they said on the Declaration of Independence." said John.

"John, you are so brave. You come home to me. My prayers go with you," said his mother, hugging him, as tears ran down her cheeks.

The next day, John showed his draft papers and was assigned under Captain Jacob Rudolph in the 5th company of the Chester County, Pennsylvania Militia for three months. The militia did not have uniforms. John wore a tan cotton shirt with brown pants from home. The continental army wore a blue wool coat and breeches. The coat collar was turned up and had a red trim. John wore his worn leather tricorn hat. He brought his hunting supplies from home. He had a flint-lock musket with a long barrel which was loaded from the muzzle using a ramrod. He carried a powder horn, bullet mold and wadding which he placed in a knapsack, along with food, clothes, blanket and canteen. John woke up to the sound of the drum. He marched to the sound of the fife and drum and engaged in battle with another sound of the drum. The soldiers found themselves singing *The Liberty Song* while they were marching.

After the three months, John went on to enlist on the *Andrew Doria,* or *Black Brig,* as the sailors called it. It was stationed on the Delaware River that spring of 1777. Last December 24, the *Andrew Doria* fought the British ship *HMS Racehorse* in a two-hour battle, capturing the ship and renaming her *Surprise.* Now the *Surprise* and *Andrew Doria* were stationed at Philadelphia during the summer as part of the forces to defend the city.

After Washington's defeat on the Brandywine River, which was his attempt to stop the British that September, John waited on the *Andrew Doria* in the harbor. As the British closed in, he saw from the deck the rush of families leaving Philadelphia in rattling wagons, loaded with crying children and frightened women. Men were on horses galloping toward Chester County. The *Andrew Doria* was then ordered to leave Philadelphia by General George Washington and go to Germantown. The ship arrived there in a heavy fog on the fourth day of the eleventh month, 1777, and fought in the battle with the British. After a few hours, defeat was near. The British had the Brig surrounded. With all the cannon blasts and guns firing around him, John froze. A large older soldier, Isaac Kirk, grabbed John and pulled him out of harm's way. All the crew, except the sailors, were discharged. Then Captain Isaiah Robinson of the *Andrew Doria* gave orders to the crew to burn their ship so it didn't fall into the hands of the British. Even with all the effort, the British captured Philadelphia, the capital and the largest city. What a terrible blow. Finally discharged, John was mad and discouraged. He went home to the family farm in Chester County.

It had been a long and tiresome day when John walked into the family farmhouse. "Father, it is so good to be home, but I don't plan to stay here long," said John.

"It is so good to see you. Your mother and I have been worried you might be dead or injured. We have prayed for your safety every night with evening prayers." Hugging his son, he then pushed him back. "Son, it is not safe for you to be here. The British have been sending small raiding parties out to confiscate supplies from the farms. You will be caught," said his father.

"The British are all around here. I passed a party on the way here and hid in the woods until they were gone. I will travel at night, staying on the back roads."

"The British have offered protection of life and property if we will swear loyalty to the king."

John gave his father a hard look. "I wouldn't trust anything they say."

"I don't, but there are farmers and traders near here who have joined the British Army. Don't trust anyone."

Upset, John rejoined the Pennsylvania Militia and was immediately hired as a substitute soldier for George Craws, a Quaker neighbor, under Captain John Lindsey for two months. He next volunteered under Captain Brady and stayed under him as such until the British left Philadelphia on eighteenth day of the sixth month, 1778. The Pennsylvania Militia attempted to control passage into Philadelphia in order to limit supplies to the enemy. Anyone coming into or leaving the city was arrested as a spy. John's next service was as a seaman on the *Walker Privateer* in winter of 1778 under Captain Matthew Rules. The ship crossed among the West Indies Isles and the sailors captured two British merchant vessels. Afterwards, the ship returned to the port at Philadelphia on the fourth month. [41]

The eight month of 1779, in the battle of Powles Hook, Major Light Horse Harry Lee made a nighttime raid on the British who controlled the fort. With the fall of the fort, the British lost control of New Jersey. John was then stationed at Allentown, New Jersey and served a two months' tour under Captain William Brooks. Then on November 26, 1780 John was assigned to the sixth Battalion of Chester County under Captain William Kirk. There inside the encampment, he saw Isaac Kirk standing outside his tent. John was overjoyed to find a friendly face. Isaac was like a father, being twenty-two years older. While John was stationed on the *Andrew Doria* in Germantown, he became friends with Yeoman Isaac Kirk, a fellow Quaker. "Friend Isaac, the English didn't kill you yet?" asked John, smiling.

"No, I'm too mean to die," said Isaac, shaking his hand. "How have you been, Friend John?" asked Isaac.

"Some dysentery, that's all. It's probably this food they give us."

"It's not my wife's cooking, that is for sure. What I would give for her homemade noodles, chicken and mashed potatoes."

"This war will end soon now that Lafayette has returned with his French soldiers."

"That is what the captain is telling us."

John stayed with Isaac in the same unit until the end of the war on the third day of the ninth month, 1783. Discharged, John went back home

---

[41] John Supler Pension file, Series M805, roll 783, image 467, file W4521, (Washington: National Archives) 6.

to the family and farm. When he got home, he was a nervous wreck and it took a while to calm down and adjust to normal life again.

Shortly after coming home, John decided to visit his friend, Isaac Kirk, on the west side of Philadelphia in Upper Darby Township. He had a farm with one hundred and thirty acres there. His wife, Rachel, met John at the front door with baby Sarah in her arms. Friend Isaac was next to her in no time.

"Friend John Supler, good to see you, come on in," said Isaac.

"I just came into Philadelphia for supplies and thought I would stop by on my way back home. It has been a while," said John as he took off his hat.

"Yes, it has. Come in and sit awhile." Isaac backed up and turned to the kitchen. "John, let me introduce you to my family. This here is my ten-year-old son, John, coming in with the wood for the fireplace. Over there in the corner is Thomas, who is eight, playing with the dog. Here in the chair is Ann, sewing. She just turned fourteen. My oldest, Phebe, is nineteen and is making a pie at the kitchen table with Rachel, who is sixteen now. And you met my wife, Rachel, and baby Sarah at the door."

John looked into the kitchen and saw the children stand and bow as Isaac called their names. As they continued to walk to the parlor, John said, "You have a delightful family."

Just then Isaac's daughter, Rachel, with her red hair pulled back in a mobcap, came into the parlor. "Father, who is this?" asked Rachel.

"This young man, friend John Supler fought with me in the war. We had some rough times together, especially in Germantown," said Isaac.

"Please to meet you, Rachel Kirk," said John as he stood up, holding his hat and bowing his head.

"Father, can John stay for dinner? We have plenty," asked Rachel.

"Yes, John, stay for dinner," said Isaac.

Rachel smiled and watched him, flirting as she returned to the kitchen, walking with a slow sway to her hips, making her dress swish. John watched her sashay across the room and his heart quickened. Turning back to Isaac, John smiled. "Yes, we did have some rough times in Germantown. The British were all around us, fighting in all directions," said John, moving his arms. "I didn't think we were going to make it out alive."

Isaac shook his head and said with a frown, "Then we got the order to burn the *Black Brig* and get out of there. It was wild, men yelling and running in all directions before it blew."

"Then you grabbed me and pulled me off the burning brig. I was disoriented with all the smoke and noise. I still have nightmares of that day. If it wasn't for you getting me off the brig, I wouldn't be here today," said John.

Isaac then said with concern, "This will get better in time. The war was a terrible experience. You need to give the nightmares to God and put it in your past. Go on with your life and plan your future."

At the dinner table, John heard Rachel whisper, "Ann, move, so I can sit across from John." Frowning, Ann moved, but was obviously not happy to give up her place at the table. John couldn't help but look at Rachel. She was so beautiful, especially when she smiled at him.

Isaac, sitting at the head of the table, said, "Let's bow our heads and say a silent prayer for God's blessing."

After dinner, John, alone with Isaac, asked, "Isaac, could I have permission to court Rachel?"

"Rachel is full of spirit. If it is fine with her, but her sister Ann would have to go along as chaperone," said Isaac, smiling.

John smiled and nodded.

Finding Rachel sitting on the front porch, he joined her. After a few moments of silence, John asked, "Are you busy next first day?"

Rachel looked at him and smiled as she straightened her apron and said, "No, I am not. Why?"

"Can I come see you then? Maybe we can go for a buggy ride."

Rachel, not sounding too excited, played with him, "If my father is fine with it."

After courting for a while, John talked Rachel into sneaking out at night. They walked around the farm, gazing at the stars. They fell in love and at times, found themselves in the hay. The following year, they were married at St Michael's Zion Church in Philadelphia on the nineteenth day of the eighth month in 1784. Since they were married outside the Quaker church, Rachel was also disowned by the church. Their first-born, Susannah, came into the world four months later on the twenty-first day of the twelfth month in 1784, and was named after John's mother. Then their daughter, Rachel, was born on the eighteenth day of the second month in 1786. Eventually, John and his wife Rachel went to the Elders in the Quaker church and repented. They were then reinstated in the Quaker community in Philadelphia.

~ * ~

The Pennsylvania government wanted the western part of the state to be settled, so they gave its soldiers from the war land bounty there. John and Isaac each received two hundred acres of land in the Western Reserve. Isaac Kirk's family, along with John, Rachel, their two baby girls and John's sister, Margaret, moved to Washington County, Pennsylvania, in the spring of 1786.

John bought a beautiful blue Conestoga wagon with red trim and got a good team of six horses. They loaded the wagon with their furniture, pots and pans, dishes, silverware, clothes, linen and supplies and took off for the west. They brought with them a milk cow, bull, chickens, wheat, rye, corn and flax seed. There was a hidden second floor in the wagon and in this space, they kept the seeds for the garden. The Kirks and the Suplers went on a wagon train across the mountains along with twelve other wagons of mostly Quakers. They continued due west for about three hundred and twenty miles over the mountains. It was a rough and tedious journey that lasted a good couple of weeks. Each night, John's wife took care of the babies, cooked, sewed, and pitched the tent, while John tended the livestock. Every fifty miles, he brushed tar on the wheels to keep the axels greased. Finally, they located in Donegal Township, about three miles southeast of West Alexander. In the midst of a great forest, they cleared the land and planted their garden. It was necessary to have it planted first, so they had food during the winter. All the Quaker families worked together, building their cabins and barns in the unbroken wilderness.[42]

As time went on, it was hard to find money. British currency was seldom seen in circulation anymore. Some of the new arrivals brought a few Spanish coins, but it was rare to see any money. John made a still to produce whiskey for currency, as did most of the farmers in the area. Then in 1791, Congress passed the first tax bill, the Distilled Spirits tax of 1791. It was to help pay the large bill for the American War of Independence. Tax collectors were sent to the area, taxing nine cents to a gallon of whiskey. The area farmers were mad and ran the tax collectors off, even tar and feathered some of them. One night, John went to the local tavern which was built onto the side of a stone house, where he met up with a group of local farmers. John went to the tavern once a week to socialize and discuss matters of the day. He walked into the tavern and took his tankard off the back shelf against the wall. Having his tankard filled with Ale, he walked to middle of the room where his neighbors sat. They were all talking loudly around small round wooden tables.

"Friend John, I hear the people of Pittsburgh are rioting in the streets. They even burnt down the tax collector's house," said one of the young neighbors.

"I'm against violence, but I can't afford to pay such high taxes. Unfair taxes was one of the things I fought against in the war," said John, raising his tankard.

"What are we to do then?" asked another neighbor.

"I will pay what I feel I can afford, and no more, but I will not become violent. It is not the Quaker way," said John.

"I will go with the protesters. We need to stand up for our rights," yelled a farmer, as he stood.

"Whiskey is our form of currency. Why, we even pay the preacher with whiskey," said another farmer, slamming his tankard down on the

---

[42] Beers, J. H. and Co., *Commemorative Biographical Record of Washington County, Pennsylvania* (Chicago: J. H. Beers and Co., 1893) 811.

table.

Several men in the room stood for what they saw as right and decided not to pay any tax. They would run the tax collectors off.

On a warm day in the eleventh month in 1793, John came out of the general store in West Alexander where the mail was delivered. Rachel waited for him in the carriage, watching the dusty road ahead. "Rachel, I received a letter from my father," choked John, with tears filling his eyes.

Worried, Rachel taking a deep breath, asked, "What did he have to say?"

John reopened the letter and started reading, "Father says, 'Mother is sick with yellow fever and I'm afraid she will be dead soon. The city of Philadelphia has been in a panic with the worst epidemic ever. Most of the wealthy fled the city and it is now shut down. No one is allowed to enter or leave. People are roaming the city at night, ransacking houses and businesses of the people who have left. Mother has been so sick for a week now. Her eyes and skin are yellow. She has terrible muscle pains, along with the high fever and chills. The doctor came yesterday, bled her and gave her a dose of mercury as a last effort. I am sick now and I'm afraid we will both be gone by the time you receive this letter.' He goes on to say the death bell rings almost constantly. They are saying a hundred people are dying every day there."[43]

"Oh, I'm so sorry," said Rachel, crying with her hands over her eyes.

"The stagecoach brought in this morning a batch of newspapers with the mail. I saw the story on the front page of the *Pittsburgh Gazette*, so I bought a newspaper. They believed it started with a ship of refugees from the Caribbean. There were some passengers onboard the ship who died from the yellow fever. One doctor blames it on standing garbage and swamps near Philadelphia. It goes on to say there was mass hysteria there. They believe five thousand people died there between August and October. What a terrible nightmare," said John, as tears ran down his face.

Rachel reached over and hugged John. "They are with God now,"

---

[43] George Childs Kohn, *Encyclopaedia of Plague and Pestilence: from Ancient Times to the Present* (New York: Facts on File, Inc.,2001) 261-262.

she whispered.

A year later, in the tenth month of 1794, John came home and saw his wife, Rachel, making bread in the kitchen. "The men at the tavern tell me President George Washington sent around twelve thousand troops to the area to stop the rebellion against the whiskey tax. As soon as the troops got here, the instigators ran off, but they did arrest a few men,"[44] said John.

"I am glad you didn't get involved," said Rachel.

"I wouldn't do that. The government needs taxes, but it should be fair and not collected at gun point," said John.

"Yes, but it must have been scary for the few farmers causing the problem."

Taking a deep breath, John said, "Yes it must have been. Changing the subject, Rachel, I am going to help build a Quaker meeting house with a group of friends."

Rachel placed the bread in the brick oven on the side of the fireplace then, turning to John, said, "It would be nice not to have to meet at each other's houses. I really don't have the room and the Quaker community is growing so fast."

"It will be a simple log house, which we will also use as a school. Friend Isaac Elliot is supplying the material. You remember, he was among the Quaker farmers in the area when we first came here who helped build our cabin. Isaac Elliott with his wife, Alice, and their eight children moved here in 1780 from York, Pennsylvania."[45]

"Oh, his son, Ben, is around here a lot, helping. He likes our daughter, Susanna."

"I will have to have a talk with him," said John with a stern look.

"Oh, John, they are only children."

As the years passed, Ben and Susanna became inseparable and ended up married in 1802 in that Quaker meeting house.

On a cold dreary day in December of 1799, a rider came down the

---

[44] Htttps://www.britannica.com/event/Whiskey-Rebellion

[45] Crumrine, Boyd; *History of Washington County Pennsylvania with Biographical Sketches* (Philadelphia: L. H. Everts and Co. 1882)176-177.

road and up to the house, yelling, "President George Washington died last Saturday night."

Everyone was very heartbroken. The whole town mourned, for weeks. The newspaper said not only the nation, but Europe mourned the lost. He was everyone's hero, the father of this country and now he was gone. The town people decided to celebrate his life with a ceremony in his honor. Everyone from around West Alexander came to the celebration. Celebrations were held all over the nation. Americans truly loved this man.

Isaac Kirk original stone in West Alexander, Pennsylvania

On a hot day in the eighth month in 1807, Rachel brushed away her tears as she saw John coming up to the house. "John, my brother was here to tell me Father passed this morning."

"Oh no. I loved Isaac as my own father," said John, finding it hard to talk."

"He lived to be sixty-eight and had a good life," said Rachel, fighting the tears.

It was a quiet, plain funeral. No one wore black or mourned openly. It was a simple graveside ceremony, and a plain tombstone was erected. It was the Quaker way. He was buried at the old Presbyterian Church Cemetery in downtown West Alexander, Pennsylvania. In his will, he left the farm to his wife, but upon her death, it was to be divided between his two sons, John and Thomas. The remainder of the personal property was to be sold and divided between his four daughters.[46]

~ * ~

In 1812, the country was in war with the British again, which lasted less than three years. John was lucky not to see any of his children go off to war. After the war, the government encouraged the settlement of Ohio, with the promise of good farmland in Ohio. Some of the children of John Supler, and Isaac Kirk, along with John's daughter's in-laws, Isaac Elliott and his family, took off in wagons to another Quaker community in Stark County, Ohio in 1816.[47] John and Rachel said goodbye to their family and friends, knowing they probably would never see them again.

Several years later, in 1820, the government built a national road, which came through West Alexander, Pennsylvania. It was a wonderful road that brought the pioneers west and growth to the area increased. Stagecoaches and waggoneers hauling supplies from the east were more frequent now. The postal service was faster. On the twenty-fourth day in the fifth month of 1825, General Marquis De Lafayette passed through the town, stopping at the Inn for dinner. John, along with the old Veterans of the American War for Independence in the area, dressed up in their old uniforms, got their weapons and marched through the center of town. They stopped in front of the Inn, where many of the townspeople waited.

John remembered how the French General Lafayette fought in Germantown along with the Continental Army. Many of his fellow soldiers felt they would have lost the war if it wasn't for General Lafayette

---

[46] Will Book, #1, Washington County, PA FHL US/Can film 863624 (will books v. 1-2 1781-1814) page 498.

[47] Crumrine, *History of Washington County*, 776.

and the French assistance. The American people loved the old general.[48] There were shouts of joy as their hero appeared on the steps. He rekindled the spirit of the American War for Independence and for love of liberty and\country. John would always remember his words. Afterwards, they renamed the Inn the Lafayette Inn.

On the first day of the eleventh month of 1832, John applied for a pension and received fifty-nine dollars and sixty-three cents per year. He died on the fourteenth day of the sixth month of 1835 and was buried at the old Presbyterian Church Cemetery in West Alexander, Washington County, Pennsylvania, not far from his good friend Isaac Kirk.

---

[48] https://www.american-revolutionary-war-facts.com/American-Revolution-War-Generals-Facts/General -Marquis-de-Lafayette-Facts.html

Genealogy of John Supler

JOHN SUPLER SR. b. 1736 England d. 1793 Philadelphia, Pennsylvania m Susannah Gray 17 November 1754 Philadelphia b. 1728 d. 1793 Philadelphia

Known children of John and Susannah:
1. John Supler b. 20 October 1756 Chester Co. Pennsylvania d. 14 June 1835 Washington Co., Pennsylvania
2. Margaret Supler b. 1759 Chester Co., Pennsylvania d. 1852 Washington Co., Pennsylvania
3. George Supler b. 1761 d. 1763

John Supler b. 20 October 1756 Chester Co., Pennsylvania m. Rachel Kirk, daughter of Isaac Kirk and Rachel, February 1784 Philadelphia b. 13 August 1767 d. 18 August 1850 West Alexander, Pennsylvania

Children of John and Rachel:
1. Susannah Supler b. 21 December 1784 Chester Co., Pennsylvania d. March 1873 or 1883 Marlboro, Stark Co., Ohio
2. Rachel Supler b. 13 February1786 d. 13 September 1830
3. Margaret Peggy Supler b. 17 March 1787 d. 7 October 1865 Adams Co., Illinois
4. John Thomas Supler b. 25 January 1790 d. 28 April 1871 Washington Co., Pennsylvania
5. Sarah Supler b. 6 May 1792 d. 15 February 1879 Washington Co., Pennsylvania
6. Samuel Supler b. 17 July 1796 d. Logan Co., Ohio

7. Ann Supler b. 30 January 1798 d. 4 September 1859 Washington Co., Pennsylvania
8. Edward Supler b. February 1804 d. July 1892 Ohio Co., (West) Virginia
9. David Supler b. 18 February 1809

Genealogy of Isaac Kirk

ISAAC KIRK b. 22 October 1735 Pennsylvania to Joseph Kirk of Delaware Co., Pennsylvania, and Anne Hood d. 1803 Washington Co., Pennsylvania m. Rachel 1763.

Children of Isaac and Rachel:
1. Rachel Kirk b. 13 August 1767 d. 18 August 1850 m. John Supler 1784
2. John Kirk b. 3 November 1773 d. 1837 m. Jane
3. Thomas Kirk d. aft. 1852
4. Phebe Kirk m. b. 1764 Chester Co., Pennsylvania 1786 d. bef. 1825 North Lewisburg, Ohio m. Nehemiah Green
5. Anne Kirk b. 1769 d. 1847 m. Mclaughlin
6. Sarah Kirk m. Alexander Monroe

Chapter Eleven
Samuel S. Poling (1767-1855)

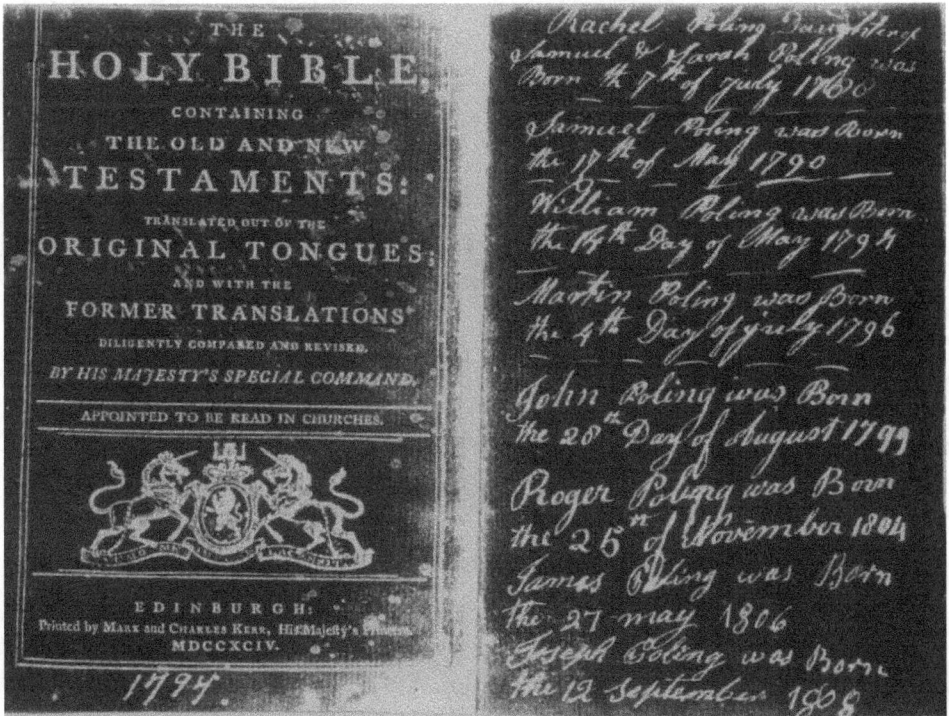

Copy of Samuel Poling's 1794 Bible

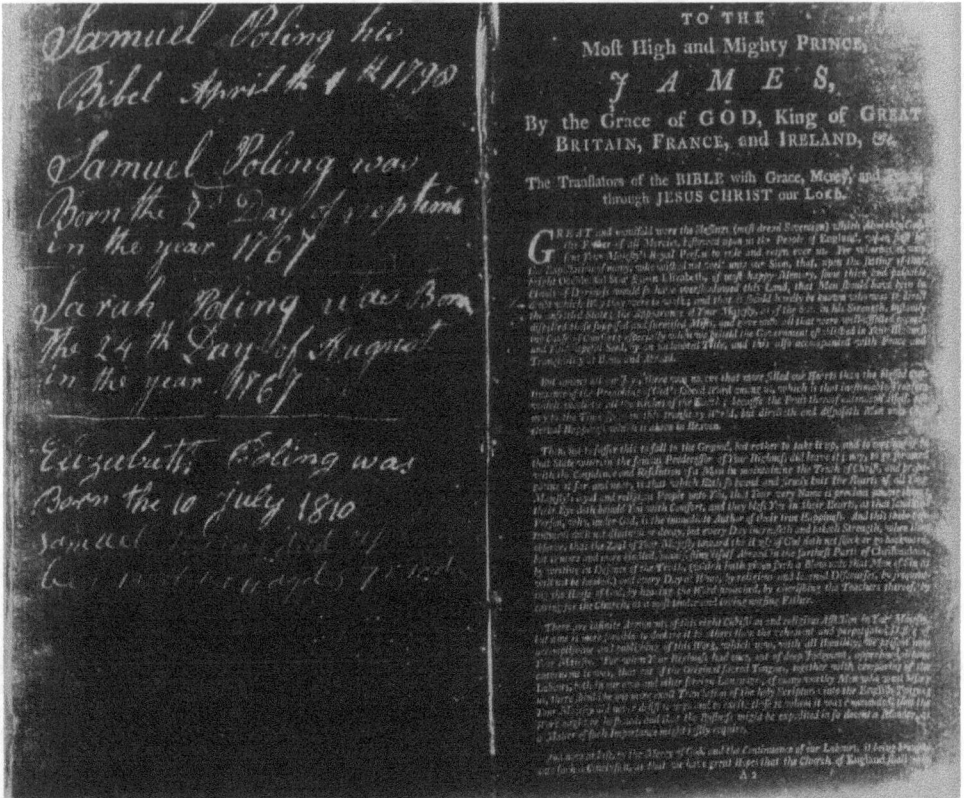

Copy of Samuel Poling's 1794 Bible

When little Samuel was only a year old and his sister, Sarah, was fifteen, their mother Lena died. She was only forty-three. This left Sarah to basically raise her little brother. Their grandfather, Martin, died two years later. All Samuel's father Samuel Sr. could talk about was moving away from New Jersey to Loudon County, Virginia.

Frightened by the way his father burst through the door, little Samuel, now four, dropped the pots and pans he was playing with on the kitchen floor. His father was so upset, shouting, "Sarah, we have to move. It is only a matter of time before this area will be in the middle of the war. Just today, the people in town told me how the citizens in Boston were shot and killed by the British Army soldiers. The newspaper had a picture of the massacre across the front page! The people of Middletown were so enraged. They were out, shouting in the streets to put an end to this British domination."

"What will happen now?" asked Sarah, as she held little Samuel, now crying.

Pausing, Father said, "War."

"Will you go fight, Father?" asked Sarah, now in tears too.

Hugging Sarah and little Samuel, Father said, "No, I have you children and no wife. Who will take care of you? Besides, this war will be fought in our own land among us."

Later that night, little Samuel stood on his tippy-toes and looked around the table. His uncles, aunts and cousins, along with his brothers and sisters, were there. His Uncle Richard stood in the doorway.

"I am taking my family and leaving for Virginia. The land is rich for farming and, hopefully, it will be far enough away to be out of the war," said his father as he gestured toward the chair, indicating for Richard to sit down.

"Some of us want to stay behind and join the New Jersey Militia. We want to fight the British," said Richard, taking the seat.

"You're young. I have young children to take care of right now," said Father.

"This war that is coming will not be easy, but this is my life. There are a lot of good men willing to fight," said Richard.

Now looking at his son, Martin, Father said, "I just want to stay out of it. Martin, son, you have a young family, you need to stay out of this war too."

"Father, I am torn between leaving with you and fighting," said Martin, rubbing his forehead.

"I have little grandchildren who need you. Come with us to Virginia," said Father, pleading.

"My family comes first. I will leave with you," said Martin.

Soon after, little Samuel left New Jersey for Loudon County, Virginia with his father, his grandmother Sary and most of the family. They sold the farm, their belongings and kept only what was necessary. At Freeport, New Jersey, they boarded a ship that would take them to Virginia. They all bought farms just south of Leesburg, along Goose Creek, which was a branch of the Potomac River. The farm Samuel bought included a two-story framed house. He grew corn, wheat, flax, tobacco and had a vegetable garden on the farm. Little Samuel's grandmother, Sary, lived with them. She loved to cook and would spend the day cooking for the family. His sister, Sarah, now eighteen, helped a lot around the farm. She was a smart and attractive young lady, who was educated in the schools back in New Jersey.

In Virginia, the towns were farther away, which made going to church not easy, so they seldom went. There was a large Quaker community in the area. They were friendly and harbored run-away slaves. Samuel's family never owned slaves, only the very wealthy could afford them. His father liked the Quakers and was against slavery.

On one breezy October day, Samuel, now six, rode on a wagon with his father. They took the corn to the grist mill on Beaverdam Branch of Goose Creek.[49]

"Father, how do they make corn meal?" Samuel asked.

"The water turns the large waterwheel and the shaft which is connected to gears inside that work the millstone," said Father.

Edward Garret, who owned and ran the mill, was just inside the door. "Hi, Mr. Poling. Who do we have here?" asked Edward.

"This is Samuel. He is asking how the grist mill works."

"Well, see those big stone wheels over there," said Edward, pointing. "The corn falls from the hopper above onto the stones, the stones turn from the water turning the wheel. As the stones turn, they crush the corn kernels."

"What is that hissing sound I hear?" asked Samuel, making a face.

"It is the grain going through the sifter. Hold your hand out and feel the grain."

"It feels so good. Now Grandmother can make corn bread when we take the corn meal back."

Just then, Samuel saw a black fluffy cat and ran after it. There in the corner under the stairs was a litter of kittens.

"We have to keep cats here to keep the mice out of the mill," said

---

[49] John T. Philips, *The Bulletin of the Historical Society of Loudon County, Virginia*, (1957- 1976): 30.

Edward.

"Father, can I have a kitten?" asked Samuel.

"When they are older, maybe, and if your grandmother doesn't mind," said Father.

"But Father, the kitten with the white face loves me," said Samuel.

When they got back to the farm, Samuel talked Sary into having a kitten. It wasn't hard, Sary had a special love for little Samuel.

Sary was seventy-two when she died in 1774. She was buried on the farm in Loudon County.

~ * ~

Even at eleven years old, in 1778, Samuel stayed close to home, for his father feared for his safety. There was no school in Virginia by their farm like there was in New Jersey. His sister taught him at home, which was very limited.

"Sarah, I don't understand this math," said Samuel, as he sat at the kitchen table.

"What don't you understand?" asked Sarah.

"When you multiply large numbers or add large groups of numbers, I have a hard time."

"If I had some school supplies, it would help to show you how to do it."

"Maybe Father will let us go down Mountain Road to The Post."

"Samuel, you know with the war going on, he wants you close to home."

"Maybe this one time, since there has been no war around here."

Later that day, Father saddled two horses. He helped Samuel on the smaller horse. Father's larger horse had a pillion, a type of cushion attached to the rear of his saddle where Sarah rode. From the pillion hung a small wooden platform for her feet. They went on to The Post, which was a cabin, a type of Trading Post, where the mail stopped. It took two hours to ride the eight miles. A stone post stood outside by the road that read Leesburg fourteen miles, Winchester forty-two miles. There were no houses in sight, just horses, wagons and carts that stopped in front. They tied their horses on the hitching rail and walked inside The Post.

"Father, I need a slate writing board to practice my math on and a slate pencil," said Samuel.

"We will get that and a new quill pen and ink for writing," said Father.

"Anything else I can get you?" asked the owner.

"I believe that is all. Is there any news from the travelers passing through the area?" asked Father.

"Yes, France has entered the war against Britain. With France helping us, this war should be over soon."

"I wouldn't count on it."

"At least most of the fighting has been up north. Wait, I have a letter for you."

Mail was expensive and took a while to get delivered, due to travel being slow and difficult. Letters were long and elaborate. Samuel's father was lucky to receive one a year. The letter came from the family back in New Jersey. Samuel's father read how the British retreated from the Monmouth County battle and marched through Middlefield. The residents were frightened and hid their food, cattle, and pigs in the thick forest. The British set up an encampment on both sides of Kings Highway, a couple miles outside the town for a week while waiting for transport to the British-occupied New York City. The letter went on to tell how the British tore out the benches at the old church and used it as a hospital. The pastor held services in the barn. Samuel's cousin, John Poling Jr, under Colonial Asher Holmes, helped capture the British Brig *Britania* off the New Jersey shore. It was such a thrill to hear from the family that Father sang *Yankee Doodle Dandy* all the way home. In the days to come, he would reread the letter several times.

News got to them that on October 19, 1781, that British General Cornwallis surrendered at Yorktown, Virginia, ending the war. Samuel Sr. died 1782 in Loudoun County, Virginia and was buried beside his mother on the farm. At the kitchen table in family farmhouse, they read Samuel Sr.'s will. An inventory of the estate was valued at one hundred and sixty pounds.[50] The farm was left to the oldest son, Martin.[51] Each of the other children were given money.

Letters were sent to the family in other states about Samuel Sr.'s death. The next month, they received a letter from their uncle William. Standing by the fireplace, the family discussed the letter.

"In Uncle William's letter, he writes he wants us to move to Maryland. Now that the war is over, land has opened up in western Maryland," said Martin.

"I know you are my older brother and Father left the farm to you, so why would you want to move?" asked Samuel.

"In his letter, Uncle William said the land there is beautiful with the Allegany Mountains in the distance. He has a farm there by Georges Creek and was one of the first settlers on the government land paid for Maryland's Revolutionary soldiers. He was able to procure a large section of land there. He said the land is an ideal spot, well-watered by many springs and small streams. The land is really rich for farming."

"So, Uncle William wants us to move to his land?"

"Yes, he does, and as soon as I sell the farm, we are all moving."

The family was so proud of Uncle William for fighting in the war and could not wait to see him again.[52]

Martin sold the farm and the family moved to Maryland in 1782. Samuel, now fifteen, was all excited about the move. His cousins also sold their farms and left for Maryland. He never was far from home, so this was going to be an adventure. They left Virginia by going up the Potomac River. When they came to the village of Cumberland, they stopped at a tavern. In front of the tavern was an old war soldier in a worn-out continental uniform. He brought his gun to order and gave a military salute. "Happy Jack at your service!" He shouldered his musket and marched into the tavern.

---

[50] Loudoun County Will Book B, 436.

[51] Samuel (Poling) Poland will (August 1782), Loudon County Will Book B: 116.

[52] *Maryland Troops* 1775-1783, Vol. XVIII, *Archives of Maryland,* (Baltimore: Maryland Historical Society) p. 49.

Samuel and his family sat by Happy Jack at the long wooden table. They ate a hearty meal of beef stew and had some whisky.

"I was one of George Washington's bodyguards during the war," said Happy Jack.

"You must have some stories to tell," said Samuel.

"Would you like to hear some?" asked Jack.

"Yes, I really would," said Samuel on the edge of his seat.

Jack went on to tell stories of his many incidents on the different battlefields in his seven years of service from Boston to Yorktown. The tavern was quiet while everyone listened. Samuel sat at the table, his chin in his hands, staring at Happy Jack, the meal forgotten. After a while, Happy Jack picked up his knapsack, placed it on his back, with his bayonet by his side and a wooden canteen, musket on his shoulder. As he left, he tipped his three-cornered hat and gave a farewell salute. Everyone wished him good will.[53]

They continued until they finally arrived at the Potomac River tributary to the Georges River, that summer of 1782. There, they found little villages along the river and, in the valley among the Allegany Mountains, was Uncle William's cabin.

Samuel lived with Martin on his farm until he married Sarah Bennett. Sarah, according to family history, was a cousin.[54] A Methodist church was nearby, and the family started going to church again. Samuel and Sarah were married there in 1787 when they were both twenty years old. Samuel ended up building a cabin on the land by Martin's. The farm became known in the area as the Poling farm. The land description stated it started at the large chestnut tree, running south to marked maple tree with ten notches, then south forty-one and half, west seventy-eight perches (perch or pole is a surveyor's tool, a length equal to five and a half yards), to a maple tree marked with twelve notches, then thirty-six

---

[53] James Walter Thomas, Thomas John Chew Williams, *History of Allegany County Maryland* (Regional Publishing Co., 1923), 151.

[54] Clerissa H. Tatterson, *History and Genealogy of the Poling Family* (Parsons, West Virginia: McClain Printing Company, 1978), 116.

degrees west one hundred sixteen perches, then a straight line to the beginning.[55]

As time went on, it was harder to find money. Some of the travelers brought Spanish coins, but it was rare to see any money. Samuel, sitting at the supper table, discussed the problem with Sarah.

"Sarah, I have a hard time finding money. British currency is seldom seen in circulation. Maryland Bank had money printed, but it's not good everywhere," said Samuel, rubbing his forehead.

"Samuel, how will I get the things I need from the mercantile?" asked Sarah, hugging her waist for comfort. She was six months pregnant.

"I will try and exchange the surplus of wheat and corn for whiskey. Whiskey, I hear, is worth twenty-five cents a quart jar in the stores. The stores are using it for money."

"That will help for now, but what will we do when there is no surplus left?"

"I heard the federal government is working on a national currency, but it will probably be a while before we see it."[56]

A son, Samuel, was born in 1787 but died as an infant. They named their second son Samuel, too, in 1790, which was not an uncommon practice. Usually, the first son was named after the father's father and if he died as an infant, the second son was named after him. A daughter and three more sons were born there in Maryland. Samuel and Sarah sold the farm and fifty acres of land on October 10, 1800, in Georges Creek, Allegany County, Maryland.[57] They profited greatly from the sale of the land in Maryland. Now with five children, the family traveled alongside the river to (West) Virginia. They put all their worldly possessions in a wagon and herded the livestock. Travel was slow. They

---

[55] *Allegany County, Maryland Records, 1795-1806* (The Genealogy Records Committee Cresap Chapter, Cumberland, Maryland, 1969), 251.

[56] *James Walter Thomas, Thomas* John Crew Williams, *History of Allegany County Maryland,* (Regional Pub. Co., 1923), p 241.

[57] *Allegany County, Maryland Records, 1795-1806* (The Genealogy Records Committee Cresap Chapter, Cumberland, Maryland, 1969), 251.

started early morning and traveled to late afternoon, hunting for game when they stopped. They stopped at a town where they restocked their supplies, had the horses shod and wagon wheels repaired. When they finally reached their destination, Samuel and Sarah purchased land by Sugar Creek, Randolph County, (West) Virginia in 1803 at a low price. There, they lived in a green valley with rolling hills framed by high mountains on either side with sheer cliffs. The valley was well-watered with Sugar Creek running through it. Since it was untamed land, there was plentiful game of all kinds. The land was so wild it was full of wolves, panthers, and wild cats. The government even paid a bounty for their fur. Only a bridle trail was in front of their farm. The closest village was Beverly, which was about twenty-eight miles away. There, they could find a hotel, mercantile store, blacksmith, boot maker, gun shop, furniture builder, saddle and leather store, a wagon-maker, and churches.

By 1810, Samuel and Sarah had ten children, nine living.

One of their neighbors was a wagon-maker, Solomon Carpenter, who paid close attention to his work and was known for his superior wagons. Samuel rode over to his house one day in 1812, finding Solomon in his barn, working.

"Hi, Solomon. I need a new wagon," said Samuel, shaking his hand.

"What kind of wagon?" asked Solomon?

"Farm wagon, about ten feet long and four feet wide."

"Do you want hickory, ash or oak wood?"

"Whatever you think. I am using it on the farm and to get supplies."

"I will see what my father-in-law, John Hill, has at his sawmill on Sugar Creek."

"Sounds good."

"I hope I can finish it before I end up being drafted into this war."

"Just when we thought our problems with the British were over."

"Well, give me a couple weeks." Just then, his two-year old daughter ran into the barn. "Polly, what are you doing out here?" Solomon asked as he picked her up.

"She is pretty. I have a son, James, who is five. I know how they do whatever they have in mind at times." Samuel continued, as he walked to his horse, "See you in a couple of weeks."

A month later, Solomon and Samuel's son Samuel III were both drafted, along with a lot of young men in the area. Samuel's cousin, Nathaniel Poling, who moved to Georgetown by Washington D.C. and owned a carriage business there, sent Samuel a letter. Nathaniel wrote about how he entered the war in 1812 where he enlisted under General Winter's thousand troops. They marched to Bladensburg six miles below Washington DC where the army was overpowered and defeated by the British in August 1814. They fell back to Washington DC where he witnessed the burning of the bridge over the Potomac, Navy and Army buildings, the president's house, and the capitol with its valuable library and handsome furniture. He described how his heart ached as the firelight could be seen for miles, as their national treasure disappeared in flames. By the time Samuel received the letter, the war was over.

After the war, Ohio opened for settlement. Public meetings were held where stories of Ohio were told. How land there was delightful with inexhaustible wealth. Much excitement over Ohio was seen by the neighbors. Samuel watched as James, now a teenager, courted Polly and went to these meetings. James and Polly married in 1831. As the years went by, Samuel watched his children and grandchildren go on the wagon trains to Ohio. By 1835, only Samuel's son, Joseph, his wife and children continued to live on the farm with his parents in Randolph County. The county was divided in 1843, which placed the farm then in Barbour County.[58] Samuel died in 1855. In his will, he left the farm to Joseph.[59] As you will see in Chapter 17, Joseph sold the farm and moved to Ohio where Samuel's children lived. He brought his mother with him.

---

[58] Tattterson, *History and Genealogy of Poling Family*
[59] Barbour Co., Virginia, *Will Book* 1, 93.

Genealogy of Samuel Poling Sr.

SAMUEL POLING b. 1725 Monmouth, New Jersey d. 1782 Loudon Co., Virginia m. Madalene (Lena) b. 1725 d. 1768

Children of Samuel S. and Lena:
1. Martin Cornelius Poling b. 1748 New Jersey d. 1819 m. Rachel Wyckoff 1765
2. Richard Poling b. 1750 New Jersey d. 1828
3. Sarah Poling b. 22 April 1753 m. Roger Parks d. 1827
4. William Barnet Poling b. 26 Dec 1754 d. 1781 Loudon Co., Virginia
5. Samuel Poling b. 02 September 1767 New Jersey d. 12 September 1854, Barbour County, (West) Virginia.

Genealogy of Samuel Poling Jr.

SAMUEL POLING b. 02 September 1767 Monmouth Co., New Jersey d. 12 September 1854, Barbour Co., (West) Virginia m. Sarah Bennett 1786, b. 24 August 1767 New Jersey, d. 22 September 1863 Union Co., Ohio.

Children of Samuel and Sarah:
1. Infant Samuel Poling b. 1787 d. 1787 Allegany Co., Maryland
2. Rachel Poling b. 7 July 1788 m. Cincinnati Jackson
3. Samuel Poling b. 17 May 1790 Allegany Co., Maryland d. 1876 Union Co., Ohio m. Elizabeth Marks
4. William Poling b. 14 July 1794 d. 1841
5. Martin Poling b. 4 July 1796 d. 1818 Randolph Co., (West) Virginia

6. John Bennett Poling b. 1799 Allegany Co., Maryland d. 1866 Union County, Ohio m Sarah Park 8 July 1725 Randolph Co., (West) Virginia
7. Roger Poling b. 25 November 1804 Randolph Co., (West) Virginia d. 29 June 1866 Union Co., Ohio m. Sarah England
8. James Poling b. 27 May 1806 Randolph Co., (West) Virginia d. 5 December 1893 Union Co., Ohio m. Mary (Polly) Carpenter 15 December 1831 Harrison (West) Virginia
9. Joseph Poling b. 12 September 1808 Randolph Co., (West) Virginia d. 22 March 1883 Union Co., Ohio m. Phoebe McKinney
10. Elizabeth Poling b. 10 July 1810 Randolph Co., (West) Virginia m. Anthony Huff

Genealogy of Solomon Carpenter

SOLOMON CARPENTER b. 1784 d. 1837 Union Co., Ohio m. Catherine Hill 1809 Randolph Co., (West) Virginia b. 1784 d. 1855 Union Co., Ohio

Children of Solomon and Catherine:
1. Jessie Carpenter b. 1810 d. 1875
2. Mary (Polly) Carpenter b. 1811-1812 d. 28 January 1881
3. Ephriam Eurem Carpenter b. 1813 (West) Virginia d. 1899 Union Co., Ohio m. Betsey Ann Allen 1835
4. Elizabeth Carpenter b.1815 d. 1854
5. Nancy Carpenter b. 1818 d. 1872
6. Peree Carpenter b. 1819 d. 1888 Shelby, Iowa
7. George Carpenter b. 1822 d. 1886 Union Co., Ohio

Chapter Twelve
Benjamin Elliott (1778-1859)

Six long days have come and gone since the Elliott family left West Alexander, Pennsylvania that early spring of 1814. They were excited about going west to Ohio, ever since they heard wonderful stories of Ohio and how beautiful it was at the Quaker meetings. How the government encouraged the people to settle on the land in Ohio after the war of 1812, by offering good fertile land, cheap. The whole Elliott family, Ben, Susanna and their five children traveling with his father, mother, brothers, sisters, and their families left together. Ben's oldest children, Ben Jr., eleven, Isaac Kirk, nine, Susan, seven, walked alongside of the wagon, which carried all their belongings. Susanna and the youngest, Wilkinson, five and Rachel, three, rode up front in the wagon. It was a hundred and twenty-four miles to Marlborough, Stark County, Ohio.

Ben rode ahead of the group, scouting the land, when he heard a loud growl and came upon a large bear in the branches of a huge chestnut tree. Shaking, he grabbed his musket from the saddle and shot the bear, killing it. The land there was full of wild animals. He settled west of Marlborough village where there was a Quaker settlement and a meeting house of the Society of Friends.[60]

Ben bought the land by paying a percentage down and paying it off in one year. When finally paid off, he received a certificate of purchase. Land there went for one dollar and twenty-eight cents to two

---

[60] William Wade Hinshaw, *Encyclopedia of American Quaker Genealogy Vol. IV* (Washington: William Wade Hinshaw 1946), 30.

dollars an acre.[61]

---

[61] Dr. George W. Knepper, *The Official Ohio Lands Book* (Columbus: The Auditor of State Jim Petro 2002), 36-37.

In 1821, Lexington Township was divided, and the western part became Marlborough Township. His parents, Isaac, and Alice, settled in Lexington Township by Alliance, Ohio and Ben's family settled in Marlborough Township nine miles away.

When first settling there, one-third of the settlers were Quakers. All of the neighbors assisted in raising Ben's cabin. The logs were too hard to raise without assistance and you were considered a bad neighbor not to help. The women prepared an abundance of food for the workers and there was a party-like atmosphere. Once the land was cleared, Ben farmed wheat and flax and Susanna planted a vegetable garden behind the cabin.

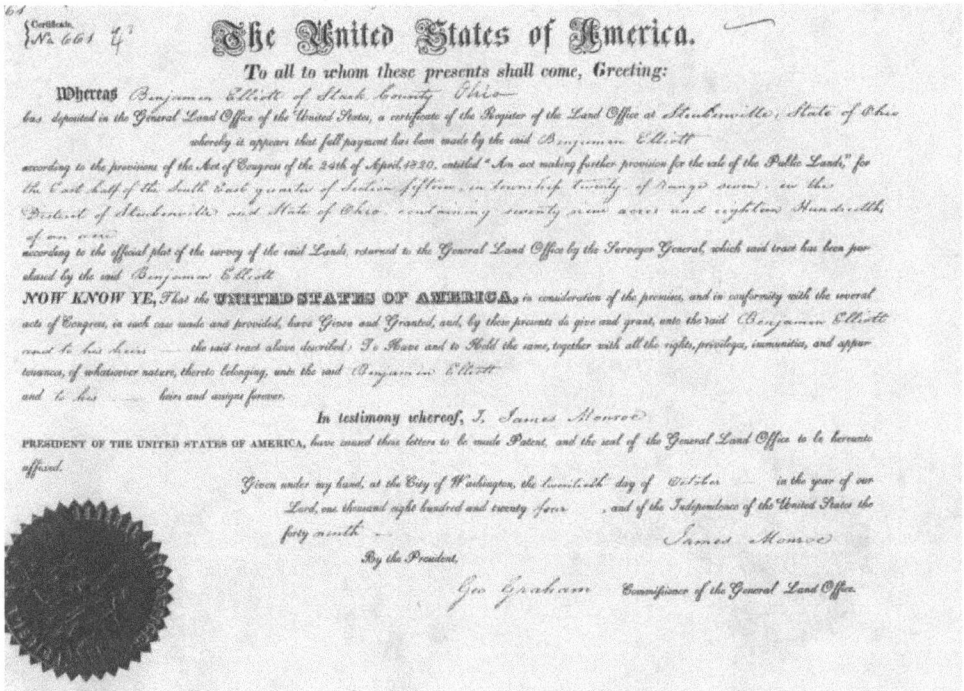

Ben went to the new land office in Steubenville where he bought seventy-nine acres and eighteen hundredths of an acre from the government in 1824. The land was along a clear blue stream called Deer Creek, where he built a grist mill and then, a year later in 1825, a sawmill.[62] He built a natural dam with rocks across the stream to race the water through the mills, making the wheels turn.

One day, Ben came home from the mills to find his wife on the front porch, waiting for him.

"Ben, I am almost out of flour, I'm afraid you will have to go without bread until I can have some," said Susanna.

"I will take a bag of wheat to the mill tomorrow, but it will take at least two days to grind the wheat into flour," said Ben, thinking about how he could make it faster as he ran his fingers over his beard.

"I will have to make do. Ben, a scary looking, but a very friendly man came by today. He was a scraggly man with dark brown hair to his waist. He wore a sack cloth and was barefoot."[63]

Worried, Ben asked, "What did he want?"

"He was selling apple seedlings he brought from his orchard. He had samples of some apples and cider. The apples were very tasty, but I wouldn't give any cider to the children. He was very knowledgeable about not only apples, but medicinal plants, also."

"Did you buy any?"

"I bought six seedlings, which was all he had with him, for five cents apiece."

"That was a good price. I will plant an apple orchard behind the barn."

"He said his name was Jonathan Chapman and if I wanted more, he would be back around in a couple of weeks."

"I heard the men talking about him at the sawmill. They called him Johnny Appleseed."

Three days later, Ben brought home the flour from the mill and Susanna made bread for the whole week. It was an all-day process, but the results were great tasting bread.

Two weeks later, Jonathan Chapman returned with more

---

[62] *History of Stark County, Ohio* (Chicago: Baskin and Battey, Historical Publishers 1881) 574.

[63] Will Moses, *Johnny Appleseed* (New York, New York: Philomel Books, 2001), 19.

seedlings. He stayed for dinner and told Bible stories which he acted out in the most entertaining way. The children really enjoyed him, he was such a happy man.

Ben's mother Alice died in 1827, at seventy-one. It was a quiet, plain funeral, and she was buried in Deer Creek Quaker Cemetery, a few miles from their farm. To Quakers, death was a natural part of life. Ben and Susanna, saddened by her death, were expected to go on with their lives.

In the early 1830s, the Quakers in the village were involved in the Underground Railroad. One night, sitting in the rocking chair by the fireplace, Ben said, "I got a message at the sawmill that a package is coming tonight."[64]

"I will be ready for them. Did he say how many this time?" asked Susanna.

"No, I don't believe he knew. He had to be quiet about it, you don't know who in town might give them away."

"Surely not the Quakers."

"No, but there are a lot of other people, not Quakers, that would tell for the reward money."

Susanna placed a quilt on the clothesline after supper and lit a candle in the window. It was a sign the house welcomed runaway slaves. Later, after they went to bed, there was a knock on the door. Ben slowly opened the door to find a tall young man with blue eyes and light brown hair tied in the back. He said, "I am a friend of the friends."

"Welcome, friend," said Ben.

Next to him, holding a sleeping young black girl in his large muscular arms, was a tall African man.

"I'm Joseph, the conductor. This is Jim and we have two women and three young children in the wagon under the canvas."

Susanna came to the door, holding a lantern, and said, "Bring them in, I made up beds in the root cellar. I will bring you some food in a little bit." Looking at Jim, she said, "Take the wagon to the barn and

---

[64] William Henry Perrin, *History of Stark County Ohio* (Chicago: Baskin and Battey Historical Publishers, 1881), 575.

hurry before someone comes down the road."

"Yesuum," said Jim.

Ben gently took the young child and led the small group to the cellar. Quietly, they went through the darkened house, not sure if someone might be watching. In a low tone, he asked, "How long have you been traveling?"

"For two days now straight through, hiding in the forests, trying to stay off the roads." Joseph sighed and continued, "The children are exhausted and hungry."

"Susanna made a large roast earlier. She will warm it up and bring it downstairs."

Ben showed Joseph the fake wall behind the shelves of canning jars. "You can hide here, if necessary, but it would be a tight area for this many."

"Thank you for taking them in, I know you can get into a lot of trouble," said Joseph.

"I am doing God's will. He will protect us. The Bible tells us to feed the hungry and clothe the naked and it said nothing about color," said Ben.

"This is mighty brave of you."

"Our ancestors have done this for years now. The Quakers helped start the Underground Railroad and work together to keep it going. Edward, another friend, will be here later, he is the conductor that will take the group to the next safe house, as soon as it is safe. He will bring food for their trip and clothing for them to change. All the friends here contribute to the cause."

"It is so wonderful the friends go out of their way to help people they do not know," said Joseph.

"This is one of the cruelest things man has done to other men. I feel it is my duty to help."

"God bless you and your family, Ben."

"Abraham, the train dispatcher, told us you were coming, so we were prepared." Ben continued after seeing how tired Joseph looked. "Get some sleep and in the morning, you can take a horse and ride back home."

Jim came back from the barn. He helped Susanna bring food to everyone. They each had a bowl of roast with carrots, potatoes and dumplings.

After coming back to the kitchen, Susanna said, "You can see the fear in their eyes. They have no shoes or clothing except what they have on and that is tattered."

"Yes, they are desperate people, with a lot of faith in us," said Ben, with a crack in his voice.

The next day, Joseph rode off after saying goodbye to his new friends. It was another two days before the group of runaway slaves could safely leave. Word was out that bounty hunters were in the area, up from Kentucky. Edward, one of the Quakers from the village, took them on to the next safe house. They traveled at night, north for fifteen miles. They were sent with clothing, good shoes, food and money. Ben and Susanna said special prayers for them with their evening prayers. Then two nights later, there was a pounding on the door. Ben opened the door to find two angry men outside.

"I hear you have a black runaway slave here who calls himself Jim," said the bigger of the two men.

"No one here but my family," said Ben.

Looking disturbed, the man yelled, "Are you sure?"

"You can come in and have something to eat, I'm sure Susanna can put something together for you."

Now confused, they came in and Susanna fixed them some leftover stew.

"Let's look around. I bet they are hiding in here," whispered the bigger man.

"Yah," said the smaller man as they walked through the house.

After they left, Susanna gave Ben a hard look. "Why did you ask them in to eat, Ben? Just to make me a nervous wreck?"

"Well, we are to love our enemies. Besides, they were less suspicious after eating."

"It is good thing I had leftovers, or I would really be upset at you."

Sometimes it would be months before another shipment came, but the community continued to gather food and clothing at their meetings for when the occasion arose, they would be ready.

Marlborough was a little frontier settlement and received mail two or three times a week by stage. The stagecoach came through on Main Street and stopped at the tavern where everyone picked up their mail. On his way home from the mill one late day in June of 1835, Ben stopped at the tavern and picked up a letter for Susanna. When he got home, Susanna was cooking supper. He said, "Susanna, your mother, Rachel, wrote you a letter."

"I'm worried it is bad news," said Susanna.

"Yes, I felt the same. We don't get much mail, as expensive as it is to send a letter."

Slowly opening the letter, Susanna read the news and, turning to Ben, said, "Mother said Father passed. He died on June 14 and was buried in Presbyterian Church Cemetery in West Alexander, Pennsylvania. She goes on to say she is doing well, and my brother John Jr. helps her a lot."

"How old was your father?"

"He was seventy-eight years, seven months and twenty-four days."

"To think he fought in the War for Independence and lived to be that old. He was a great man to know."

"Yes, and my mother is sixty-seven, I wonder if I will see her again," cried Susanna.

Ben hugged her and said, "God willing, you will."

On June 18, 1839, Ben's father Isaac died. He was eighty-one and was buried by his mother in Deer Creek Quaker Cemetery. Just as Isaac's father passed his silver-handled cane on to Isaac, now it was passed on to Ben. After his father's death, in the 1840s, Ben's brothers, Isaac Jr., Moses, his sister Elizabeth, his daughter, Susan, sons, Wilkinson, Absalom and their families all moved to Logan County, Ohio to the Goshen Quaker Community near Mt Victory, Ohio.

Downtown Marlborough was booming by 1850. A carriage factory came in, then a clothing business, a hotel, a mercantile store, post office and foundry which made steam engines. That fall, Ben picked up a Pittsburg newspaper at the post office on his way home from the mill.

"Susanna, I read in the paper that the fugitive slave act went into effect, penalizing anyone found helping runaway slaves a one thousand dollar fine and up to six months imprisonment if you are caught."

"Ben, we are getting too old, we are in our seventies. We can still help, but we should be less active."

"It also stated the abolitionists marched in the cities, calling for the end of slavery."

"That's good, but the Quakers are quiet, simple people. They do their part as they see fit."

Marlboro Cemetery

BENJ. ELLIOTT

Died Aug 4, 1859

Aged 81yrs 2 days

Susanna Supler Elliott[65]

---

[65] Find A Grave, online<wwwfindagrave.com/memorial/75132505susannah-elliott>.

Genealogy of Benjamin Elliott

BENJAMIN ELLIOTT b. 31 July 1778 York Co., Pennsylvania d. 31 July 1859 Marlboro, Ohio m. Susannah Supler 25 December 1802 Washington Co., Pennsylvania b. 21 December 1784 d. March 1883

Children of Benjamin and Susannah:
1. Benjamin Elliott b. 1803 Washington Co., Penn. d. 1880 m. Sarah Grewell
2. Isaac Elliott b. 1805 Washington Co., Penn. d. 1870 m. #1 Ann Bowman #2 Mary Norton
3. Susannah Elliott b. 1807 Washington Co., Penn. d. 1892 m. James Rochelle #2 John Rossell
4. Wilkinson Elliott b. 1809 Washington Co., Penn. d. 1895 m. #1 Sarah Taylor #2 Nancy McCreory
5. Rachel Elliott b. 1811 Washington Co., Penn. d. 1880 m. #1 Abraham Vanscoyoc #2 Isaac Cope
6. James Elliott b. 1812
7. Absalom Elliott b. 1814 Stark Co., Ohio d. 1857 Union Co., Ohio m. Rosella Hope Rossell
8. Jonathan Elliott b. 1816 Stark Co., Ohio d.1873 m. Mary Keller
9. Edith Elliott b. 1818 Stark Co., Ohio d. 1875
10. Enos Elliott b 1820 Stark Co., Ohio d. 7 May 1837
11. Ann S. Elliott b 1822 Stark Co., Ohio d.1907
13. Agnes Elliott b. 1823 Stark Co., Ohio d. 1895

Chapter Thirteen
John Rossell (1785-1858)

Outside the meeting hall, in 1844, after the Quaker meeting, John looked over to see his daughter, Hope Elliott, standing next to an attractive lady.

"Father, I want you to meet Susannah Rochelle, she is my husband's sister," said Hope, smiling.

"Nice to meet you, Susannah. Absalom is a good man," said John, as he removed his hat and bowed slightly.

"Yes, he is. I have seen you around town, John," said Susannah, looking at his blue eyes.

"My daughter tells me we have both lost our partners in life," said John.

"Yes, my husband James Rochelle died in 1841, he was only twenty-seven. He had a hard life." Susannah explained to John how her first husband James lost his parents as a young child. He was bound over to a farmer by the name of Rawls who took James from Virginia in 1819 when he was ten years old to Marlboro, Ohio. Rawls treated James badly. He was abusive and a neighbor took James away from him. "When we married, the only thing he owned was an ax."[66]

John sighed. "God has allowed some awful hard things in this life."

"Yes, and far too much heartache. My three children took it extremely hard when he died. Benjamin was seven, James was six, and Harriet was only four." Susannah looked up at him, her eyes filling with

---

[66] Chapman Brothers, *Portrait and Biography Album Hillsdale County* (Chicago, 1888), p281.

tears.

"Sorry, it must have been rough," whispered John. "I lost my wife a few years ago. We had a good life together. My children are all older and some even have families of their own now, but it is still hard."

"Hope is so sweet. You must be proud of her; she is such a good mother."

"Yes, my grandchildren are blessed."

"John, would you like to come over for supper?"

Next week, John came over for supper. Susannah fixed rabbit stew. After supper, they took a walk along the country road.

"John, where did you originally come from?'

"When I was nine years old, we left Northampton,[67] Burlington County, New Jersey, and moved to Fayette County, Pennsylvania. I came on the wagon train with my father, Job, and stepmother, Mary, along with my brothers and sisters. There were twelve wagons going west. Some of them were my aunts, uncles, and cousins. A good month later, we made it to Fayette County. I remember the large mountains were beautiful, but hard work climbing on the simple roads available. Father drove a team of horses that pulled the large wagon. I walked along the side of the wagon with my older brothers, Thomas, and Job Jr., while my sisters rode in the wagon. Father received the land for fighting in the War for Independence."

"I bet your legs were sore from all that walking."

"You better believe it. Then when we finally got there, we had to clear the land and plant crops with the seeds we brought."

"Sounds like a lot of work."

"Well, Father had our membership transferred to the Redstone Quaker Community and they were a great help to my family. They also helped build our cabin."

"What year was that?"

"The spring of 1790. I remember how apprehensive my father was of the Iroquois Indians in the area when we first arrived. He kept his rifle close by, but there was no real trouble with them. We would see them

---

[67] What is now Mount Holly was originally formed as Northampton on November 6, 1688.

coming and going on the trails to their hunting trips, but always staying away from us."

"That does sound scary. How did you meet your wife?'

"I met her at the Redstone meeting house, and when I was twenty-five, I married Phebe Duly on sixth day in the third month in 1807 at the Quaker meeting house.[68] Soon after our marriage, though, we moved to Columbiana County, Ohio, with my older brothers, Job Jr. and Thomas, and my sisters, Mary and Hope, and their families. We purchased land for one dollar an acre then in 1808 in Franklin Township, Columbiana County, Ohio. We had eight children together. After Phebe died, I moved to Marlborough, Ohio with my children."

"You never know where God is going to lead us."

"Susannah, would you mind if I court you?"

Susannah reflected on that awhile and said, "I would like that."

John reached to her hand and held it. "There is a barn dance this Saturday to raise supplies for the Underground Railroad. Would you like to go with me?"

"Yes, I would. What should I bring?"

"Any used clothes or extra food you may have."

"John, my brother, Absalom Elliott, is talking of moving to Union County, Ohio. I have brothers and sisters living there already. They tell me what great farmland it is. There is a wonderful Quaker community there too."

"Yes, my daughter talks about it too. I love those grandchildren, so I would have to leave with her."

When John's daughter Hope decided to move to Ohio, John asked Susanna to marry him in 1845. Shortly after they married, John and Susanna along with Benjamin, now eleven, James, ten and Harriett, eight, moved to Union County, Ohio along with his daughter, Hope, and her family.

John and Susannah had a daughter, Susan, in 1846, their only child together. They moved to a farm two miles southwest of Mt. Victory

---

[68] US Quaker Meeting Records, 1681-1935, Pennsylvania, Fayette, Redstone Monthly Meeting, Minutes 6th day of 3rd month 1807.

in Union County.

Susannah's daughter, Harriet married Abner Kirk Elliott, the son of Wilkerson and Sarah Elliott, in 1857. Then two years later, John died in 1859, leaving Susannah, her sons Benjamin and James, and their daughter, Susan, now thirteen. Benjamin enlisted on May 2, 1864, in the 136th Ohio National Guards Company D for one hundred days.

Benjamin Rochelle

Harriet Rochelle

In 1870, Susannah was living next door to her daughter, Susan, and her husband, Job Shirk. Later in life, she lived with her daughter, Harriett, in Logan County, Ohio and died in 1885 at the age of 78. She is buried in an unmarked grave by her daughter, Harriett, at Rush Creek Cemetery in Union County, Ohio.

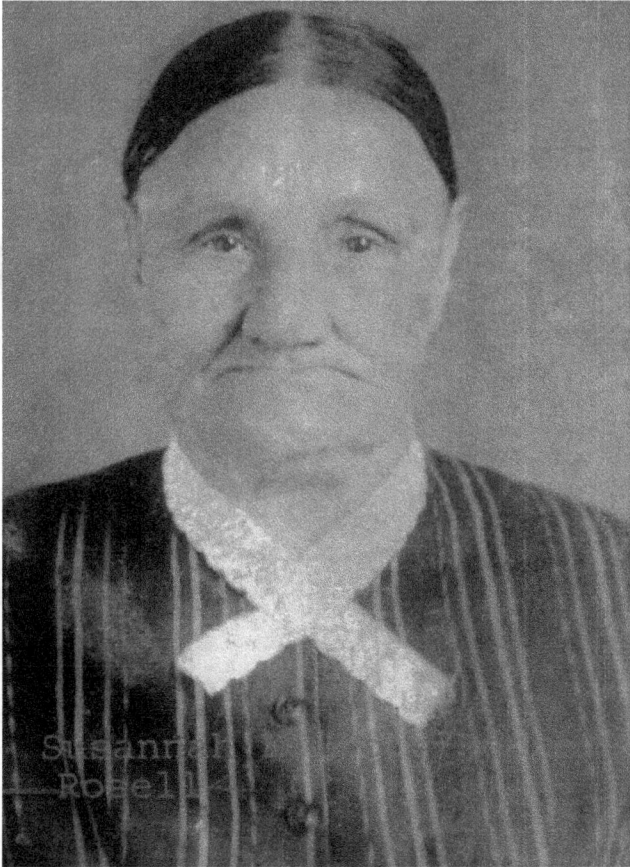

Susannah Elliott Rochelle Rossell

Genealogy of John Rossell

JOHN ROSSELL b. 25 Oct 1785 Burlington Co., New Jersey born to Job Rossell and Huldah Kemble d. 6 Dec 1858 Union Co., Ohio. (1) m. 1807 in Fayette Co., Pennsylvania to Phebe Dooley. (2) m. November 14, 1844[69] in Marlboro, Ohio to Susannah Elliott Rochelle b. 31Aug 1807 Washington Co., Pennsylvania d. Sep 1885 Logan Co., Ohio daughter of Benjamin Elliott and Susannah Supler. 1st marriage to James Rochelle b. 1813 Courtland, Virginia d.1841 Ohio.

John and Phebe children:
1. Anne Rossell b. 1813 Columbiana Co., Ohio m. William Meek in 1835.
2. John Alonzo Rossell b. 6 Mar 1815 Columbiana Co., Ohio d. 20 May 1888 Tustin, Michigan. M Susannah Underwood 1837
3. Rosella Hope Rossell b. 1818 Columbiana Co., Ohio d. 1898 Osceola, Michigan m. Absalom Elliott 19 Feb1838.
4. Mary Jane Rossell b. 1820 Columbiana Co., Ohio d. 1869?
5. Sarah Jane Rossell b. 1823 Columbiana Co., Ohio d. 1905 m. Amos Underwood 1842.
6. Enoch Rossell b. 1826 Columbiana Co., Ohio d. 1890
7. Phebe Rossell b. 1827 Columbiana Co., Ohio d.1904 Osceola, Michigan m. Joseph Whitecotten.
8. James Rossell

John and Susannah child:
Susan S. Rossell b. 1846 in Union Co., Ohio d. 1892 Logan Co.,

---

[69] Ohio County Marriages 1781-2013 Stark marriage records 1836-1851 B p.230

Ohio m. Job Shirk 1863 Union Co., Ohio.

Susannah and James Rochelle children:
1, Benjamin Rochelle b. 18 Sep 1834 Marlboro, Ohio d. 23 Jan
   1896 Hillsdale Co.,
   Michigan m. Sarah Fowler 1862.
2. James Lynes Rochelle b. Sep 1835 Marlboro, Ohio d. 1909 m.
   Rachel Jane Grubb
3. Harriet Rochelle b. 1837 Ohio d. 1892 m. Abner K. Elliott 1857

Chapter Fourteen
John Shirk (1787-1873)

John Shirk died July 28, 1873 aged 86 y 5m 25d

Watching the sun set over the magnificent North Fork Mountain in (West) Virginia, while sitting on the front porch with his family, John told his wife, Sally, and the children about his grandparents.

"Long ago in Switzerland, in a beautiful valley with a view of the Alps Mountains, lived a group of farmers who were devoted Mennonites. They lived peacefully until the government decided the country's religion would be the Protestant Reformed Church and no other religion was accepted. To make matters worse, the Mennonites refused to pay taxes and objected to military service. The government felt it was treasonous and persecuted them. Finally, they tried to kick the Mennonites out of Switzerland. In Switzerland, the name Shirk was spelled Schuch and they were from the village of Sumiswald in Canton Bern. My father, Henry, came from these devoted Mennonites," John explained.

"How did they come to America?" Sally asked, sitting next to their ten-year old son, Levi.

"When it became intolerable, a group of Mennonites with my grandparents came over to America around 1729 when they heard Pennsylvania was open to religious freedom. They came down the Rhine River to the port of Rotterdam, Holland. At that time, there were about twenty stops along the way where boats were stopped by local governments and inspected. They were frightened they would be hauled off at each stop and thrown in prison for being Mennonites. From Rotterdam, they crossed the Atlantic Ocean to Philadelphia, Pennsylvania on a big ship. The whole journey lasted around six long hard months. From Philadelphia, they made their way down to Lancaster County, Pennsylvania. Around 1750, my grandparents traveled from Lancaster area with large group of families to this part of (West) Virginia."

"We have so much to be thankful for, living in this country with religious freedom," Sally commented, as she struggled with the two-year old twins in her lap. Then she added a thought, "No one tells you what you have to believe or what you can or cannot say."

"My father, Henry, grew up here in Hardy County, Virginia, not far from Moorefield. He met and married my mother, Mary Caty Catrie, here. She was born in Ireland," John said.

"I remember your brothers, John. Your mother must have had her hands full."

"Yes, she did, but talking about family, I was so afraid of your grandfather, John Jacob Brake. He seemed larger than life to me. Your father, Isaac, was different. He was a humble man, but I thought I would never get around to asking him to let me court you," John said.

"John Shirk, my father admired you for your strength and character in kindness and justice. You are a very moral man and I love you for that," Sally said. "You are always out helping the neighbors with their crops when they are sick, not to mention you're so tall, handsome and muscular."

"You're so sweet, I love you." Looking down at his ten-year old son, John stated "Levi, we are going on an adventure, a journey into a new land called Ohio."

"Are we going by ship, Father?" Levi asked.

"No, we are going by a covered wagon with a large group of people on what is called a wagon train."

They left the following week on the wagon train to Ross County in 1818 with his in-laws, Isaac, and Rossana Brake, along with twenty other families from the area. The wagons took turns being in first place since the dust from the road flew on the rest of the wagons. The second floor of the wagon was a space for seeds and vegetables. When someone died in route, everyone donated a board from the second floor for the coffin. Every two weeks or after a good rain, the wagon train would stop to dry and air out. This was the time the women would do the laundry. The men were always in fear of a stampede of the cattle they brought with them. Every night, they had two hours of social visits. Sometimes someone would play the fiddle and there would be dancing. Most Sundays were a day of rest. Every fifty miles or three days the men would have to tar the wheels to keep them moving. They traveled an average of fifteen miles a day. Three years later, in 1821, they made it to their destination in Liberty Township, Union County, Ohio after a two year stop in Chillicothe, Ross County where the land office was located. (More of this in the Isaac Brake story.)

In Union County, they settled in Liberty Township on the Joshua Judy farm his father-in-law, Isaac Brake, bought. John bought seven hundred thirty-three acres of wild land, heavy with forest, for one thousand dollars, two miles west of Newton (now Raymond) in the same township. There, John made a permanent house, to which he added rooms to as they were needed. He cleared the land and grew corn, wheat, and flax for making clothes. It was hard work, removing the tree stumps to plant crops, but the land was so rich with black soil, the crops grew larger and faster than they did in (West) Virginia where the soil was rocky and well used.

A few years later, there was scarcity of corn throughout the land. John had an abundance to spare. He always felt that the true value of corn was twenty-five cents a bushel and did not raise it. John found many poor people throughout the area and sold it to them for twenty-five cents, where others were selling corn at fifty cents a bushel. One of his neighbors, Joshua Judy, came by one day to John's farm, driving up in a wagon.

Finding John working in his barn, Joshua asked, "John, I hear you are selling corn for twenty-five cents a bushel. Is this true?"

"Yes, I am," replied John with a stern look on his face and his arms crossed in front of him.

"Well, I will take all you have, then," said Joshua, with a sharp grin on his face.

"Do you have the money, Joshua?" asked John. Then looking out at his horses, John continued "That is a fine team of horses you have."

"Yes, they are, I am very proud of them," he stated.

"Well, Joshua, you can drive further on with your good team of horses and your money. I will keep my corn for those who have no team or money," John commented.

John thought Joshua wanted to buy all his corn to turn around and sell to make a profit.[70]

In 1822, John watched from his farm for his brother, Adam Shirk, and wife, Anna. He received a letter that they were coming on the next

---

[70] *Memorial and Biographical Record of Delaware, Union and Morrow Counties* (Chicago: The Lewis Publishing Co., 1895) p. 317.

wagon train. They brought their mother, Caty, and his sister, Mary, who they called Polly (Polly was a common nickname for Mary then) who was fourteen.

John was taken back on how much his mother had aged since he last saw her. She lost a lot of weight and her hair was white now. "Oh, Mother," said John as he helped her down and hugged her.

"I have missed you so," said Caty.

"It's so good to see you, Adam. I see you grew a beard since I last saw you," said John.

"I have had this awhile, Anna likes the way it tickles her," laughed Adam.

"John, Henry died on August 10, 1819. He wanted to stay at his farm until the end," said Caty.

"We sold the farm, and I brought the money Father left you," said Adam.

"I will build a cabin for Mother on my property with the money. There, she can live out the rest of her life close by," said John. Polly lived with her until she married Michael Brake, John's brother-in-law, who was also a neighbor.

Caty lived to be 88 years old and died on January 10, 1843. She was buried in the first cemetery in the area, Baughan Cemetery. In 1850, John's sons, Levi, Isaac, Henson, and Silas all lived in houses next to him. John had his family all around him in Union County.

John was a member of the Disciple Church, also called the Christian Church, and donated the land to erect a church. The members met at each other's house until they had their own church. They started a cemetery right behind the church and John was one of the first to buy plots of land. It is called New Mill Creek Cemetery by Raymond, Ohio. On the bottom half of the tombstone in small script is "Therefore, my beloved brethren, be ye steadfast unmoved, be always abounding in the work of the Lord for as much is ye known that your labor isn't in vain in the Lord."

Genealogy of Henry Shirk

HENRY SHIRK b. abt. 1758 (West) Virginia d. 10 Aug 1819 m. Mary Catherine (Caty) Catrie b. 21 Apr 1754 in Ireland d. 10 Jan 1843 Union Co., Ohio

Children of Henry and Caty Shirk:
1. Patsy Shirk b. 1780 d. before 1819
2. Susannah Shirk b. 1782
3. Elizabeth Shirk b. 1784 m. Samuel Argo
4. Jacob Shirk b. 1785 m. Catherine Kimble
5. John Shirk b. 03 Feb 1787 m. Sarah Brake
6. Adam Shirk b. Oct 1791 m. (1) Anna Dox (2) Charity Mann
7. Henry Shirk Jr. b. 1800 m. Rebecca Van Meter
9. Mary "Polly" Shirk b. 1806 d.1868 m. 1829 Michael J. Brake
10. Johnathan Shirk b. 1795 m. Elizabeth Edger
11. Caty Shirk b.1793 d. before 1819
12. Job Shirk

Genealogy of John Shirk

JOHN SHIRK b 3 Feb 1787 Hardy Co., (West) Virginia d. 28 July 1873 Union Co., Ohio m. 2 Aug 1805 Sarah (Sally) Brake b. 2 Jan 1790 (West) Virginia d. 25 Sep 1869 Ohio.

Children of John and Sarah Shirk:

1. Levi Shirk b. 1808 d. 1873 m. Martha Patsey Taylor b. 1812
2. Elizabeth Shirk b. 1809 d. 1898 m. (1) Calib Orahood (2) Ezekial Clements
3. Aaron Shirk b. 1810 d. 1887 m. Rosanna Tobey
4. Nancy Shirk b. 1811 d. 1884 m. Daniel Johnson
5. Jemma Shirk b. 1814 d. 1883 m. (1) Abraham Grubb (2) Wm Davis
6. Henson Shirk b. 1816 d. February 17, 1888 (cancer) m. Nancy Wilson
7. Hiram Shirk b. 1816 d. 1883
8. Jonas Shirk b. 1819 d. 1853 m. Olive Harrington
9. Silas Shirk b. 1821 m. (1) Sara Stow (2) Christina Hamilton
10. Lucy Shirk b. 1824 d. 1896 m. Matthew Johnson
11. Isaac Shirk b. 1823 d. 1895 m. Mary Jane Dillon
12. Adam Alfred Shirk b. 1826 d. 1883
13. John Shirk b. 1828 d. 1884 m. Amelia Clemens
14. Sarah Shirk b. 1831 m. James Miller

Chapter Fifteen
Adam Shirk (1791-1876)

Adam Shirk's house

The War for Independence ended eight years ago. The years following, there was a post war baby and building boom. There on the family farm, in a lovely green valley among high mountains with its beautiful trees and rough terrain, on a fall day in 1791, Adam was born in Hardy County, (West) Virginia. Caty (nickname for Mary Catherine), Adam's mother, already had six children, but loved them all dearly. Adam, throughout his childhood, looked up to John, his older brother, and they did everything together, from hunting to working on the farm.

When John got married and moved out of the family home, Adam was over to his house frequently. One day in 1812, while at John and Sally's house, Adam sat in a chair by the fireplace. John looked at Adam across the room, worried, and said, "Adam, President James Madison ordered United States Congress to declare war with Britain yesterday."

"I read in the *Virginia Gazette* that Britain imposed a blockage and seized sailors on American ships, forcing them to work on British ships." Adam sighed. "It also said they were trying to seize the Ohio Great Lake Region and provide support to Shawnee Indians against the American settlers. This makes me so angry. They have no right to do this!" Adam stood up.

"Just when I was feeling safe and getting ahead, we are at war again. I'm afraid I will have to leave Sally and the children to go fight," John said as he rubbed his forehead.

"It would be a hardship for Sally, left with small children and your farm with the cornfield doing so well this year," Adam said, thinking out loud.

In September, John Shirk was drafted, but Adam substituted in his brother's place. He was single and wanted to go, he was mad at what the British were doing to the new country. Besides, Sally was beside herself since they got the news. Adam rode his horse to Petersburgh, Virginia, which was twelve miles around the mountains. He enlisted under Captain Michael Yoakum in 1st regiment Virginia Militia commanded by Colonel Connell.[71] Adam was given a Virginia uniform, which consisted of a blue wool hunting shirt trimmed with red fringe, dark wool trousers and black leather boots. On his head, he wore a low-crown hat. He also had a leather girdle around his waist, in which he carried a tomahawk, a knife, cartridge box, a bayonet and a quart size canteen. He was armed with a musket and carried a shoulder linen knapsack which held extra uniform and extra clothes. A blanket was lashed to the top. Over the knapsack was an oil cloth to protect it from the wet weather. This all weighed an additional thirty-five lbs. The command was to go to Northern Ohio to help build a fort. The regiment marched three hundred and thirty-five miles to the Maumee River rapids that fall and averaged twenty-five miles a day. Adam's legs were so stiff and sore at the end of each day's march, he

---

[71] Adam Shirk file, no. 4844 War of 1812, micropublication 8456 (Washington: National Archives).

could hardly walk.

Once in Ohio, the regiment had an engagement with a small band of Shawnee Indians. Shots were fired, but no one died. The Shawnee took off running and the men continued to march on to the river. Finally, after a good two weeks, they reached the head of the rapids. There, they assisted in building Fort Meigs. It was on a beautiful area, overlooking the Maumee River, where fish and game were abundant. The blockhouses where half done, the Pennsylvania Militia were already there with about five hundred men and were employed building the fortifications. The Virginia Militia joined them, building the blockhouses and completing the stockade.

Adam battled winter weather and disease in the camp and continued to build the fort. He lived in a tent with several other soldiers and at night, it was so quiet, he could hear the sentry at the fort pacing.

Adam, standing outside the tent, said to the soldier next to him, who was also from the Virginia Militia, "A soldier in the next tent died of lockjaw last night."

"That is terrible, how did he get it?" asked the soldier.

"He was on horse detail and got a bad cut on his arm. Then he got horse manure in it, from what I heard," Adam said, frowning. "Last night, he just stopped breathing in his sleep."

"I have had that assignment," said the soldier, concerned.

"Yes, me too," Adam shook his head. "A man came down from Detroit yesterday, General Harrison thinks he is a spy. They placed him under a guard for now."

"I pray we finish the job we came to do and leave before the fighting begins. Every night, I expect the Indians and British to attack the fort. This is nerve wracking."

Worried, Adam said, "I heard gunshots across the river earlier. I heard it was some Indians."

"Scouting party, probably. The shots stopped as soon as they began. I haven't heard anything since."

The spring rains brought mud up to their knees, but they continued to get the fort built. There was mud all over and there wasn't a dry foot in camp. They dug up the ground to build a trench in front of the block houses on north side of the fort and found ancient human bones, piles of bones and they took out twenty-five skulls in one pit. This must have been an ancient battlefield, Adam thought, and wondered what must have happened here years ago.[72]

Adam knew the fort was important in winning the war with the British and it kept him going to get the fort built. After the fort was completed, their job was done. He looked out over the river that spring, thinking, this is the most beautiful place. The river rapids flowing down through the meadows was so charming.

Adam was honorably discharged there, since it was the end of his service. He set out for home on Aril 9, 1813. Before the Virginia Militia left, Major Ball made it to the fort with two hundred men which brought the number up to sixteen hundred men left there.

The militia from Virginia marched the long trip home together. Adam could hear the cannons going off in the distance as they marched and were glad they were headed home. The militia passed ashes and charred cinders where cabins once stood. They passed the Shawnee wigwams, torn and left in a hurry and passed fresh mounds of dirt and knew the dead slept there. Through the swamp and woods, they marched. It seemed longer going home, but when Adam saw the mountains, he knew he was getting close. Finally home, Adam was worn out and so were his uniforms.

Caty saw Adam coming down the road and yelled at him, "Adam, is it you!" She ran to Adam and hugged him; she did not want to let him go. "I have waited for this day. I was so worried you would never make it home."

"There were days I thought I might not make it back," Adam said.

"Adam, you have lost so much weight."

"I need a good home-cooked meal, Mother. I dreamt of your meals for the last six months."

"Well, I will have Henry kill a hog and we will have a feast and

---

[72] Harlow Lindley, editor, *Fort Meigs and war of 1812,* (Columbus, Ohio: The Ohio Historical Society, 1975), 129.

invite the family over."

"Where is Father?"

"He is out working in the fields."

"How are John and Sally and their children?"

"They are all doing well. Sally is pregnant again." Caty smiled.

That evening with the whole family there, Adam told of his adventures in the Ohio Territory.

"Thank you again for going in my place, Adam. I will forever be in your debt," said John.

"I would do it again, John. The land there is so beautiful with lovely winding streams, large forests and flat with rich black soil," said Adam.

Later that week, Adam went to Petersburgh, Virginia to get supplies and met the lovely Anna Dox.

When he got home, Adam said, "Mother, I am going to ask Mr. William and Mrs. Rachel Dox if I could court their daughter, Anna. I believe she is twenty-one."

"Adam, do you know who they are? They are a very proper and well-to-do family in Petersburgh."

"I just want to court their daughter, not to take their money."

"Adam, courting is a very serious matter; it is the uniting of families. I hear Rachel Proctor Dox, Anna's mother, is the niece of General Thomas Proctor," Caty continued.

"Mother, Anna makes my heartbeat faster, just talking to her and I need to move on with my life."

Adam and Anna, after a proper courting period, were married January 26, 1817 in Petersburgh and their first child, Lydia, was born a year later.

Adam came home from his brother's house for supper. Once inside the kitchen, he saw Anna placing the dishes on the table. "John and Sally are leaving for Ohio with the wagon train out of Moorfield next month. This hilly, mountainous land is so hard to farm. Ohio is mostly flat with dark rich fertile land."

"You want to go too; I can see it in your eyes, but Lydia is a tiny infant, Adam," Anna said.

"Yes, and Father is ill. I am afraid he won't live long with his heart giving him problems. When the time is right, we will go to Ohio."

Henry died. In early 1819 they buried him in Shook cemetery in Smoke Hole, Hardy County, Virginia alongside his son, Absalom, and daughters, Caty (who was named after her mother) and Patsy. Henry owned one hundred eighty-six acres at Burkett's Hole, close to Smoke Hole and Shirk Gap.

The farm was auctioned off and the money divided among the family, as instructed in the will.

In 1820, Adam, Anna, little Lydia and his mother Caty, along with his sister, Polly, who was fourteen, left for Ohio. Jonathan, Adam's younger brother, married Anna's sister, Elizabeth Dox, and came along to Ohio. His brother, Henry Shirk Jr., was the only member of the family to stay in (West) Virginia and lived with his wife Elizabeth in Pendleton County a few miles away.

Adam hitched up the team of horses to the wagon and turned to look at Anna. "Did you finish packing our possessions?"

"Yes, dear."

"Anna, let me hand you Lydia and let's get these horses on the road," said Adam.

When they got to Moorefield, they paid the wagon master. Adam had a limited education, but he could read, write and do some arithmetic. He knew when the cost of an item was too much, but he paid the wagon master it anyway.

They crossed the Ohio River at Sistersville on the ferry and went on Zane's Trace through Fairfield County then into Union County, not far from his big brother, John. Adam and Anna had their second baby, Hannah, shortly after settling in Liberty Township, Union County.

Looking down the road from the porch of the farm they rented, Anna said, "Adam, it is so nice to be here with our family just down the road."

"I know, my brothers Johnathan and John along with your brothers Adam and Michael Brake, are just within a stone's throw," said Adam.

~ * ~

In 1826, Anna looked at Adam over dinner with Lydia, now eight, and Hannah, now four, sitting on a bench next to her. She said, "Daniel is not quite a year old, and I think I am pregnant again."

"That is great. If it is a boy, I want to name him Stephen, I always liked that name," said Adam.

"I don't know where we are going to put everyone."

"I think it is time to have a farm of our own."

Adam bought land just down the road in 1829 in Taylor Township, where he built first a cabin in 1831 then a frame house later, which he added on to as the family grew. He planted oats, corn and wheat and had sheep and pigs. There were so many Shirks in the area, they named the school Shirk School. About half the children in school had the last name of Shirk.

Adam and Anna had a total of twelve children. One child, Adam Jr., died in infancy and was buried at Baughn Cemetery.

Adam was in the barn, tending to the livestock, when Anna came into the barn, crying. "Adam, your mother just died at home." The cold January wind blew the barn door shut, making Anna jump into Adam's arms.

Holding her with tears in his eyes, Adam said, "Anna, she was eighty-eight years old and we knew she would die soon. Even so, it is hard not to grieve the passing of a dear mother."

The family buried her in the Baughn Cemetery beside baby Adam Jr.

Adam never received his land grant from the government for the war of 1812 until after the Act of 1850, when he received eighty acres of land.

Then on April 25, 1859, Anna died. Adam put a large black ribbon on the door and had her showing in the parlor off the living room. She was so loved; people poured through the house. Everyone brought food and Adam had enough food to last a month. The family friend, Charity Mann, who was loved by the family, was especially helpful, giving Adam emotional support. He married Charity the next year on June 8, 1860.

Back in January, that year on the tenth, Adam went to Columbus, Ohio to the Old Soldier's Convention. About a hundred men, veterans of war of 1812, attended. They marched to the capitol where they received military honors. Then in 1861, war broke out again, but this time, they fought the South.

Adam was a member of the Christian Church, also called Disciple Church, where his son, Stephen, was pastor. After the Sunday services in 1864, Adam and Stephen stood at the church door, talking. "The women in Marysville are all up in arms about women's rights now. They are marching up Main Street with their banners," Adam said. "They want equal rights for women along with equal rights for African Americans."

"Their husbands need to get them back in the house, taking care of their families," Stephen said.

"Well, maybe, but you want to keep your wife happy." Feeling tension, Adam changed the subject. "The roads are all muddy from the rain we have been having. It is almost impossible to get a team of horses and a wagon through."

"I hear they are finally going to improve the roads, now that the railroad is coming through," Stephen said. Then looking up at his father, he said, "Father, I am thinking of enlisting in the union army."

"You are thirty-two years old with a family. Do you think that is wise?" Adam said, worried.

"I preach almost every week about the evils of slavery; I don't think it is enough."

"This war won't last long. The South has no factories, little money and since Gettysburg, they have lost almost every battle."

"Yes, but I really feel the calling to join the army."

"Stephen, I can't stop you, especially if your mind is made up." Adam threw his arms up in the air. Upset with the conversation, he left.

Stephen enlisted a few days later in 1864 and left for Camp Chase in Columbus, Ohio. Stephen came home to his family a few months later but was never the same. (More to come in Stephen's story)

Starting February 14, 1871, Adam received pension from the government of eight dollars a month. The average farm laborer at the time made twenty-three dollars a month.

One very hot summer in 1873, there was a typhoid epidemic. Just the word typhoid terrorized the people of the community. Several in the area became sick and some died. Then Charity became sick, but the doctor said she had consumption[73] (TB). He believed it was contagious, so they quarantined Charity in the bedroom. She had coughing spells and hard time breathing and each day, she became sicker. Adam got out word to all his children she was dying. The next day, she died. Then his brother, John Shirk, who he loved dearly, died that summer too. Grief-stricken, Adam lived for another three years.

Finally, after fifty years on the same farm, Adam died at his home, July 29, 1876, of old age. Eighty-seven years of a well-lived life, ten of his children still living and well over fifty grandchildren, along with a large number of great-grandchildren. It was a huge funeral. Adam was buried at New Mill Creek Cemetery. On April 1, 1877, his youngest son, Aaron, legally took over his farm.[74] The farm is still owned by the great-grandchild of Aaron.

---

[73] Charity Shirk entry, Union County Death Records Vol. 1-3, 44, no. 115, Probate Court, Marysville, Ohio.

[74] W. H. Beers, *History of Union County Ohio* (Chicago: W. H. Beers and Co., 1883),676.

Genealogy of Adam Shirk

ADAM SHIRK b. 22 October 1791 Hardy Co., (West) Virginia d. 29 July 1876 Union Co., Ohio m. #1-26 January 1817 Anna Dox b. 5 August 1796 d. 25 April 1859, #2-1860 Charity Mann d. 1873

Children of Adam and Anna Shirk: [75]
1. Lydia Shirk b. 1818 m. 1843 George Draper
2. Hannah Shirk b. 1822 (never married)
3. Daniel Shirk b. 1825 m. 1847 Sarah D. Brake
4. Stephen Shirk b. 1826 d. 1910 m. 1848 Mary Brake
5. John W. Shirk b. 1828 d. 1899 m. 1859 Sarah Safford
6. Henry Aaron Shirk b. 1828 d. 1921 m. Elizabeth Myers
7. Sarah Shirk b. 1831 d. before 1876 m. Joseph Snodgrass
8. Aaron Shirk b.1834 d. 1906 m. Mary E. Baughan
9. Adam Jr. Infant son b. 1835 d.1835
10. Rachel Shirk b. 1837 d. 1878 m. #1-1860 Nelson Draper #2-1864 Ira Belville
11. Clarinda Shirk b. 1838 d. 1924 m. 1857 Andrew Hisey
12. Nancy Jane Shirk b. 1844 d. 1932 m. 1865 John C. Hisey

On Sunday September 3, 1918, the Shirk family held a reunion and one hundred sixty-five relatives attended at the home of James Davis. These were the children, grandchildren, great grandchildren, and second great grandchildren of Adam and John Shirk.

---

[75] Will of Adam Shirk April 1, 1877

Shirk Reunion September 3, 1918

Chapter Sixteen
Adam Brake (1794-1870)

It was not easy for Adam to live in the shadow of his grandfather, John Jacob Brake, who was well known in Hardy County, (West) Virginia. His grandfather was wealthy, but also overbearing and always pushing his ideas on the family. He acted like his way was the only way. Grandfather's third wife, Catherine, was even more condescending toward the family, after his grandfather Brake died and left everything to her. Adam's father, Isaac, was never good enough in her eyes and she went out of her way to say hurtful things. Adam stayed away from her as much as possible. When the offer to go to Ohio with his father, Isaac, came up, Adam was more than willing. At the age of twenty-six, in 1818, he left with his parents, Isaac and Rosanna Brake, along with his brother and sisters for Ohio on the wagon train. In Chillicothe, Ohio, where the land office was, they met up with Mordecai Baughan's family, as well as other families going to Liberty Township, Union County, Ohio. There was a long stream of wagons converging there, waiting for land in Ohio.

Standing next to his family's wagon, Adam saw a tall, distinguished man with a beard and mustache who was standing at the next wagon. He walked over, holding his hand out, and said, "Hi, my name is Adam Brake."

Mordecai shook hands with Adam and said, "Mordecai. Nice to meet you."

Smiling, Adam said, "Mordecai, where are you from?"

"Our family moved from Culpepper, Virginia, to North Carolina a few years ago, when land opened up. It was a mistake. Now that land is opening in Ohio cheap, we want to try farming here. I hear the land is perfect for farming, flat land with rich black soil."

"I know what you mean, the land in Hardy County, (West) Virginia is mountainous and rocky. The soil is used up and there is overcrowding of families in the area," Adam said with his hands on his hips.

"In North Carolina, the soil is red," Mordecai said.

"I don't think I ever saw red soil. Is it any good?"

"It is a poor-quality soil and doesn't hold water well. Not only poor soil, but everything it touched had a red cast to it," Mordecai continued. "My children ran through the house with red muddy feet, tracking it on everything."

"Are these children running around the wagon yours?" asked Adam, grinning.

"Yes, this is William running by who is five, and Mary, who is chasing him, is eight. My wife, Mary, is at the campfire, cooking dinner, and our daughter, Eve, the pretty little brown-haired girl helping her, is eleven. I have three older children, out looking for wood for the campfire."

"I think I saw my sister Elizabeth hanging around your son, Jeremiah, yesterday," said Adam.

"Yes, I noticed that too. They seem to enjoy each other's company."

Smiling, Adam nodded. "Yes, they do."

After they moved to Liberty Township, Isaac purchased one of the farms Joshua Judy owned. Adam stayed with his father and helped work the farm. He removed the many trees, planted crops, and helped with the many farm animals they accrued.

Jeremiah and Adam's sister were married three years later by the justice of peace. Adam would run into Eve on and off over the next six years, watching her grow up. Adam eventually fell in love with her and when she turned seventeen, he married Eve in 1823. They lived the first few years in a rented house in Marysville, Ohio. Their daughter, Mary, was born a year later and named after Eve's mother. Isaac came along two years later and was named after Adam's father.

Adam walked home from downtown and found Eve rocking the baby. "Eve, Dr. Thompson sold us the farm next to his. It is in the same settlement area where a large group of our family and friends live in Liberty Township."

"Thank God, this little house is very crowded with the new baby. It will be so good to be back closer to our parents," said Eve.

Their family grew with four children by1833. Then one day, after riding home from town, Adam found Eve on the front porch, churning butter. "Marysville was busier than usual today, with horses and carriages up and down Main Street. Children were out skipping rope and a lot of adults were standing around, talking," said Adam.

"What were they talking about?" asked Eve.

"A group of ladies from Steubenville, Ohio have gone to the streets, protesting against forcing the removal of the Indians."

"There is a group of Indians living a few miles northeast of here."

"I have read in the *Marysville Tribune* there are almost two thousand still living in Ohio," said Adam.

"The Wyandot Indians live in small cabins in a settlement, not hurting anyone. Why does the government want to remove the Indians, haven't they done enough to them?"

"I see Andrew Jackson won the presidency. Four more years of him running the country."

"He caused so many problems with the Indians, I dread another four years."

"I know what you mean. Oh, by the way, one of the neighbors stopped by and gave me some white corn on the cob."

"I see it has small hard kernels on it."

"He told me to put it in a pan with little fat and heat it up over the fireplace. It is called popped corn."

Eve got out a cast iron pan and put in some butter she churned earlier that day. She took a knife and scraped the dried kernels into the pan. She watched as the corn sizzled in the pan. Then all at once, the kernels started exploding. Corn was flying all over the room.

Eve screamed as she got out of the way. "Adam, is this corn supposed to jump out of the pan like this?"

"I bet you're supposed to put a lid on it," Adam said, laughing. "What is left tastes good. The neighbor said he got it from the Indians a few miles from here. If we like it, we could have some more to plant."

In 1843, the Wyandot Indians were forced to leave Ohio for Kansas after they signed a treaty in 1842 with the Federal Government. Early morning on July 13, while Adam was out in the barn, he heard the neighbor come over, yelling, "The Indians are on the trail, marching south."

Adam came running into the house. "Eve, hurry, get the children and come get in the buggy, we are going over towards Bellefontaine. The You will never see anything like this again in your life." Wyandot Indians are marching in large numbers from Upper Sandusky south to

Cincinnati.[76]

As they got close, they saw people lined the streets all the way along to say goodbye.[77]

"Look over there down the road, there are hundreds of Indians," said Adam as he pointed with his right finger. As far as Adam could see north and south there where Indians and there was no end to that long line. The tall Indian chiefs on horses came; the aged and sick Indians, wrapped in bright colored blankets, were in wagons. Wagons went by, loaded full of belongings. Then came the long line of Indians who wore light brown tunics with red and white beads around their arms and wore dark leather leggings with beaded leather moccasins on their feet. Their dark black hair was tied in back of their head, two feathers came from the top of their headbands which were decorated with colored glass beads.

"Adam, you can tell how proud the Indians are by the way they sit tall on their horses with broad shoulders and straight backs," said Eve.

"Yes, and look at the tiny heads of the babies peeking through the small bundles tied to the women's backs," said Adam.

"I am amazed how well-dressed they are. Why, they look so much like us," said a man from the crowd.

"Yes, and such a parade of fine buggies," said Adam.

"Look at the brown-faced little children with big black eyes in the baskets tied to the horses beside their mothers," said Eve.

The long feathers on the horses' manes swayed in the wind. More Indians walked on down the road with still proud brown faces. They rode their beautiful horses, carrying skins, food and cooking pots. It was a sad scene. Some of the Indians and village people cried as they waved goodbye.

"Where are they going?" asked Eve.

"According to the *Marysville Tribune,* there are steamboats in

---

[76] John J. Vogel, Ph.D., *Indians of Ohio and Wyandot County* (New York: VantagePress, 1975),66

[77] Mary Stockwell, *The other Trail of Tears* (Yardley, Pennsylvania: Westholme Publishing, 2014), 314-315.

Cincinnati that will take them to their new reservation in Kansas," said Adam.

"This is too sad to watch."

"We will never forget this day."

~ * ~

The years went on and they had three more children by 1848. In no time at all, their oldest, Mary, was twenty-one, grown and married to Stephen Shirk. They rented a farmhouse down the road. Adam started to walk out of the kitchen as Mary came in, upset, stomping her feet.

"Are you alright?" Adam, thinking to himself, Stephen must have brought another dog home and didn't tell Mary, again.

"No! Does Stephen always have to have his way?" shouted Mary. "Now he wants his favorite dog back in the house."

"You are a little too headstrong for your own good."

"Men!"

"I'll leave you with your mother," said Adam as he continued to the barn.

The following year, Adam came in from the barn and found Eve in tears, "Adam, little David's throat is red and swollen. His body is hot, and he cries constantly," cried Eve.

"I will go for the doctor," said Adam. By the time the doctor got there, David was burning up with fever and small red spots appeared on his arms and legs.

"Keep him cool by sponging him with cool water and hope for the best. He has scarlet fever, which is contagious, so keep him away from the other children," said the doctor.

Their little three-year old son, David, died after being sick with scarlet fever for ten days and was buried in Baughn Cemetery,[78] the cemetery Eve's father started with part of his farmland. Eve cried until her eyes were puffy and red. Mary came over frequently to help her

[78] David Brake entry, Union County Death Records Vol 1-3, Probate Court, Marysville, Ohio.

mother. "Fevers have taken many children away from their mothers in the area," said Mary.

"The poor mothers, I know how their hearts hurt," said Eve. Only time healed Eve's broken heart.

By 1850, Adam and Eve owned thirty acres of improved farmland and twenty-three acres of wooded area. They also owned one mule, two cows, four sheep, eighteen pigs and crops of rye, oats, and Indian corn.

A year later, at 42 years old, Eve's prayers were answered with another baby. Amanda brought joy back into Eve and Adam's life.

On July 4, 1860, Adam and Eve decided to go to Marysville to the 4th of July Celebration. Adam hooked the horses up to the buggy and picked up Eve and their daughter Amanda at the front porch. Eve carried out a basket with fried chicken in it. Amanda carried a basket of sugar cookies. Once they were in the buggy, Eve asked, "Adam, are we going to get there in time?"

"Yes, it only takes two hours to get to the Marysville fair grounds. They are expecting a large crowd today," Adam said.

"It is going to be a glorious day, the children and their families are going to meet us there and they are all bringing food," Eve said.

"Eve, did you remember to bring blankets to sit on?"

"Oh, I need to get some cloth napkins also."

"I will get them for you, Ma," said Amanda.

"Hurry," Eve said as Amanda ran into the house.

"Amanda is so good for an eight-year-old," said Adam.

Once there, they found Mary and Stephen and the grandchildren among the large groups of people. They joined them and sat on their blankets. The president of the committee called the celebration to order, followed by Reverend J. Smith giving a proper prayer. The Marysville Brass Band played *Hail Columbia.* The Declaration of Independence was then read while the crowd remained silent, except for a few babies crying.

Speeches by prominent men were given of the struggles which the heroes of The Great War (Revolutionary War) endured, that we might secure and perpetuate the blessings of civil and religious liberties. Also, of the great blessings God bestowed on this country. The evils of slavery were also brought up. After several more pieces of music by the band, everyone left for refreshments that were provided, along with their own food they brought, in the shade of the trees. Most of the crowd returned to town after eating. Some men brought whiskey and a little fight broke out.[79] That was when Adam and Eve left for home.

"You would think the men would have good sense to abstain on a day like this," said Eve.

"That is the problem, they don't have good sense," said Adam.

"I hope the government passes laws to stop consumption of alcohol soon."

"I believe the government is worried more about the slavery issue right now."

"Yes, the constitution should be for black people as much as white people."

"I am afraid war is coming and that means our children will probably be drafted."

Adam's fears came true when their son William, twenty-six years old, went off to enlist September 1861 in Union Army Company F 31st Ohio Infantry. Then their son, George W., was drafted when he was thirty and went off to war. He came home long enough to marry Elizabeth Lewellen on July 4, 1863, then he returned to the war, only to die November 1, 1863. Their son-in law Stephen Shirk enlisted (more in Stephen's story). Adam's nephews were drafted and fought from Harper's Ferry all the way to Atlanta. Eve's brother, William moved to Illinois and became Captain of Company C unit 63 Illinois Infantry. Almost everyone in the area had family members in the war. So many died and many others came home injured, if not physically, then emotionally.

~ * ~

Adam and Eve rode into the small town of Broadway to do some trading, a day in August of 1866. Money was hard to come by after the

---

[79] "The Celebration of the Fourth at Marysville" *The Marysville Tribune,* Marysville, Ohio, 11 July 1860, page 2, column 2.

Civil War, so Eve made a large rag rug to take to the General Store in exchange for material to make a new dress. As they rode into town, they saw a wagon unloading grain at the grain elevator by the railroad station. Across the street was a man taking his horse into the Livery Stable and then there was the Harness Shop, where they sold horse equipment. A lady was looking through the window at the hats at a millenary shop. Next came a shoe and boot shop. Adam thought about how he should get his boot repaired. *The Enterprise* newspaper office was across the street next to the post office and finally the general store. Adam tied the horse and buggy to the hitching post and carried the rug into the store. After Eve got her material, she stopped at the post office and picked up a letter.

"Adam, I received a letter from William in Illinois. He says my father died July 25 there," said Eve, as tears fell from her eyes.

"I am sorry you did not get to see your father again," said Adam as he hugged Eve.

"Mordecai was eighty-five years old. He lived a long and good life, "said Eve.

A year later, their son, Isaac moved back home with his two children, seven-year-old son, Winfield and two-year old daughter, Adora. He had struggled to make it for several years, but with the death of his wife, he gave up in 1867.

Adam died three years later, at the age of senenty-six and was buried in Baughn cemetery. Stephen Shirk, the son-in-law, gave the funeral sermon. Adam, as a child, belonged to the German Reformed Church, but when their daughter Mary's husband became a minister, he became a member of the Christian Church and went regularly.

Eve signed the farm over to Isaac after Adam's death, stipulating Eve and Amanda stayed on at the farm.

An outbreak of typhoid fever in 1873 caused several people to become ill and die. Amanda died of gastric fever on May 9, which was probably typhoid fever.[80] She was only twenty-one.

Eve continued to live with her son Isaac until her death in 1875. She was sixty-six years old.

---

[80] Amanda Brake entry, Union County Death Records Vol 1-3, 42, no. 72, Probate Court, Marysville, Ohio.

Genealogy of Adam Brake

ADAM BRAKE b. 15 July 1794 Hardy County, (West) Virginia d. 15 May 1870 Union County, Ohio m. Eve Baughan 19 January 1826 b. 1809 North Carolina d. 19 July 1875 Union County, Ohio, daughter of Mordecai Baughan and Mary Zimmerman.

Children of Adam and Eve's:
1. Mary Brake b. 17 February 1827 Union Co., Ohio d. 4 January 1903 Peoria Ohio m. Stephen Shirk 12 August 1848
2. Isaac Brake b 1829 Union Co., Ohio d. 22 June 1914 m. Talitha Whittaker b. 1836 d. 1867
3. Sarah Brake b. 1830 d. 25 February 1910 m. Daniel Shirk 12 October 1848
4. David Brake b. 1831 26 January 1849
5. George W. Brake b. 1833 d. 1 November 1863 m. Elizabeth Lewellen 4 July 1863
6. William Madison Brake b. 6 May 1835 d. 30 September 1898 m. Almira Perry 1874
7. Susan Brake b. 1837 m. John Bault 23 December 1856
8. Amanda Brake b. 27 November 1851 d. 9 May 1873

Chapter Seventeen
James Poling (1806-1893)

James Poling, abt. 1888

James looked back around the Conestoga Wagon at the beautiful mountains he was leaving behind. In the streets were his family and friends, waving as he went down the gravel road. They passed the little white church, where he and Polly were married back in December of 1831. Their pastor was upset with them then and their parents were not happy either. They waited until baby Eurem was over 2 months old before they got married. They lived with James's parents since Polly's family left for Ohio over a year ago. Polly's given name was Mary, but her father nicknamed her Polly and she loved it.

His brother Joseph was at the edge of the road, waving. Joseph promised to come to Ohio someday, but right now, he was going to take care of their parents, Samuel and Sarah, and their large farm. In the wagon were James and Polly's four-year old son, Eurem, and their one-year-old daughter, Sarah Ann. Polly was keeping them busy by letting them play with the pots and pans.

"Polly, I am so excited about going to Ohio. I hope I can get the land next to your parents. I really feel good about this move," said James.

"Yes, I do too. Can you believe my parents have been there in Allen Township for five years now? They write that they have a fine home there," said Polly.

"Did you tell me he received a land grant from the government, from being in the war of 1812?"

"Yes, but he doesn't talk about the war much," said Polly.

"It probably brings back bad memories," said James.

"I am glad your brother Roger and his wife Sarah are able to come along with us," said Polly. "It makes traveling so much more pleasant. I hope their small wagon is big enough for them and their three children."

The next day, they met up with the wagon train, going to Ohio. It took several days of traveling over rough roads, across rivers and through the wilderness to get to their destination.

The land in Ohio was flat, except for hills here and there. Large areas of woods with large ancient trees were everywhere. There was an abundance of animals and the streams were full of fish. Large herds of deer could be seen in the fields and woods. Turkeys could be shot from the cabin door; they were so numerous. James and Polly were able to buy the land next to his in-laws, near Darby Creek, not far from Woodstock, Ohio. The land was about eight miles from Marysville, the county seat.

James and Polly lived with her parents until they could build a cabin. Finally, moving into their first small cabin, Polly looked at James. "I am so glad our cabin was built before the baby was born."

"Me too, your parents' house was getting crowded, and I was getting uncomfortable there," said James.

"Why?" asked Polly.

"The way your mother looked at us every time the children got into her things," said James.

A year later in 1837, Polly's father, Solomon Carpenter, died. Solomon's death was especially hard on Polly since she saw him almost every day. She would frequently run next door and spend time with her parents. As Polly sat in church and cried, her family gathered around her and her mother. The pastor gave the eulogy.

"Solomon was a friend to everyone he met and no one was a stranger. He was the best carriage and wagon maker around. The Carpenter family has been in this country for a long time. His forefathers first came to America in the late 1600's from Wiltshire, England and settled on Long Island, New York. From there, the family migrated to Barbour County, Virginia. Solomon and Catherine were among the first pioneers here in Union County, Ohio. He and his wife had niner children, of which two died young. He will be deeply missed by his family and many friends."

"James, Father left me fourteen dollars and thirty-five cents in his will (today, it would be approximately equal four hundred and eight dollars). I am putting it towards building our larger cabin," said Polly.

"I know; I built this first cabin too small," said James.

A year later, James' and Polly's son, Eurem, came down with a fever just before his seventh birthday and died. It was so hard to lose their firstborn.

"Lord, help us get through this difficult time," cried Polly as she watched her little boy buried at Buck Run Cemetery.

"We will, it just takes time," choked James, as he hugged Polly.

Later that year, on October 30th, 1838 their son, Orsamus, was born and brought joy back into their lives.

The next year in 1939, Polly came home from her mother's house and found James tending the horses.

"James, my mother received a letter from a lawyer stating her father died leaving her a hundred dollars from his estate (today, it would approximately equal two thousand nine hundred and fifty-four dollars)," said Polly. "He lived to be over eighty years old."

"I'm sorry," said James.

"James, do you remember my grandfather, John Hill?" asked Polly.

"Yes, didn't he own a sawmill and a homestead on the west side of Sugar Creek in Virginia?"

"That was him. Grandfather was in the Maryland Militia in the War for Independence. He was born in Frederick County, Maryland in 1759. He never moved to Virginia until after he married my grandmother Barbara."

James Poling's Cabin

James built this cabin by 1840 on his land, off a dirt road that ran between North Lewisburg and Marysville (route 245 now) close to Darby Creek. It was a labor of love. He hewn logs and split slabs to shape the cabin. He used nice large straight beams of the Cucumber Tree Wood across the ceiling of the main room. The logs were chiseled out with simple hand tools of a broad ax and a chisel. Walnut stairs were next to the back wall that went up to the second floor where there were bedrooms. The lovely stone chimney was built with skill, so the smoke went up the chimney and not back into the room. Over the front door were two deer horns fastened to the wall with a rifle hanging on the horns. The rifle was a thing of beauty. The walnut stock was polished until it shined. The silver plate was beautifully hand carved. A homemade pouch made of deerskin with attached powder horn hung on one of the antlers.

Shortly after the cabin was finished, their son, Rueben, was born there in 1841. Then four years later, Polly was talking to James as they were getting ready for bed.

"Mother wants us to join a new church she has been going to lately," said Polly.

"Catherine is going to church again?" asked James.

"Yes, Mother speaks so highly of the church they built over in Woodstock," said Polly.

"Really? What is this church called?" said James as he sat on the edge of the bed, watching her.

"Universalist Church," Polly said, as she brushed her long brown hair.

"Universalist? What kind of church is that?"

"Well, Mother said it is an open religion; they believe in the freedom of beliefs," said Polly.

"What is wrong with the Christian Church we go to now?"

"Nothing, James. Mother feels this is more open to different views and her friends really like it. This church allows children to the services too."

James shifted on the bed. "I am not worried about the older ones, but do you think the baby will stay hushed?"

"I will nurse Angernsia just before we go and she will sleep through the services," said Polly.

"If your mother likes this church that much, I think we can go and find out more about what open religion is about," James said, kissing Polly on the forehead. They felt comfortable there and continued with

Universalist Church for the rest of their lives.

In 1854, James received a letter from his brother Joseph, telling him that his father, Samuel, died. Joseph sent information on the will in the letter.

"Samuel leaves 344 acres of land to his son Joseph Poling, plus all his horses, cattle, sheep, hogs and farming equipment, all household furniture and bedding. Joseph is to take care of Samuel's wife, Sarah, during her life. Joseph is to pay to the other sons and daughters: four sons, Samuel, John, Roger and James, all of Union County, Ohio, all my wearing clothing to be divided equally between them. To daughter Rachel Jackson one dollar, to my son William's heir one dollar to be divided equally. To Martin's daughter Sarah one dollar. To my daughter Elizabeth Huff of Union County, Ohio, all my wife's wearing clothing at her death." [81]

"Joseph writes that father died in his sleep. He was eighty-eight," said James, sullen.

"I am so sorry about your father, James," said Polly as she rubbed his arm and tried to comfort him. I miss your mother, Sarah. Does he say how she is doing?"

"Good enough to travel. As soon as he sells the farm, they are all coming to Ohio," said James.

"It will be so good to see them again; it has been ten years now," said Polly.

Sarah and Joseph sold the farm on Sugar Creek in Barbour County, Virginia on September 13, 1860. Sarah came with her son, Joseph, and his family to Union County, Ohio.

"Polly, come out here. Joseph is coming up the road with Mother," said James.

"I'm coming," said Polly.

"Oh, Mother," said James, as he ran to the wagon. "I am so sorry to hear about Dad."

"Thank you. James, you look so much like Samuel," said Sarah, as James lifted her out of the wagon.

---

[81] Samuel Poling's Will, Barbour County, Virginia Will Book I, 93.

James was so happy; he couldn't stop hugging his mother.

"How are you doing, Joseph?" said James as he walked over to hug him.

"Good, it is so good to see you again," said Joseph.

"There is a farm near here you should be able to get at a good price, said James, "until then you can all stay here with us."

"Thanks."

"The fishing is good here, we should go fishing Sunday and take the boys," said James.

"That sounds like fun," said Joseph. "We have a lot of catching up to do."

"I also have quite an arrowhead collection. I find them in the fields when I am plowing," said James.

"Oh, how interesting," said Joseph, smiling.

"Yes, Cyrus and Orsamus both got married and left home this year to start their own families," said James.

"Our children are growing up so fast."

"So much is happening. The railroad goes through Woodstock now and the town is growing."

"James, there is talk of war, I have a feeling it will be here soon."

"I know, I fear for our children."

MARKINGS:

Reuben Poling

President Lincoln called for thirteen regiments of troops of young men in Ohio to fight with the union army. James and Polly's worse nightmare came when their son, Reuben, at twenty years old, who was 5'6" tall, with dark brown hair and gray eyes, told them he wanted to enlist for the war.

"James, Rueben is very determined to take up the cause and fight for what is right," said Polly.

"I know, he is talking about walking to Woodstock to enlist and join Company H of the 66th OVI there. Some of his friends have already left," said James.

"I hope he changes his mind, even if he did promise to write often," said Polly.

The next day, Rueben started to the school by Woodstock as usual that January day in 1862, but when he learned the regiment was leaving, he walked on into Woodstock, where he enlisted and left with the army.

Rueben wrote his parents letters regularly, although they were a long time coming, telling them about the war. With the letter, Rueben sent a picture of himself as he appeared on the day of his enlistment. James could see the fear in his eyes from the uncertainty of what he was going to face. Rueben was ordered to New Creek, Virginia, where he was placed under the command of Colonel Charles Candy. From New Creek, he went on to fight at Shenandoah in March of 1862 and by May had advanced to Winchester, Virginia. He kept his letters simple, just mainly telling them of the different places he fought. In the next letter, Polly read how he crossed the Rappahannock River in June. The bridge was gone so they placed pontoon boats across the river to get into Fredericksburg, Virginia. He fought at the battle of Port Republic under General Shields, then from August 28-30, he was at the battle of Bull Run.

In a letter in September, Rueben stated the Battle of Antietam was the worst battle he was in yet. He fired over the shoulders of a fellow soldier. He saw one soldier shot in the chest with the bullet coming out his back then falling over dead. Each letter told of his travels and the battle in which he found himself. He fought in the battle of Chancellorsville in May and in July 1863, he went to Gettysburg, Pennsylvania, where he was placed in reserve. From there, his unit went in pursuit of General Robert E. Lee to Manassas Gap, Virginia. In his next letter, he talked about how, in August, his company was placed on a train to New York

City by order of President Abe Lincoln to stop the draft riots and get control of the city. The buildings and stores were looted and burned with hundreds of citizens of New York being killed in the riots.

Then the next letter came. He was back at war in a skirmish at Garrison Creek, Tennessee. From there, he marched to Chattanooga. He stayed at Bridgeport, Alabama, down the Tennessee River for the winter from December 1863 to May 1864. Then in May of 64, he was part of the Atlanta campaign. Rueben drove a team of horses from Atlanta to the seaboard of North Carolina to get supplies for General William Tecumseh Sherman. There he picked up a Bible. In his last letter, from June 10 to July 2 of 1864, he was at Kennesaw Mountain and the occupation of Atlanta. Then no more letters and James and Polly feared the worst. They waited and waited, but no more letters came. They never gave up.

Rueben was mustered out (discharged) at Goldsboro, North Carolina on April 3, 1865. He took the train back to Woodstock, Ohio. Back in town, he was disoriented since the town changed so much in the three years he was gone. Remembering the farm was by Darby Creek, he walked to the creek and then waded part of his way home due to the heavy brush. James and Polly did not recognize their son as he was walking up the path to the farm; he was so ragged and haggard. He lost a lot of weight and it had been a long time since he had a haircut or a shave. It was only when he yelled, "Ma!" that Polly realized Rueben finally came home. She hugged and kissed him as tears rolled down her cheeks. Rueben collapsed in her arms from lack of food. It was a miracle he escaped being wounded or captured, although he had the measles and spent six months in a hospital in Cumberland, Virginia.

A few days later, James went to Marysville and heard about President Lincoln being shot in the head at Ford's Theatre in Washington City on April 14, 1865. It was on the front page of the Marysville newspaper and everyone in town was talking about it. He came home to find Polly. "Polly, sit down, I have some bad news," said James. "President Lincoln has been shot in the head at a theater. He was taken to a house across the street, where he died the next day."

"Oh, no," Polly cried. "No, not our President."

"Yes, it hit me like a ton of bricks," said James, as he hugged

Polly.

"How can this happen?" cried Polly. As the tears ran down her face, she realized their beloved President was dead. Her heart ached and she knew she would never forget this day as long as she lived.

April 29, the funeral train of Abe Lincoln left the State Capital Building in Columbus, Ohio after an all-day showing of his body. The scheduled stops were published in the newspaper as the Lincoln Special. James, Polly and the family went to Woodstock to watch for the train.

"The newspaper stated it would stop in Woodstock to take on water and fuel around 9:30 tonight before going on to Urbana," said James.

"James, look, there must be over five hundred people here, lined up along the tracks to see the train. I did not know there were so many people in the area," said Polly.

"Some might have come from miles away. They feel this is the least they can do, to show the respect and honor he deserves," said James.

"Look at all the bonfires, you can see them for miles," said Polly.

Then at 9:46 p.m., the train came slowly down the tracks at five miles an hour and stopped. A group of women took bouquets of flowers onto the train and laid them on Lincoln's coffin. Some of the women were crying while the men stood back with a stern sad look on their faces. The Woodstock Cornet Band played *Pleyed's Hymn* along with other hymns.

Crying, Polly said, "Look, James, how the American flags are hanging on both sides of the engine and black drapes are hanging on the windows."

The train whistle went on continuously. The people were just standing there after the train left, too overwhelmed to leave. "This is truly a moment in history," said James.

"Poor Rueben, this must be harder for him," said Polly.

"He is being comforted by a girl," said James.

"Yes, her name is Sarah Faulkner."

In June of 1866, James's brother Roger died, and they buried him by their mother Sarah in Buck Run Cemetery.

Standing by his grave, James said, "Roger was such a good brother, we have been through so much together. He was only two years older than me. Now he is here with our mother." James looked over to his mother's grave, which was closer to the road. "I cannot believe it has been three years now since my mother died."

"Yes, we were in the middle of the war and everything seemed so depressing then," said Polly.

"So many young men, relatives and neighbors, died in the war. It makes you wonder how many more years we have," said James.

Genealogy of James Poling

JAMES POLING b. May 27, 1806 Randolph Co., (West) Virginia d. December 5, 1893 Union Co., Ohio m. Mary (Polly) Carpenter December 15, 1831 Harrison, (West) Virginia.
b. Bet. 1810-1811 Virginia d. January 28, 1881Union Co., Ohio

Children of James and Mary:
1. Eurem Poling b. 1831 Virginia d. August 1838 Ohio
2. Sarah Ann Poling b.1834 d. 29 March 1919 m. Edward Ryan 1855
3. Cyrus Poling b. 1836 Marysville, Ohio d. 1898 m. Samantha
4. Orsamus Poling b. 30 October 1838 d. 1922
5. Rueben Poling b. 6 April 1841 Union Co., Ohio d. 1929 m. Sarah Frances Faulkner 14 October 1865
6. Angernsia Poling b. 1845
7. Jerusha Poling b. 1848 d. 1894 m. Lester Clark 1870
8. Jeremiah Poling b. 1851 d.1945
9. James Albert Poling b.1857

Chapter Eighteen
Stephen Shirk (1826-1910)

Stephen and Mary Shirk, 1895

Stephen lived with his parents, Adam and Anna Shirk, where he worked hard on the farm until he was twenty-two. At that time, he wanted to start a family of his own, so he rented a farm nearby. Stephen was a good-looking man, at six feet three inches, black hair with blue eyes and muscular from all the hard farm work. He had been a devoted member of the Christian Church since he was fifteen.

Stephen and Mary Brake were childhood friends and neighbors. They lived a short distance from each other on the same road and as time went by, became sweethearts. One fall day, Stephen asked Mary if she would go for a buggy ride with him and she agreed. Stephen saw that Mary had pulled her pretty chestnut brown hair, which came to her waist, tightly to the back of her head in a bun. She was so pretty in her long calico dress. That night, while they were riding in the buggy, Stephen asked, "Mary, have ever thought about your future?"

"Stephen, I have been helping my grandfather so much lately, I haven't had time to think of the future. You know my grandmother Rosanna just died and it has been hard on Isaac. He wouldn't eat if I didn't go over and cook for him."

"That was strange how Rosanna died," Stephen said. "Do they know what she died from?"

"The doctor said it was a strange disease in which you are constantly thirsty and pass water a lot; he said it is always fatal. I miss my grandmother; she was always there for me."

"How is Isaac otherwise?" Stephen asked.

"He is lonely. He loves to talk about the past when I come over. Do you know his mother was a Lenape Indian. I guess that makes me one eighth Indian. My father never talked about it. I guess he does not want people to know. There are several in the area who hate Indians."

"Really, I didn't know he was part Indian."

"My sister Sarah has been going over, too, to help. She loves cleaning house."

"My older brother, Daniel, is in love with Sarah, I wouldn't be surprised if he asked her to marry him soon," Stephen said, smiling. They continued the buggy ride to a little trail back to a charming lake. There they sat and watched the deer near the lake.

"The stars are really out tonight, along with a beautiful full moon," Mary said, with her head on Stephen's shoulder.

Stephen held her hand. Turning, he asked, "Mary, will you marry me?"

"What! Not with all those dirty dogs you have that run through your house," Mary said a little too loud. "Animals are supposed to be outside, not running through the house. How many dogs do you have now?"

"Only four, and a cat. They are a lot of help around the farm."

"Why don't you let them live in the barn?"

"If you marry me, I'll put the animals in the barn."

"You will have to ask my father for my hand in marriage."

When they got back to Mary's house, Stephen nervously approached Adam Brake, who was sitting in the parlor smoking a pipe.

"Sir, I would like to marry your daughter," Stephen asked, fast before he lost his nerve.

"That is up to Mary," Adam said. Then with a smile on his face said, "Stephen, you are a fine young man, I would be proud to have you for a son-in-law."

He married Mary Brake on August 10, 1848. There was a barn party after the wedding. Everyone brought food and gifts. A large table was made with boards on stands. Clean hay was placed to sit down on and large area in the middle was cleared for dancing. The young children were running around, pretending to dance. The area fiddler player was there, playing square dance music, while one of the neighbors called the dance moves. A group of men were talking just outside the barn with Stephen.

"I voted for Zachary Taylor, he is talking of keeping us from war and holding the states together, even if he is from the Whig Party," said the neighbor.

"I fear this issue of slavery will lead to war someday," Stephen said, thinking out loud. "I'm really worried."

"Some of our neighbors are harboring runaway slaves," the neighbor said.

"They are in grave danger if the law finds out. They are brave souls, doing God's work," said Stephen.[82] Then turning, he saw his brother Daniel dancing with Mary's sister, Sarah. Stephen thought they were courting when he asked Mary to marry him.

Later, Stephen stopped Daniel. "Daniel, you and Sarah look serious."

"Yes, I'm going to ask her to marry me on the way home tonight," Daniel said.

"Good luck," said Stephen.

Daniel married Sarah Brake later that fall.

~ * ~

As time passed, Stephen purchased fifty-six acres of land. In 1852, he built a farmhouse and purchased thirty-two more acres. Amanda, their second daughter, was born the next year. Emily, three years older, loved her new sister and they were inseparable.

One Sunday afternoon in the summer of 1853, Stephen's neighbors, the Brakes and Shirks, came over. As usual, they did not knock on the door, just walked in to find Stephen playing with his two little daughters, Emily, four, and Amanda, six months. Emily was chewing on her straw-colored hair and held her rag doll. Amanda, with a little round face and light brown curls, placed her toes in her mouth. Sarah came over to visit her sister Mary and brought her two little daughters.

Stephen, happy to see Daniel and Sarah said, "Make yourself at home."

"Let's play a game of horseshoes," said Daniel.

Stephen's favorite pastime was playing horseshoes. "Okay," said Stephen, jumping up from the floor. "I have some old horseshoes from my big black mare. She needed new shoes, so I have four more to play with now."

Next thing, they were out back, playing horseshoes. Daniel, John, his younger brother, and David Brake, Mary's brother, all teamed up.

---

[82] Future generations would marry into the Quakers who lived there.

"Let's say Daniel and I against John and David," said Stephen.

"That sounds great. Stephen, do you have any hard cider?" asked David.

"Yes, there is some left over from last fall in the root cellar. Let me go get some," said Stephen.

Daniel threw the first shoe and got a ringer. "Three points," he yelled. He threw the second shoe and it leaned against the ringer. "Two points."

John threw the next shoe and knocked Daniel's leaner off. "That cancels your two points," said John.

It was a close game since the men were muscular from hard farm work and played a good game. They continued to play and talk about the abolitionist who had been preaching in the area against slavery.

"Mary bought a copy of Harriet Beecher Stowe's book, *Uncle Tom's Cabin,* when she went to Marysville last week," Stephen said. "Do you know Harriet lives in Cincinnati with her husband? Her book is the top seller, the storekeeper said. They can't keep the books on the self."

"I can't believe Franklin Pierce became president. The democrats just want to keep slavery.

He is so against the abolitionists," said Daniel. "You can go to jail if you believe slavery is a sin and do anything about it."

"I'm so against slavery. I can't believe the majority of people voted for him in office. I hear he drinks heavily. How can you run a country drunk?" said Stephen.

The family grew with William Shirk, born 1854, then twins, Angeline and Cornelius, were born January 11, 1856. Stephen and Mary's hearts ached for little Cornelius, he was so small and had a hard time breathing. Nine days later, little Cornelius died, too immature to live, and was buried at Baughn Cemetery.

A heavy frost killed the young corn crops on June 5 of 1856. Stephen lost his crops and prayed for an answer. Finding Mary in the parlor, knitting, Stephen said, "Mary, I am thinking of being a minister in the Christian Disciple Church. I really feel this is my calling."

"Really, Stephen, is this what you want to do, but what about the farm?" asked Mary.

"I will go on with the farm, it just will be a smaller farm. I can do both."

"The congregation at the church loves you, I think you will make a great minister, Stephen."

Stephen went on to become minister of the Christian Church for eighteen years and enjoyed his work there.

One day in 1858, Stephen came home from a town meeting, "Mary, I put a bid to work on building the gravel roads of Union County. With the trains coming through, the township wanted the dirt roads around the area improved."

"Sounds like a lot of hard work," said Mary.

Stephen graded and graveled nine miles of road. They were blessed with two more sons, Lewis Frank in 1858 and Joseph in 1860, but Joseph died when he was two years old. His death made a hard knot inside Steven. He wished for the power to change things.

As Stephen paced back and forth on the living room floor in 1864, he told Mary how he was thinking of joining the army. "Mary, I really feel this calling to join the army. Most of the young men in the area have joined the Union Army and are fighting in the War Between the States. Father feels the war will be over soon and I want to be a part of it. I preach every Sunday on the evils of slavery; this is a small part I can do to stop this."

"I will miss you, Stephen, but I should be able to manage. Emily is fourteen, Amanda is twelve and William is ten now. They are a lot of help with the farm and the three smaller children."

"I am only going to sign up for hundred days, then I will be back."

"Be careful and don't get shot, I want my husband back," Mary said, with tears in her eyes.

Stephen took the train to Camp Chase by Columbus, Ohio where he enlisted on May 2, 1864. He trained there for eleven days and on the evening of May 13 he left for Washington City as a private in Company D of the 136 regiment of OVI, commanded by Colonel H. Smith. He was placed on garrison duty at Fort Ellsworth, Fort Lyons, and Fort Williams. They were part of the defense of Washington City, south of the Potomac River. The forts were earthen works with some timber.

On July 15, 1864, Stephen was then placed at Fort Lyons, Virginia doing garrison duty. Part of the duty was infantry and part was heavy artillery. The men were practicing firing the artillery, anticipating an attack by the enemy. They were testing the shells and fuses and practicing target shooting under orders of the commander. While Stephen was on drill, practicing with heavy siege guns, a shell exploded at the mouth of the cannon the instant it was lit, near where he stood. Stephen and several of the men around the cannon were thrown to the ground. Stephen was knocked out and as he lay on the ground, blood flowed profusely from his nose and ears. The explosion caused Stephen to have a terrific concussion. There was no hospital in the area. He tried to walk to the barracks with the help of a fellow soldier, Nathaniel Brooks.

Stephen stated, "It's like a train of cars going through my head. My eyes are so sore, and I can barely see from them."

Nathaniel said, "Stephen, just stay quiet and keep walking to the right, we will make it." It was difficult for Stephen to understand ordinary conversation after the blast.

Nathaniel stated loudly, "The 1st Lieutenant in charge is too sick and our doctor Burkay, who was in charge of the sick at the post, has been dead for quite a while."

"Let me just rest for now, I am so dizzy," Stephen stated weakly.

Next day, he complained of buzzing in his head as if machinery was running in the middle of his brain. He attempted to get out of bed, but the dizziness caused him to fall back down. Quite feeble, he stayed in bed for several days and then was sent back to Camp Chase in Columbus, Ohio when he could travel. He was honorably discharged at Camp Chase as Sergeant Stephen Shirk on August 31, 1864 at expiration of his term of service.[83]

Mary, happy to see Stephen, cried, "I have missed you so much!" After hugging and kissing him, Mary stated, "Your eyes have sores on them, Stephen. Can you see me?"

"Just barely," said Stephen. "I can hardly hear you."

---

[83] The National Archives, soldier's certificate 356969, can No. 7463, roll 98, film # 0882311

"Oh, God, you're almost deaf."

"I am so happy to be home to you and the children, I have felt so bad for so long. My head hurts, my eyes hurt, and my ears have a constant ringing in them," said Stephen.

"You must go see the doctor, Stephen. This isn't right!"

Stephen's doctor found the right tympanic ruptured and the left tympanic thickened from the shock. This left Stephen totally deaf in the right ear. He also had some loss of hearing in his left ear. The doctor wanted to do surgery on Stephen's eyes, but he would not have anything to do with surgery. Some days, Stephen would feel so bad he would have to lay down for half the day. He was not able to work much on the farm, only able to do half the work he did before leaving for the war and was never able to do heavy work again. One day, after working a little, Stephen fell down and lay unconscious for some time. Afterwards, he was not allowed to go away from home without someone being with him. This went on for several months and then Stephen started to feel better. He decided to go back to preaching the gospel and joined the Ohio Central Christian Conference in August 1866.

Stephen watched his wife as she broke down and cried as he gave the eulogy for Adam, his father-in-law. Mary hugged her mother who was also crying with grief. This dreary day in May, 1870 seemed like such a long day and Mary was five months pregnant. Afterwards, Stephen, family and friends gathered around Mary and her mother, Eve, offering their condolences. Uncle William Baughan, who was a Union Captain in the Civil War, came over from Olney, Illinois when he got word his brother-in-law was gravely ill.

"William, it is so good to see you, we haven't seen you for so long," said Stephen.

"It seems like the only time I see you now is at funerals and weddings," said William.

"I know, it's hard," said Mary.

"Are these little ones yours running around?" asked William.

"Yes, that one running by is Charles who is six, that one over there by the tree is Mary who is four, and this little one holding my dress, Rhoda, is two. I have six older children around here somewhere. There must be over a hundred people here and most are relatives," said Mary.

"What is going to happen to your mother, Eve, now?" asked William. "It is too much for her to take care of the farm by herself."

"My brother, Isaac Jr., lives with her and Amanda," said Mary.

"How old is your sister now?" asked William.

"Amanda is going to be nineteen this year," said Mary.

"William, you come back and see us again, you're always welcome at our house," said Stephen.

"You have to make it to Illinois sometime and stay with me also," said William.

Adam was buried in the cemetery behind the church. Stephen stood at the grave and looked at Mary with a heavy heart and said, "Your father died of old age on his farm, what more could one ask."

"Now that Father is dead and just last year, your mother died, we are becoming the older generation," said Mary.

"That is scary, but I want to go on doing as much as I can," said Stephen.

"What were you thinking of doing?"

"Mary, I am going to run for Liberty Township Trustee. I feel I just have to do something."

"Well, the people of the township respect you," said Mary. Stephen went on to be Trustee of Liberty Township for ten years.

On Friday, October 9, 1889, Stephen attended Pioneer's meeting. Forty men met in a room at the courthouse. They discussed the good old days and how the younger generation have it too easy. They were from the original families that came into Union County on the wagon train back in early 1800s.

~ * ~

Stephen and Mary celebrated their golden wedding anniversary in August of 1898. Their children threw them a party. Charles, Cora, Cornelius, Joseph, and Emily already passed on. There were still seven children living with their spouses, and over fifty grandchildren.

Stephen and Mary really enjoyed their family. Sitting in chairs in the lawn with several grandchildren around him, one of his grandchildren asked, "Grandpa, tell us a story when you were young."

Stephen smiled. "When I was a young child, about eight years old, I stumbled upon a small black panther as I played in the woods. Thinking the cub was a dog, I brought him home to give it to my father. As I approached the house, the beagles came running and barking. When the panther saw the other dogs, he tried to get down. Still thinking it was a dog, I grabbed it by the neck and held it close. The animal hissed and blew its hot breath in my face, then it pulled away and climbed the nearest tree. I felt the hair on the back of my neck stand on end."

"What did you do then, Grandpa?" said his grandson with his eyes wide and sitting on the edge of his seat.

"Well, scared to death, I ran to the house as fast as I could. The panther jumped out of the tree and sprinted to the front porch after me. The dogs came to my rescue, but they got under my feet and knocked me down to the ground. A big fight between the dogs and the panther developed around me. My father, Adam, came running from the barn when he heard the commotion. He got me and the dogs inside the house, but the panther stayed until daylight frightened him away."[84]

"Tell us another story, Grandpa."

"Well, let me see, when I was a teenager, there were a large number of turkeys that ran wild in the area behind the farm which was covered with a dense forest. I remember in one week, I killed thirty-nine wild turkeys with forty-one shots and then took them into Marysville, where I sold them for twenty-five cents apiece to a local store."

"Wow, you could really shoot well."

Smiling, Stephen said, "In those days, I was really good, and my vision was perfect."

Mary's brother, William Brake, died at the Grand Army of the Republic encampment in Cincinnati, Ohio in September of 1898. He had a wart cut off while being shaved and died of blood poisoning. There were over three hundred and five thousand men, still members who fought in the Civil War.

---

[84] "Pen Pictures of Pioneers" *Marysville Tribune*, Wednesday, March 21, 1900

In 1908, Mary died of a heart condition and was buried at Oakdale Cemetery in Marysville. Stephen had been gradually going down in health with congestion of the liver and congestion of the lungs. Several months before he died, he went to live with his son on East Fourth Street in Marysville, Ohio. A few days before his death, he walked downtown and visited with his friends for the last time. Stephen died at his son Louis Frank and Delia Shirk's house, Wednesday evening, January 26, 1910.[85]

Oakdale Cemetery, Maryville, Ohio section E row 30 lot 169

---

[85] Stephen Shirk obituary, *Marysville Tribune,* Marysville, Ohio, 2 February 1910.

Genealogy of Stephen Shirk

STEPHEN SHIRK b. 21 October 1826 d. 26 January 1910 m. 12 1848 Mary Brake b. 17 February 1827 d. 3 January 1903

Children of Stephen and Mary:
1. Emily Shirk b. 1850 d. 1897 m. Benjamin Hisey
2. Amanda Shirk b. 1853 d. 1907 m. (1)1 James Thompson (2) Orsamus Poling
3. William Henry Shirk b. 1854 d. 1926 m. Belinda Welch
4. Angelia Shirk b. 11 January 1856 d. 1933 m. Charles Holycross
5. Cornelius Shirk b. 11 January 1856 d. 20 January 1856
6. Lewis Frank Shirk b. 1859 d. 1928 m. (1) Delia Poling (2) Eva Loucke
7. Joseph W. Shirk b. 5 December 1860 d. 12 February 1864
8. Viola J. Shirk b. 1862 d. 1933 m. Luther Corwin
9. Charles L. Shirk b. 1864 d. 1895 m. Laura Hill
10. Mary E. Shirk b. 1867 d. 1959 m. James W. Davis
11. Rhoda Shirk b. 1868 d. 1951 m. Amos Blush
12. Cora Shirk b. 1870 d. 1895 m. Thomas J. Hinton

Chapter Nineteen
Job Shirk (1836-1899)

Job with daughter Sarah Andrews and granddaughter Mary 1896

Steering his horse down the winding country road, Job looked at the white farmhouses and lush farmland from his seat on his buggy. A warm breeze brushed his face. His thoughts went back to his childhood. Job was the second born among seven children to Levi and Patsy Shirk. They lived next door to his grandfather, John Shirk. Life was hard then for his four brothers and three sisters. It seemed as if they were constantly sick with influenza, scarlet fever, measles, whooping cough or something else going around at the time. Mother died when he was fourteen. At that time, he left home to work as a hired hand at Andrew Thompson's large farm there in Union County, where he also bunked.

Pulling the horse to a stop, he parked the buggy in front of the porch of his son's farmhouse. He looked out at the house and remembered the day he met Susan Rossell, and how she was from a Quaker family in the area, in a farmhouse like this one. How pretty she was and how he loved the way she talked, so proper with thees and thous. They married on May 21, 1863, against her mothers' wishes. To marry outside the Quaker religion meant you were disowned by the church. They rented one of Andrew Thompson's farmhouses and continued to work hard as a farmhand on Andrew's large farm.

Job, rubbing his beard, continued to remember his life as he stepped down from the buggy. Through the years, he moved from one rental farm to the next throughout the area. By 1870, they lived in Bokes Creek Twp., Logan County by Susan's half-sister, Harriett, and husband, Abner Elliott. Those were good years when he planted oats, corn, wheat and raised sheep and chickens. The year Evie was born, in 1873, the country went into a depression. They had four children by then, and Susan was eight months pregnant. The bank he had his money in went bankrupt and he lost it all, but at least there was food from the farm. Throughout his life, he had financial difficulties, which made his life with Susan a strain.

Now coughing and short of breath, Job realized how weak this consumption left him. He realized his life was coming to an end and he was compelled to live with his oldest son, Jim. He named him James, but everyone called him Jim since he was young.

Thinking back to August of 1885, his daughter, Louie, married

William Austin and moved to Liberty Center in Henry County, Ohio. That was when Susan and Job separated. Susan went to live with Louie and William. Elmer, their youngest, now eleven, wanted to live with Jim.

Job remembered how lonely he was then and had an affair with Evelina Heath. They had a daughter who died after she was born on March 22, 1893.[86] His wife, Susan, died the next month in April of 1893. Job and Evelina never married and broke up after the death of their baby. Job then went to live with his daughter, Sarah.

Jim opened the front door and said, "Father, you're here, I thought you were coming next week."

. "Jim, I felt I better come now. I'm getting weaker from these coughing spells," said Job.

"Let me help you," said Jim, as he grabbed his arm and held him up as they walked up the porch steps.

"I have been so weak lately. So short of breath. It takes all my energy just to do little things."

"Cora made up the bedroom downstairs for you. It is close to the front porch and dining room; my wife worried you would need something close."

"Thank you for letting me stay here. Your sister, Sarah, has her hands full lately. I felt such a burden staying there." Job sat down on the rocking chair on the front porch. He watched Jim sit in chair next to him.

"I know Sarah's your favorite, but I would like some time with you too."

"Ah, I love my children equally."

Later, Job was looking at pictures by the light of the oil lamp in the parlor. Elmer came in to visit with his father. Job said, "This picture of the wagon. Reminds me of the time it rained almost every day. The month Sarah was born. Louie was eleven. She was a little momma to Sarah. My father died that same year." Job looked towards Elmer and continued, "I had all four horses to haul the wheat in the wagon along East Liberty Road. The rains made the roads wet and awful. I passed wagons stalled in the mud. I stopped to help. I was plastered with mud

---

[86] *Union County Death Record Book 3 1886-1908* #144

from head to toe."

"I heard about that. Everyone thought you were a mud monster and went around the house, screaming," said Elmer.

Job ran his hand down his beard, wheezing. "It was quite a commotion. Your mother made me clean up in the barn."

"I will have dinner ready soon," said Cora as she came in the room.

"What are you fixing? It smells good," Jim said as he grabbed her.

"Jim, you always want to grab me when I'm fixing dinner." Pushing him away, she said, "Chicken and dumplings are in the oven."

"Your mother made good chicken and dumplings. It was always one of my favorite meals," said Job.

"Yes, but with all those brothers and sisters, there was never enough," said Jim.

"It was even harder, being the youngest," said Elmer.

"I wish things could have been better. I did the best with what God gave me," said Job.

Job died six months later Dec 22, 1899, in Jim's house and was buried at Mill Creek Cemetery by Raymond, Ohio.

Genealogy of Levi Shirk

LEVI SHIRK b. 1808 (West) Virginia d. 1873 Union Co., Ohio m. Martha Patsey Taylor September 1832 Union Co., Ohio[87] b.1818 d. abt. 1850

Children of Levi and Patsey Shirk:
1. Henson Henry Shirk b. 1833 Union Co., Ohio d. 1888 Lincoln, Logan, Illinois
2. Job Shirk b. 1835 d.1899 Union Co., Ohio
3. Susanna Shirk b. 1839
4. Elizabeth Shirk b. 1842
5. Hiram Shirk b. 1844 d. 1929 m. Amorimth
6. Aaron Shirk b. 1845 d. 1911 m. Josephine
7. Hannah L. Shirk b. 1849 d. 1931

Genealogy of Job Shirk

JOB SHIRK b. 27 Dec 1835 Pottersburg, Ohio d. 22 Dec 1899 Union Co., Ohio m. Susannah Rossell 21 May 1863 Union Co., Ohio. Susannah b. 1846 d. 1893.

Children of Job and Susannah:
1. Mary Lucretia "Louie" Shirk b. 6 Apr 1864 Mt. Victory, Hardin Co., Ohio d. 9 May 1937 Liberty Center, Ohio m. William Austin 1885.
2. James Marion Shirk b. 18 Sep 1865 York Center, Union Co., Ohio d. 10 Apr 1929 m. Cora Poling 1895.

---

[87] Ohio County Marriage records, 1774-1993, Union 1820-1854 p 125.

3. Abner Clint Shirk b. 17 May 1869 Union Co., d. 1955 Defiance, Ohio m. Mary Mansfield 1898.

4. Evaloanna 'Evie" b. 8 Oct 1870 Liberty Twsp, Union Co., Ohio d. 1941 m. Lafayette 'Lafe' Thompson 1893.

5. Sarah Evalina Shirk b. 25 Jun 1873 Marysville, Ohio d. 1961 m. James 'Harve' Andrews 1891.

6. Laura Alice Shirk b. 23 May 1875 d. 1935 m. Frank Spain

7. Josephine Shirk b. 1876 West Mansfield, Ohio d. 1952 Richwood, Ohio m. George Smith

8. William 'Guy' Shirk b. 2 May 1878 Liberty Tsp. Union Co., Ohio d. 1951 m. Bertha Betty

9. Elmer Allan Shirk b. 16 Apr 1881 Union Co., Ohio d. 1948 m. Maude Norviel 1908.

Chapter Twenty
Orsamus Poling (1838-1922)

Amanda, Lura, Albert and Orsamus Poling

Sary lay in bed, burning up with Typhoid Fever. She was lethargic now, after fighting the disease for over a week. Orsamus sponged cool water over her, hoping to bring the fever down. There were so many in the area sick with Typhoid Fever. The doctor looked exhausted at his last visit, trying to keep up, so it would do no good going after him again.

As Orsamus looked at his beloved wife lying there in her bed, he thought of how she was slipping away and only thirty-three years old. He remembered their wedding day back in June of 1860, how beautiful and young she was, then only nineteen. How was he going to raise their five children without Sary, the nickname he loved to call her, even though her name was Sarah.

He watched as she took her last breath. Now she is with our babies, Frenchie, who died when she was a little over two months and Samuel, who died of the Cholera, when he was only six months old. Orsamus' heart was broken, it hurt so bad, he could hardly breathe. How could Sary be dead and leave him? How could life be so cruel? First his babies and now his wife.

Orsamus found himself crying at night when he should be sleeping. There was not a moment in the day he didn't think of Sary and missed her. Even though he was still grieving, he went on with his life. His unwed sister, Jerusha, came over to help take care of his children, now three to twelve years old. Orsamus thought about Amanda Shirk, who he knew before she married James A. Thompson. Her father, Stephen Shirk, was a good friend of the family. Amanda's husband died of pneumonia at the age of twenty, earlier this March. Orsamus remembered his funeral. It was a month before his wife died and he felt so sorry for Amanda, who had been married less than a year. Stephen Shirk, the Christian Church pastor, gave the eulogy that sad day.

A couple of months after Sary's funeral, Orsamus went over to Stephen's farm and found Amanda there. She was living with her parents since her husband's death. Orsamus felt awkward, being fourteen years older than Amanda, but felt an attraction for her.

"Amanda, it is so good to see you again," said Orsamus as he walked into the front room.

"I am so sorry to hear about your wife dying. I wasn't feeling well and was not able to go to the funeral," said Amanda as she got up from the chair.

"Yes, we had the funeral at the Universalist Church in Woodstock. I have gone there since I was a young boy," said Orsamus.

"I know how hard it is after your loved one dies," said Amanda.

"It is especially hard on the children."

"How old are the children now?"

"Delia is twelve and she is so much like her mother. She helps with the younger children. Jerusha, named after her aunt, is ten and Perrie is eight. They help on the farm. Edward is six and tries to help, but gets in the way most of the time. Serena is three and looks for her mother every day. My sister Jerusha is staying with us and helping out."

"Those poor children. If I can help in any way, let me know."

"Thanks, only time will heal the pain," said Orsamus.

"I know what you mean."

"It's so nice talking to you."

"Yes, I really enjoyed talking to you too."

Then, thinking he should do something before he left, Orsamus asked, "Would you like to go for a buggy ride next Saturday evening?"

"I would like that; it has been a sad year for both of us."

Orsamus and Amanda gave each other emotional support with their long buggy rides and long talks. They comforted each other in their sorrow and a deep bond grew between them. They enjoyed each other's company day after day until they no longer wanted to be apart.

Later that same year, they were married on December 31. It was a simple wedding with only the immediate family. Nine and half months later in 1875, they had twin girls, Cora and Flora.

Orsamus operated the large Miller farm near Milford, Ohio. It was a big operation owned by two spinster ladies. He would get up before sunrise and work on his own farm before going on to work on the Miller's farm. At harvest time, the neighbors held a threshing ring to help each other with the wheat or oats. The grain was pitched by a man on the ground to another man on a wagon drawn by a team of horses. The steam engine was connected to a grain separator. Wagons of grain were lined up and the men tossed the bundles into the separator. The grain wagons received the grain and it was hauled to the grain elevators that were by the railroad. A box was placed by the separator in case the grain wagons did not get back in time. It was a big operation which required several men.

~ * ~

One morning in July in 1876, Amanda's parents rode over in the buggy. Amanda came out to the front porch as soon as she saw her parents. "Ma, what is it?'

"Amanda, we have some sad news," said Mary, crying.

"What is wrong?" Amanda said, scared.

"Grandpa Adam died yesterday," said Mary. "He died in his sleep at his home."

"Oh, Ma, I loved him so," said Amanda.

"Yes, a lot of people did," said Mary. "He was well known, and his funeral will be huge."

Adam had ten children, over fifty grandchildren and a large number of great grandchildren. Most of the family turned up for the funeral. His son, Stephen, gave the eulogy and Adam was buried at Mill Creek Cemetery. The little church in front of the cemetery overflowed with people into the cemetery.

The next year, Amanda came home from the doctor, large with child. "Orsamus, I cannot believe we are having another set of twins," said Amanda.

"You're kidding?"

"No, the doctor heard two heartbeats today, surprise."

"Cora and Flora are very active two-year olds, this is going to be too much work for you," said Orsamus.

"Delia is helpful, but I do need some extra help. Do you think Jersuha could come over and stay with us again?" asked Amanda. "She is wonderful help and is still single."

"Yes, I will ask her. We are going to have to add on to the house," said Orsamus. "This house is going to get crowded fast."

They named the twins Ai, for the boy and Abi, for the girl. As time went on, they had another boy in 1883, Albert, and baby girl, Lura, in 1886. When Lura was about two years old, Amanda came home from visiting in Marysville.

"Orsamus," Amanda called from the barn door.

"What?" he asked as he walked to the door.

"They opened a photography gallery on Main Street in Marysville," said Amanda.

"It is amazing how they can capture your picture on cardboard like that. Science has come a long way," said Orsamus.

"Do you want to get our pictures taken with the children?"

"Yes, that would be great."

"S.C. Adams is the photographer. He is supposed to be exceptionally good, but he is charging one dollar to four dollars a picture. Which is a lot of money."

"How many pictures did you want?"

"I would like several to give to the family. There is a photographer in the back of the drug store, he might be a little cheaper."

"We will go to the best in Marysville, not a back-room man, it will be worth it."

"Can you get the older children together from your first marriage? I would love to have their pictures too."

"Yes, I will try."

"It helps they stayed in the area after they married."

"Yes, just set a time and place."

"I will dress the children in their Sunday best."

Ai, Cora, Flora, Lura, Albert and Abi Poling 1888

The following year, they had another baby, Nellie. Their beautiful baby girl only lived to be one year old and died of lung trouble.[88] She was laid out in a little white casket on the table in the parlor. [89] Family and

---

[88] Union County, Ohio Death Records Book 3 1886-1908 # 115.

[89] Polen, Nellie Obituary, *Marysville Tribune,* Marysville, Ohio, 5 March 1890.

friends paraded through their home to see the little girl one last time and give support to the grieving family. Each family brought their favorite dish of food for the funeral.

"Another death in the family, some days are just too hard to bear," said Amanda.

"God had a plan for her, she is his angel now," said Orsamus.

Amanda's brother, Lewis Frank Shirk, married Orsamus Poling's daughter, Della, by his first marriage. They lived in Marysville with James, Orsamus' father, who was getting too old to live by himself. Orsamus and Amanda went to visit him, fearing he would not be around much longer. Amanda made him her apple pie that he loved.

"Father, you lived in such an exciting time, coming from Virginia in a covered wagon when the land was a wilderness," said Orsamus.

"Yes, but the civil war was a terrible time. A lot of our young men died and our beloved President Lincoln was shot and killed," said James.

"The world is changing so fast, now there are factories, electricity, telephones, and automobiles. Nothing like the pioneer days. You have seen so much in your life."

"It has been a hard life, but a good life. I have my family and friends and your apple pie, Amanda," said James.

Lewis brought to Amanda and Orsamus news that James died few days later.

Enoch Davis on Orsamus's steam tractor 1890

Flora married Enoch Davis on September 3, 1894 and her twin Cora married James Shirk the next month. Cora and Flora stayed close, visiting each other frequently. Seven months after getting married, Flora gave birth to a son Lewis. She developed consumption shortly after the birth. She died two years later on her father's farm, where they were living. [90] James and Cora settled on the land next to Orsamus by North Lewisburg, Ohio.

Amanda started losing weight and having stomach pains. When she started vomiting blood, she finally went to the doctor. She had cancer of the stomach and the treatment was of no help. She suffered failing health for some time. Amanda died in 1907. Orsamus, sad with her death, was relieved her suffering was over. He buried her by his first wife in Oakdale Cemetery in Marysville.

---

[90] Davis, Flora obituary, *Marysville Tribune,* Marysville, Ohio, 17 *November* 1897.

~ * ~

Orsamus bought a Ford Touring automobile in 1909. It was one of the first in his community and he was the talk of the town. He was so proud of the car and would drive it almost every day. He visited relatives and took them for rides. He lived on the road between Raymond and East Liberty, the last house on the left before the railroad track when leaving Raymond.

Orsamus's daughter, Serena, by his first wife, married Henry Newlove. For several years, they lived in Marysville while Henry worked in the harness business. Hearing about a better paying job, they moved to Jeffersonville, Indiana, where he worked in the arsenal plant. After working there for a year, Henry's mind was affected by the chemicals, so he quit, and they moved back to his father-in-law's farm in Ohio. Orsamus had Henry go to the family doctor who sent him to Columbus State Hospital for the mentally ill for treatment. After Henry was discharged, he and Serena continued to live with Orsamus on the farm. Then a few weeks later, Orsamus saw Henry acting deranged, talking to the kitchen wall.

"Henry, are you okay?" asked Orsamus.

"Orsamus, I feel like I am losing my mind," said Henry.

"Have Serena take you back to the family doctor, maybe he can help you," said Orsamus.

"I am afraid he will send me back to the State Hospital again. That place was a living nightmare," said Henry, walking in circles and rubbing his head. "They did horrific treatments, restraining me, then shocking me with hot and cold water. If I refused, they beat me and placed me in solitary confinement. At night, they locked you in a room with ten other patients. The windows had heavy metal bars on them, and I worried what would happen if there was a fire. I believe criminals are treated better."[91]

On Wednesday, December 7, 1910, at 6 a.m., Orsamus was sleeping when he heard loud arguing in the kitchen, waking him up.

---

[91] https://www.nlm.nih.gov/hmd/diseases/professional.html

Before he could get out of bed, he heard a loud bang. Having this gut-wrenching feeling, he hurried out of bed. Dressing fast and running into the kitchen, he saw Serena, his daughter, screaming and frantically running outside.

"Oh no, Henry, what have you done?" said Serena, half-screaming, and half-crying.

"Henry, oh God, no," Orsamus screamed, reaching his son-in-law lying in the snow. "He is still breathing," Orsamus yelled, as he saw the bullet hole in the side right of his head with blood oozing out.

"Henry, Henry," Serena cried, as she reached his side, lifting his head out of the snow. She put her arms around him as the tears ran down her face.

"Serena, you grab his feet and I will get under his arms," Orsamus said, and they half-carried and half-dragged his unconscious body into the kitchen. Grabbing the kitchen towel and handing it to Serena, Orsamus said, "Serena, hold this towel over his head to stop the bleeding while I call the doctor." The telephone was hanging on the wall in the living room, but Henry was dead by the time the doctor got there.[92] Henry was only thirty-seven years old.

Serena continued to live with her father until he died at the age of eighty-three of cancer of the stomach on February 13, 1922. They found years later that there was a high incidence of stomach cancer among those who ate preserved meat with salt, which was common practice before refrigeration.[93]

---

[92] "Fired Bullet into Head," *Marysville Tribune,* Marysville, Ohio, 7 December 1810.

[93] https://www.wcrf.org/int/blog/articles/2016/04/salt-shaking-link-stomach-cancer.

Marysville Oakdale Cemetery section D row 2

Genealogy of Orsamus Poling

ORSAMUS POLING b. 30 October 1838 Union Co., Ohio d. 13 February1922 m. #1-Sarah Ann Ream 7 June 1860 b. 1840 d. 4 April 1874 #2-Amanda Shirk 31 December 1874 b. 23 June 1852 d. 1907

Children of Orsamus and Sarah:
1. Della M. Poling b. 1862 d. 9 March 1904 (consumption) m. Frank Shirk
2. Perrie Poling b. 1864 d. 1930 m. Melvin Tarpening
3. Jerusha Poling b. 1866 d. 1957 never married
4. Frenchie Lillie Poling b. 4 July 1867 d. 12 September 1867
5. Euriem Edward Poling b. 1868 d. 1938 m. Mary Buckner
6. Serena Lenora Poling b. 10 November 1871 d. 11 July 1948 m. Henry Newlove 1899 b. 1872 d. 7 December 1910
7. Samuel J. Poling b. 1874 d. 1874

Children of Orsamus and Amanda:
1. Cora Poling b. 12 October 1875 d. 1943 m. James Shirk
2. Floria Poling b. 12 October 1875 d. 3 September 1894 (consumption) m. Enoch Davis
3. Abi Poling b. 31 October 1877 d. 1910 m. George W. Knotts
4. Ai Poling b. 31 October 1877 d. 3 April 1922 m. Letta Stubbs
5. Albert Poling b. 18 September 1883 d 22 June 1939 m. Lydia Weaver
6. Lura Poling b. 21 November 1885 d. 4 May 1896
7. Nellie Poling b. 1889 d. 15 March 1890

Chapter Twenty-one
James Marion Shirk (1865-1929)

Jim Shirk

James was never called by his name, but by Jim. His grandmother, Susanna Rossell, a widow, lived in a small house next door to them. Jim would run over frequently and help her around the house. His grandmother talked funny, always saying *thou* and *thine*, as the older

Quakers in the area talked. She loved to sit in the rocking chair and smoke a pipe, which Jim thought was funny for a lady. She sat there in her little house, in her rocking chair, and told him between puffs how he came into the world.

"It was one breezy day in September when your father, Job, ran to my house, shouting it was your mother's time. It was 1865, and we just came through a terrible war and was happy it ended earlier that year," said Susanna.

"Uncle John Rossell was in the war and talks about it," said Jim, excited.

"Yes, I was so happy to have my son home again."

"Was I a good baby?"

"Yes, but you came screaming into the world. Your father was ecstatic, they had their first son. They loved your older sister, Mary, but Job wanted a son. I helped many a woman birth a baby into this world, but you were special."

"How was I special?"

"Your father prayed so hard for a healthy son and here you were, my perfect little grandson."

~ * ~

Jim lived and worked on the large Miller farm under Orsamus Poling in 1884. There he met Orsamus Poling's daughter, Cora. First time he saw her across the farm, talking to her father, he knew she was going to be his wife one day. As the days went by, he would stop and talk to her and got to know her better. When he got the nerve, he went to talk to Orsamus by the barn.

"Orsamus, can I court your daughter, Cora?" asked Jim.

"I knew this was coming," said Orsamus with a smile. "What does my daughter want?"

"When I asked her earlier, she said yes, if you approved."

"Okay, but always have her home by dark."

"Yes, sir." Jim was so happy; he went to find Cora.

Cora's identical twin sister, Flora, loved to confuse him. If Cora was not close, Flora could pass for Cora, which she got a kick doing. Jim came to pick up Cora and Flora came out of the kitchen, teasing him as if she was Cora.

"I can court you now," said Jim.

"Why, Jim, what would Enoch say, we are to be married this September," said Flora.

"You did it again," said Jim, laughing.

Just then Cora came in the room, frustrated over her sister. "Leave Jim to me, Flora," said Cora.

"Cora, you and your sister look so much alike, I can only tell who's who when you are close or when you talk," said Jim.

"How can you tell?" asked Cora.

"You have a stronger voice."

Jim and Cora were married the following year at the Quaker church at Mt Victory, Ohio, October 13, 1895. They sent a letter of attention to the clerk of the meeting house, which was posted at the market. The following week, the couple sat in front of the meeting house for several minutes, which seemed like forever. Cora wore a new dress she made; light brown satin, floor-length with matching bonnet. Jim wore a new suit. Then out of the silence, they stood up, held hands, and exchanged their vows in front of the members.

"In the presence of God, Friends, I take this my friend, Cora, to be my wife, promising with God's help to be unto her a loving and faithful husband, so long as we both on earth shall live," said Jim.

"In the presence of God, Friends, I take this my friend, Jim, to be my husband, promising with God's help to be unto him a loving and faithful wife, so long as we both on earth shall live," said Cora.

They signed a wedding certificate. Friends came forth and gave the couple their blessing and signed the certificate as witnesses. They celebrated with a meal afterwards. Then they went to Marysville where a professional photographer took their wedding picture.

Cora and Jim wedding picture 1895

Jim and Cora lived on the farm next to Orsamus, which was two miles northwest of North Lewisburg on Middleburg Road. Later they joined the Methodist Church nearby, Cora never felt comfortable with the Quaker religion, it was Jim's grandparent's religion. Together, they had eight children: Robert, Leroy, Lura, Emerson, Dana, Della and two children who died as infants.

Jim and Cora saw Orsamus from the front porch as he rode over to the farm in November of 1897. His head was down, and he was crying as he got off the horse.

"It is with a heavy heart, I tell you, Cora, your sister Flora passed," said Orsamus, standing on the porch, shaking his head.

"Oh, Father," said Cora, as the tears rolled down her face.

"She has been sick with consumption for a while, but I had hoped she had more time."

"I have been over to Flora's house helping her, praying she would get better soon. What will happen to her baby, Lewis? Will Enoch be able to raise him?"

"He will have help from the family. It will be hard at first."

"If there is anything we can do, let us know," said Jim.

"I felt her presence in the middle of the night," said Cora, biting her lower lip.

"You didn't wake me up," said Jim.

"I thought I saw her standing at the bedroom door, but when I went to get up, she was gone."

"You two were always close, she probably wanted to say goodbye," Jim shook his head then changed the subject. "I wanted to ask you if you would mind if my brother Elmer came and lived with us for a while? Just until he can get his own place."

"That is fine. I enjoy your brother's company."

Jim's father became too ill with consumption to take care of himself, so he lived with Jim and Cora. Not long after moving in, just before Christmas in 1899, Job Shirk died at their home. Jim and Cora left the farm in the buggy to get the doctor, who was also the coroner.

"Jim, so many are dying from consumption. Why can't they find a cure?" asked Cora.

"Maybe someday they will," said Jim.

"My sister and now your father, will this ever stop?"

Lura and Robert, 1906

Jim was well known in the area and made a good profit with his farm. Once a week, Cora and Jim would get into the horse-drawn carriage and go to town with the children. Down the road was a covered bridge over Darby Creek they passed through on the way. They took eggs and garden produce into the grocery store in North Lewisburg to trade for flour, along with other necessities. When they walked in, they were very aware of the smell of the wooden oiled floor. There were open barrels with pickles, flour and bulk goods sitting on the floor. The children would get a stick of candy from a glass jar on the counter.

The next day, Cora and Jim overslept. They hurried upstairs to the boys' bedroom.

"Robert and Leroy, get up and get ready for school," said Jim.

"I will wake up Lura," said Cora. Cora always worried about Lura since she was born with a heart defect. "Robert, watch over Lura as you walk to Johnson School and behave yourself. Your teacher has twenty students to watch over in the little one-room schoolhouse."

"I will, Mother, don't worry," said Robert.

Front row left to right: LeRoy boy sitting, Lura standing next and Robert sitting.

One beautiful fall day in October, Jim started out to harvest the fields with Robert and LeRoy when Emerson came running, asking to come along.

"Father, please can I go too?" asked Emerson.

"Son, you are little too young, you better stay home with your mother," said Jim.

"I have grown two inches since last fall. Please can I go too?"

"Let's ask your mother."

"Jim, I'm not sure, he may have grown some, but he is young and will probably get in the way. I don't feel good about it," said Cora, standing on the front porch, watching James hitch the horses to the wagon.

"He will be okay, I'll watch him," said Jim

Later that evening, as Jim came home, he saw Cora walk out and peer down the road. He could see she was anxious, as if she knew something terrible happened. Cora looked and looked. "Where is Emerson?"

Jim wiped the tears from his wet face. He wanted to appear strong as he pulled up and got out of the wagon, but his countenance showed otherwise. He watched Cora run up to him. Jim sent Robert and LeRoy into the house; he told them he would be in shortly.

"Where is Emerson? What is wrong with Emerson? What is wrong? Jim, talk to me…"

"Let's go in the house, Cora," Jim said, shaking.

"No, because you are going to tell me something happened to Emerson."

"There has been a terrible accident," said Jim, putting his hands to his face and couldn't hold the tears back anymore.

"What happened?" Cora said, frightened.

"We were taking the hay to the grain elevator in the wagon with the team of horses. Emerson and I were on top of a bale of hay in the wagon. Robert and Leroy were up front. When turning at the corner of Union Chapel, the wagon cramped, throwing Emerson and I off onto the road. The back wheel of the wagon ran over him, crushing his little body," said Jim, crying. "I am so sorry, I never thought it would happen."[94]

"How badly is he hurt?"

"He died in my arms a few minutes after I picked him up off the road."

"No, no, no, he can't be dead!" Cora said, screaming.

Jim held Cora, both shaking and crying. Robert and Leroy came over for a group hug. The tears were running down their cheeks too.

After a while, Cora said, "I want my baby here at the house."

Later that evening, sitting in the kitchen with the family, Cora said, "Jim, I've felt uneasy all day. My sweet baby boy, Dana, was fussing all day. He is only one, but it was uncommon of him. He has been more than a handful. Lura was so good; she changed his diaper and rocked him."

"My little angel," said Jim, hugging Lura, trying not to cry.

"I knew you were gone too long. I paced on the front porch for the longest time."

"We are going to have to pull together and hold each other up." Jim said, as he looked at his sad little family.

---

[94] Marysville newspaper, Marysville, Ohio, November 6, 1912.

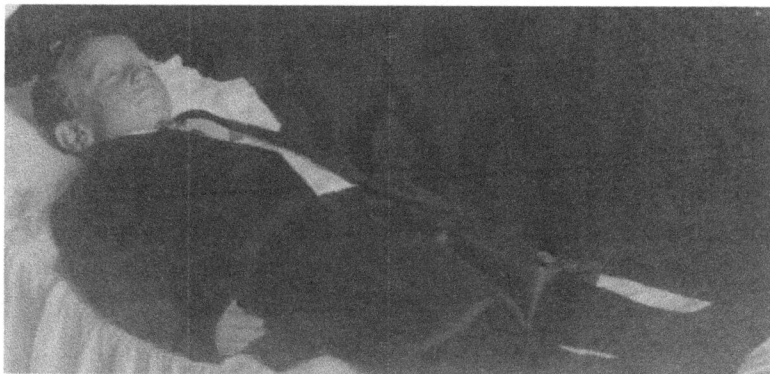

Emerson

Jim brought Emerson back from the coroner the next day. He watched as Cora cleaned and dressed him in his best outfit. Jim stood and looked at him with tears in his eyes. He looked so precious, as though he was just sleeping. Jim picked him up and laid him on a satin bed in a small coffin on the table in the parlor. They had a picture taken of him, by a photographer, since they never had a picture taken of Emerson. Jim placed a big black ribbon on the front door to let everyone know there was a death in the family, and they were in mourning.

~ * ~

In the summer of 1916, Della Mae was born. She was such a joy. Lura, now twelve, was so good with the baby.

Watching Lura playing with Della from the large kitchen that opened with a large arch doorway into the dining room, she turned to Jim and said, "I don't know what I would do without Lura. She is such a little mama," said Cora.

"She is such a help, we are blessed with such loving children," said Jim.

"It worries me that our boys may end up fighting in the war in Europe," said Cora.

"I know. I just heard that Italy has declared war on Germany. It won't be long before we are involved.

In the spring of 1918, the soldiers brought home the terrible flu epidemic. People were dying in great numbers, especially in the eastern United States.

Jim was sitting in the parlor, reading the Marysville Tribune paper. "Cora, the paper states they are closing all schools as of October 9th in the area due to the influenza epidemic," stated Jim.

"It is about time, so many children have been coming home sick. I could not bear to lose another child, Jim. I do not want our children going anywhere until this epidemic is over," said Cora.

"Maybe we should stop going to church. I can hear people coughing there. The paper said it is spread by people coughing."

"How did this ever start?"

"It states it started with the soldiers. It would be best if we just stayed here on the farm and try to do without going to the store for a while."

"I pray for all the sick, but especially for God to spare us."

Robert, Leroy, Lura, Dana

Later in the same month, on October 15, Jim and Cora's daughter, Lura, became sick with a high fever, coughing up bloody mucus and having pains in her legs. Worried sick, they took her to Dr. Freeman. He told Jim and Cora she had the terrible influenza that was going around and gave her medicine to keep her comfortable. So many of their friends and neighbors came down with the disease and died. Scared, they took her home and isolated her in her bedroom. Then at seven pm the next night, Lura died. Her lungs filled up with fluid and she couldn't breathe. Cora found her lying on her bed with a blue cast on her face. Jim heard screaming coming from Lura's room and he ran in to find Cora standing at the foot of her bed. The death was too sudden. The funeral was private and Lura was buried at Oakdale Cemetery in Marysville, beside her brother Emerson and Cora's stillborn infant son who died in 1915.

Everyone was in a state of shock and no one talked about Lura's death. It was too much, and other families had it worse. It wasn't until January 2, 1919, before the children went back to school and life seemed more normal. Still, no one talked about the death or the influenza epidemic.

"Cora, you're slowly withdrawing from life," said Jim, as he saw her sitting in the chair with her head down.

"I feel so empty. I can't cry," said Cora.

"I'm worried about you. It has been six months now."

"Working keeps me sane."

"What about the children and me?"

"I love you and the children, but what if I lose you too?" Cora said, tears filling her eyes. "Grief blanketed me these last six months. I'm so sad that all I can do is work."

"We are not going anywhere.'

"The haunting memories of Lura and Emerson's deaths keep me up nights."

"Try praying."

"God doesn't hear me. I believe I'm losing my faith, Jim."

Later that night, Jim watched Cora in her rocking chair with two lanterns lit. She picked up the Bible and started reading it. He felt comforted, knowing she was trying. It had been a long time since she read the Bible.

~ * ~

Leroy, Dana, Millie, Robert, Della, Jim, Cora and baby Betty 1928

Years later in 1928, Robert became seriously ill and brought his family home to his parents' farm (More of Robert in Chapter One).

After Robert died of consumption (TB), Jim bought a farm just three miles north of East Liberty. They just moved when Jim was taken seriously ill with nephritis and myocarditis. He was confined to his bed for a week and then died of a heart attack. The only children still at home were Dana, now sixteen, and Della, thirteen. The funeral was held in the pallor of their home. He was buried at Oakdale Cemetery in Marysville.

Cora died of cancer of the stomach while visiting her daughter in Akron, Ohio February 14, 1943.

Genealogy of James Marion Shirk

JAMES MARION SHIRK b. 18 September 1865 Union Co., Ohio d. 10 April 1929 m. Cora Poling 13 October 1895 Mt. Victory, Ohio b. 25 September 1875 Union Co., Ohio d. 14 February 1943.

Children of James and Cora:
1. Robert J. Shirk b. 30 April 1900 d. 31 January 1929 Union Co., Ohio
2. Leroy Orsamus Shirk b. 18 April 1902 d. 7 November 1987 Parkman, Ohio m. Irene Nelson 2 February 1946 Covington, Kentucky
3. Lura N Shirk b. 29 March 1904 d. 16 October 1918
4. Emerson E. Shirk b. 21 May 1907 d. 30 October 1912
5. Dana R. Shirk b. 1911 d. 1985
6. Della Mae Shirk b. 22 July 1916 d. 1972 Akron, Ohio m. Robert Leonard Jackson 1932
7. Infant son b. 26 February 1915 d. 26 February 1915
8. Infant female b. 22 March 1898 d. 1898

Chapter Twenty-two
Betty Shirk (1926-2000)

Betty Shirk 1945

Working on the family tree with my mother Betty, I positioned the charts on the dining room table. Betty looked at the charts and said, "You are always asking about the old family history. Maybe I should tell you some of mine, because when I die, nobody is going to know anything about me."

"Mom, that would be a great idea," I said, as I sat down on the dining room chair.

Betty, with a smile on her face, sat down on the chair next to me and said, "Well, let me begin when my mother went back to Toledo, Ohio after Robert, my father's, death in 1929. We stayed with Mother's sister, Aunt Minnie, and her husband, Uncle Albert. That was when I was three. Next thing I remember is we moved to Frank Danz's farm in southern Michigan, where Mother did housework. Mother never loved anyone as much as she loved Robert, but she tried to make a life for us. She met Rubin Corbin at the farm and married him in 1930. Mother and Rube never got along, and he was always leaving her. Then we moved to Ridgeway, Michigan in 1933, where Rube worked in the fields. He never made any money and blamed it on the depression. We moved back to Toledo on Upton Avenue, not far from where I was born. They divorced in 1934 when I was eight years old."

I looked at my mother, wondering why this was the first time I heard of this. I guess I was never curious to ask. "Did you ever see him again?"

"No. Mother got a job at a garment factory. She also had an ongoing affair with a married man, Arlie Weaver, whose wife was in an insane asylum. Mother would go off with him and leave me to take care of the house, which also meant to take of the fire in the stove. The last time she left, I waited three or four days and she didn't come back. I was twelve and so frightened. I had a job, babysitting for Albert and Florence Schaub. They worried about me and didn't want me to go home where I would be alone. They asked me to come and live with them. When Mother came home and couldn't find me, she was mad and knew I was over at the Schaub's house. She came over and told me to get home right now. Albert stepped in and told her he would call the police and have her cited for child neglect. She left and wouldn't speak to me for years. The Schaubs gave me everything I needed and a couple dollars a week spending money for watching their children on evenings and weekends."

"Grandma did that! I remember you told me years ago you had a hard childhood, but I never thought it was this bad. Grandma always seemed like a nice person to me," I said, feeling sad for Mom.

"She was to you. Theresa, I didn't want you to think bad of her then. As she got older, she became a nicer person."

"I don't remember Grandma hugging you, like she did us kids, but you were always friendly." Then changing the subject, I said, "You did a lot of babysitting back then."

"This was during World War II, everyone worked day and night. I worked for money to pay school fees. We had to pay for our schoolbooks back then. Without Florence and Albert Schaub, I would have never gone to school and school was especially important to me. I wanted to someday have a better life and a good job. After a few years, the Schaubs moved to East Harbor. It meant changing schools for me, and I didn't want to, so I decided to stay with my mother during the week and weekends with the Schaubs. This worried Albert to death. After the summer was over, they moved back to New York Avenue, about four blocks from my mother, and I went back with them. I didn't see my mother again until high school graduation. I asked her if she wanted to come and, to my surprise, she did."

"Did you go back to your mother then?" I asked as I rubbed her hand.

"For a while. Soon after I got out of school, I went on a trip to Galveston, Texas with a girlfriend and stayed a few weeks. I wanted to stay there, but my friend had to come home, so I left with her. I thought it would be nice to go back and stay."

"Whatever happened to Arlie?"

"Arlie died in 1945. Shortly afterwards, Mother married Bill Miller. Bill was married before and had a son, Fred, and daughter, Wilma, both grown. Millie and Bill never learned to drive a car. They took the bus or went shopping with Minnie who had a car and drove. Millie lived with Bill in the house on Edison Street in Toledo, Ohio until she died in 1967."

"Mom, what happened after Texas?"

"As soon as I got back to my mother's house, the girl next door, Betty Prater, was in desperate need of a babysitter. Her husband was in the war and she worked. I wasn't in the mood to babysit, but I went over and ended up staying with her. I got a job at the Western Union and forgot about Texas."

"How did you meet Dad?"

"Through Betty Prater. She was a good friend of George. He would come over and we played cards together. Meeting George was the best thing that ever happened to me. We got married on February 8, 1947, and Al and Florence Schaub stood up for us."

"Was Grandma there?"

"Yes, Aunt Minnie and her husband Albert, brought her."

"Mom, where did you get married?"

"Since George was married before to Ella Graber and had a three-year old son, Norman, we couldn't get married in the Catholic Church. We ended up being married by George's mother Thelma's Presbyterian pastor."

"How did you come about to be Catholic?"

"Mother stopped going to the Protestant church years ago, I believe after my father died. The Schaubs were Catholic, and I started going with them. I really felt close to God there and joined while I lived with them."

"Where did you and Dad live?"

"After we were married, we lived in Perrysburg, where we rented an apartment on the corner of Fifth Street and Louisiana Avenue from Mr. Smith, next door to George's parents. We built our first house at 511 West Seventh Street not long afterwards; it was a Sears catalog house. George worked on Front Street at Albertson's gas station, there in Perrysburg by Perry's Monument.

I always wondered about my father's family, especially after I married George. I received a few letters from Cora and Dana through the years. Being an only child, I never had much family growing up and had a great desire to reconnect with my father's people. George drove to the farm where I once stayed as a small child and found Robert Shirk's brother, Dana, his wife, Ruth, and their small son, Jim, living there. Dana told me his brother, Leroy, lived on a farm near Middleburg, Ohio, and his sister, Della, lived in Akron, Ohio. Dana then showed us where my father's and grandparents' graves were in Marysville. I was so happy to find the family.

"In 1956, I decided I wanted to learn to drive a car. We only had one car: a Chevy. George always bought a Chevy. Finally, being able to drive, I had some freedom. It felt so wonderful to go to the store and not have to wait to have someone take me.

"After I married George and started having children, I became closer to my mother. We spent the holidays together and went on trips during the summer with her. She died in 1967 after being in St Charles hospital in Oregon, Ohio for several months from bowel problems. I took my baby Walter up to hospital so she could see him."

Millie and Bill Miller, 1963

Feeling sad, I said, "I remember the funeral and going to Woodlawn Cemetery afterwards." Looking at Mom, I asked, "Did you love my dad?"

"I loved him. We had three beautiful children (Theresa 1947, George in 1950 and Robin in 1955). I always wanted three children at least. I was an only child, and it was very lonely growing up. I had a good life with George. He was a World War II veteran, but he would never talk about it. He would get this certain look on his face and I knew it bothered him. He went to the VFW to talk to the men there about it."

"What happened that you met Clarence Snyder and divorced my father?"

"I was lonely. Your father worked two jobs and his construction business kept him gone most of the time. I started taking piano lessons from Clarence's wife, Bernie. Clarence paid me a lot of attention. I found myself falling for him, but I always loved your father. I found myself pregnant with Walter and I pretended it was George's. It tore his heart when I finally told him, and he filed for a divorce in 1967. Even then, he would have taken me back, but I left."

Holding Mom's hand, I said, "I remember how hard it was then, everyone was upset."

"I married Clarence Snyder after his divorce with Bernie. We rented a farmhouse on Route 582 and then in 1977 Clarence retired from Heinz and we moved to Florida. By then, we had another child, Michelle, in 1971."

"I remember how happy you were to move to Florida. You called it your Shangri-la."

"Yes, I dreamed of moving here for years."

"At first, it was hard because we missed you, but it was fun to look forward to visiting you. We had some amazing trips around Florida. One of my favorites was tubing down the Ichetucknee River in Northern Florida, although Larry got sunburned."

"That was fun. One of my favorites was camping in the Keys and going on the glass bottom boat in Key West. I especially loved amusement parks and riding roller coasters. I also enjoy collecting dolls, especially older Cabbage Patch dolls and making doll clothes for them. But it has been hard since 1985 when Clarence died of a stroke. I tried working again after not working for sixty-two years. I ended up having a heart attack in 1987 and almost died. They had to do emergency triple by-pass. Only one took, so I have been living with a weak heart. The doctor didn't give me much time to live, so every year is a blessing."

Genealogy of Betty Jean Shirk

BETTY JEAN SHIRK b. 18 August 1926 Toledo, Ohio d. 30 December 2000 Ocoee, Florida m. (1) George Clarence Jones, Jr. 8 February 1947 b. 14 April 1922 d. 23 May 1995 m (2) Clarence Snyder 1970 b. 27 October 1912 d. 10 April 1985.

Children of Betty and George:
1. Theresa L Smith b. 1 December 1947 Toledo, Ohio m. Larry L. Smith 25 September 1969 b. 6 February 1948 Elk Valley, Tennessee
Children listed in chapter 23.

2. George Calvin Jones b. 2 August 1950 Perrysburg, Ohio m. (1) Joanne Clark 1970 (2) Diane Shields 28 May 1994 Los Vegas, Nevada b. 26 September 1954 Oregon, Ohio
Child of George and Joanne:
Timothy George Jones Sr.b. 5 August 1974 Toledo, Ohio
Child of Tim and Danya Plantz:
Timothy George Jones Jr. b. 20 May 1995
Child of Timothy George Jones Sr. and Lori Raab:
Raelaigh Mae Jones b. 9 July 2010
Child of Timothy George Jones Jr. and Katie Steele:
Oliver James Jones b. 16 July 2018

3. Robin Marie Jones b 23 August 1955 m. (1) Bill Birtwhistle 1971 (2) David Burnette 14 March 1975 b. 7 July 1954
Child of Robin and Bill:
Roxanne Marie Birtwhistle b. 13 October 1971 m. Robert Todd Spraetz 25 Sept. 1999

Children of Roxanne and Todd:

Zoe Ella Spraetz b. 1 June 2004 Tacoma, Washington

Jacob Robert Spraetz b. 17 August 2006 Tacoma, Washington

Children of Robin and Dave:

David Earl Burnette Jr. b. 1 November 1984

Kristen Nicole Burnette b. 26 June 1980 m. (1) Brandon Estep 6 September 2002 (2) Jason Culver 28 April 2010 b. 26 September 1985

Child of Kristen and Brandon:

Angela Michele Estep b. 18 September 2000

Children Kris and Jason:

Annabelle Julie Culver b. 31 March 2010 Toledo, Ohio

Zachary Alexander Culver b. 2 October 2019 Toledo, Ohio

Children of Betty and Clarence:

1. Walter Christopher Snyder b. 25 May 1966 Toledo, Ohio

2. Michelle Rene. Snyder b. 28 June 1971 Toledo, Ohio m. (1) Russell Roberts Sr. 10 June 1990 b. 4 June 1968 d. 4 August 1996 Bulls Gap, Tennessee (2) Reid Fletcher 24 December 1995 Orlando, Florida b. 8 January 1955 Rockwood, Tennessee

Child of Michelle and Russell:

Russell David Roberts Jr. b. 10 October 1987 Orlando, Florida m. Melissa Nicole Glass 27 April 2013

Children of Russel and Missy:

Hayden David Roberts b. 12 October 2013

Linkin Alexander Roberts b. 12 November 2017

Chapter Twenty-three
Theresa Lynn Jones

Theresa Jones 1966

I was too young to remember everything, but bits and pieces come to me now and then. It was seventy years ago. I remember coming home with my parents to our house to see Uncle Arle and Aunt Charlotte sitting on the couch in our little house on Seventh Street. My parents left the door unlocked and we were surprised. Arle picked me up and threw me in the air, hitting my head on the ceiling and scaring me. I remember standing at the foot of my brother Norman's bed, thinking he was dying. He had German measles then and I just got over the three-day measles. We were so sick. Later, Mom told me I was three years old then. My dad, George Jones Jr., was a World War II veteran, but he never talked about it. He would say, "Don't you worry your pretty little head about it. I want you just think of the good things in life." Dad was married before to Ella and had a son, Norman, by this marriage. He was four years older than me.

Mom loved to sew and made most of my clothes up to junior high. When I was two, Mom went to the hospital in Perrysburg on the corner of Second Street and Maple Street to have my brother George. The hospital was a box-shaped two-story building, privately owned.

I got a large tricycle when I was four and was told to stay in my own neighborhood on West Seventh Street, but one day, I took off down the street and crossed the street at the corner away from our house. I ran right into our insurance agent's car. He got out of the car, grabbed me and my tricycle and took me to my house where my dad gave me the first spanking I remember. Most of the time, our punishment was to stay in our room and sit in our rocking chair.

When I was five, I went to kindergarten at Elm Street School on the corner of Elm and Seventh Street. They changed the name to Toth School after their beloved principal. I walked half a mile to school with other children in the neighborhood. Mom did not drive then, and we had only one car, a Chevy, which Dad took to work. He worked on Front Street at an Albertsons gas station. I remember one winter day, I decided to make a large snowball, rolling it home until it got too big to roll. It was getting late, and Mom was worried to death. A girl about my age was kidnapped in Michigan and they were on the lookout for the kidnapper.

I had friends in the neighborhood, and we would play with our dolls. Susie and Diane had a good size playhouse their father built that was fun. Linda lived across the street. We made mud pies for our dolls. Joyce lived three houses down and we would trade doll clothes to dress up our dolls. When we played with my brother George, he wanted to play cowboys and Indians. Norman would pull George and me around the block in our little red wagon and pretend we were going on vacation.

Then in 1954, I went to first grade at St Rose School. Sister Mary Arthur was my teacher and I just loved her. She was young and very loving and was like a second mother when I was in school. Norman was in the fifth grade there at the time. After school, we would walk to Perry's Monument on front street and play on the steps. We were to go straight to the gas station where dad worked and wait until he got off from work. It was on the way and Dad never found out.

Then in the second grade, the nun was older and sick a lot, so we had a lot of substitute teachers. One of my substitute teachers was Lulu Rossbach. She said she was the first teacher in the area to have her master's degree and taught in a one room schoolhouse. We were preparing for first communion that year. Every morning, we would go to Mass first thing. We would stand in line, a nun with a clicker would click it and we marched to church. Click, go to the pew, click, go to the seat, click, kneel.

Everything I did and thought was a sin, or so I thought. Mad at my mom, punched my brother, stole a dime from his piggy bank, etc. I had my first confession and found it was not scary at all, but someone I could talk to about the things that bothered me. The priest, Monsignor Waltz, gave me good advice and made me feel good. I had a group of friends and we decided to see who could get the most holy cards. We made it a point to go to the funeral home across the street from the school, almost every day to get holy cards. Had no clue who died.

First Communion was so special. Mom bought me a beautiful white dress and veil. I felt like a princess. We had a little party afterwards where I received religious presents. I remember my great grandmother Lulu Jones was at my party and she seemed so old to me; she was eighty.

First Communion

My mother did not work outside the home and had a tight schedule. Mondays were laundry day. She changed the sheets on the beds, washed clothes and hung them out on the clothesline. Tuesdays, she would iron. Wednesday was mop floor day. Thursday was clean the bathroom, clean the kitchen, and refrigerator. Friday was sewing and mending day. Mom cleaned the living room every day! Mom really got crazy in the spring with cleaning and airing out the mattresses and pillows. Every room was stripped from furniture and cleaned. I told Mom I was going to put on her tombstone, 'she kept a clean house'.

Saturday was grocery shopping day; Mom didn't drive, so we had to wait for Dad. Mom also ran the house, cut the grass, helped us with our homework and played Bunco with a group of ladies once a month. Sunday was church day and visiting family, usually Grandma and Grandpa Jones, who lived a mile away on Fifth Street. Mom and Dad played euchre with Grandma and Grandpa while we played in their living room. Grandma kept a box of toys for us in the dining room closet under the stairs. Grandpa played a wild game of euchre; I can still hear him slam his hand down. Grandpa smoked in those days. When my uncles were over smoking, I would see layers of smoke in the house, and everyone was in a fog. My parents never smoked or drank alcohol.

In the third grade, they came through the schools and vaccinated everyone against polio. It was a big deal then. Polio was so frightening at the time. Mom thought it was from swimming. After being vaccinated, I could finally go to the Perrysburg pool in the summer. We would ride our bikes to the pool. It was the place to be then. We would also go downtown and go to the little theater on Saturdays. It was twenty-five cents. They showed two shows, usually westerns. We walked or rode bikes everywhere. Perrysburg was a small friendly town then; everybody knew everybody.

A few months before my eighth birthday, Mom went to the hospital to have my little sister, Robin. Right from the beginning, I loved her and helped take care of her. Around this time, Norman went to live with the Grabers, his mother Ella's parents. He came to visit on the weekends, and I thought he was everything. Mom finally learned to drive a car, which gave her more freedom.

When I was in the fifth grade, I came down with hepatitis A. They thought it was from drinking contaminated water. I went to Dr. Pugh's office on Second Street three times a week for penicillin shots, turning my bottom black and blue. He charged three dollars a visit and my mom worried about the cost. Dr. Pugh's office was on the side of his home. He had one nurse working for him. It always smelled like rubbing alcohol in the rooms. There was a waiting room, two exam rooms and his office, where you got your prescription. The waiting room had these ceramic heads of people on the wall, and it creeped me out. Dr Pugh was very nice, and I really liked him. Mom isolated me from the family in my bedroom. I ate my meals in there, away from everyone. Dad brought me homework from school and presents often, like coloring books and paper dolls and his stamp collection. I remember feeling so weak I could hardly stand up at the time. Once Mom came in the bedroom and I was staring at the dust particles from the light coming in the window. She started screaming, thinking I was dead. That was the first time I realized how sick I had been.

In the center of our living room was our black and white television set. I watched *Father Knows Best, Leave It to Beaver* and *Lassie* whenever I got a chance. When the TV broke down, Mom would take out all the bulbs and take them into the hardware store and test them to find out which one blew so she could replace it.

Somewhere around the fifth grade, my father worked for the city of Perrysburg for a while, then quit and started his own business, George Jones Construction. He got a job, working as a night janitor at the Perrysburg high school. He felt more secure, working two jobs.

When I was in the sixth grade, we moved out to the country. Dad built a house on Roachton Road by Thompson Road. My life changed. We got a colored television; it was such a big deal. Norman came back and lived with us. We played baseball with the neighbors; they were mostly boys. We played so much baseball, there were baseball lines in their yard. No grownups and we made our own teams and rules, it was so much fun. We loved to play in the woods by the house. George would pretend he was Tarzan. We picked wild mushrooms in late April, wild strawberries in June, wild black raspberries in July and hickory nuts in the fall. Our next-door neighbors had square dances in their barn. They taught us to square dance.

Dad worked two full time jobs. We saw him in the morning and at ten o clock at night, but he usually had the weekends free and we always took a vacation in the summer. When I was twelve, we went to Hubbard Lake in Michigan to a cabin owned by my great Uncle Gerald McGill. It was a great time; from there, we went to Mackinac Island for a day. Next summer, we went to Niagara Falls, coming back through Canada. We also took trips to The Smoky Mountains, Buck Lake Ranch by Angola, Indiana. Vacations were the one time we were together as a family.

When I was thirteen and in the eighth grade, Mom wanted a piano and to take lessons. She said she would teach me as she took lessons. She had Robin go with her and as time went on, the piano teacher, Bernie, her husband Clarence, Mom and Dad became friends, going square dancing every Saturday night. Around this time, Mom started singing with the suburban singers, a group that put on operettas there in Perrysburg.

Norman joined the Air Force right out of high school my freshman year. I wrote to him often. He trained at Lackland base in Texas, and afterwards was stationed in England when the Beatles were just starting to get popular. I was crazy about Elvis and the Beatles. I wanted the new forty-five record as soon as it came out. I babysat around the neighborhood to get money. It was so much fun.

My mom and I were always arguing then. One day, when I was fifteen, I came home and found Clarence and Mom kissing in the kitchen. Clarence left right away. Mom and I had a terrible fight. I told her I couldn't stand living there anymore and ran out of the house. Down the road and into the woods. I ran until I found a small clearing and threw myself on the ground, crying. For a long time, I cried.

Suddenly, a bright light shone down around me, and I felt like a bubble of love encircled me. I knew at once it was God. I felt him telling me to get up, go home and forgive my mom. Also, I felt he was telling me one day I would be a nurse. It was a powerful feeling. I got down on my knees and told God my life was his.

I must have been there quite a while because it was getting dark and my mom was driving down the road, looking for me. She pulled over and told me to get into the car. I remembered her saying I couldn't run away because I would end up a prostitute in a city. She said Clarence was like an older brother she never had. I asked her to forgive me and went back home. I felt an urge to read the Bible, so I saved my allowance, bought my own bible and started reading it. We had a large fancy family Bible, but Mom was always afraid I would mess it up. I told my best friend Dana about what I experienced, and she thought that we should become nuns, but after a couple weeks, we changed our minds. Her grandmother was Lulu, my old substitute teacher. She was retired now, but did some tutoring. I would have her go over my English papers, because I had a hard time with English. I found out I needed a high-grade average to get into nursing school.

While in high school, I went to religious instructions and CYO (Catholic Youth Organization) at church every Thursday night, and afterwards, we would go to Broske's and get pizza. It was so good then. Margaret Broske made it from scratch and shredded lots of cheese on top.

Everyone knew Margaret and loved her. I walked to my grandparents' house those nights since they lived a block from the school on Fifth Street. It was a short distance to the church. My grandfather loved to tease, and my grandmother loved to fuss over me. Those nights were always fun.

I enjoyed going to the high school football games. We were the Yellow Jackets. Just before our big game with Maumee, we would have a snake dance through town, going in and out the stores, yelling cheers, then end up with a large bonfire in front of the football field. I would go around, selling candy at the game for the pep club, throwing the candy up to the people in the stands and them handing money back down to me. Several people said keep the change. Pep Club mothers always wondered how I sold so much candy and always had too much money.

Sock hops after the games were so popular then and we would go to the old courthouse. It was called the Bee Hive. It was a place teenagers could hang out and it had a large hall for dancing. The last time I went there, there was a large crack in the wall on the left side. It was rock'n'roll dancing then. The floor and the crack would move with everyone dancing. Later that week, in 1963, when no one was there, the roof caved in. We were so upset we lost our Bee Hive. We decided to go house to house, collecting money for a new one and having fundraisers. It was finally made in 1965, by the firehouse, but was never the same. It is the senior center now.

Perry Dairy Bar was a hamburger diner across from the school. During lunch hour, a lot of kids would run over there and pile into the little booths. We played the jukebox and shared fries.

My sophomore year, on November 22, 1963, John F Kennedy was shot. My family really liked him. It came over the PA system when I was in English class he was shot in the head. The teacher asked us to say a prayer for him. I started crying hard and left the room. I ran in the hall to the stairs and sat there, crying. The guidance counselor found me, tried to console me and called my father. Everyone was so upset and hurt.

When I was sixteen, Mom and Dad went with Bernie and Clarence for a long weekend in Stratford, Canada while I watched Robin and George. I did so well that they went the following year to California, leaving me in charge for two weeks. Grandma and Grandpa Jones checked up on us, but it was scary being left alone for so long. A couple of migrant workers' car broke down in our front yard and they were out there at night for a long time. Our parents told us to stay away from the field workers, they could be dangerous. We brought the mattress from our beds and slept in the living room on the floor. George slept against the front door with a kitchen knife. The migrant workers fixed their car and left. For the rest of the two weeks, we slept on the mattresses on the living room floor.

When American Bandstand came on the television our world stopped. We ran into the house, sat on the floor and watched Dick Clark announce the latest band and watch teenagers dance to the new dances. Then we would practice the dance moves.

My favorite class in high school was Latin. Mrs. Bauer made the class interesting with a lot of class participation. At the end of each school year there was a Latin Banquet. First year students were slaves and we dressed in Burlap bags. Second year we were masters and wore our Sunday best. Third year we were gods and goddesses and wore formal outfits. The second-and third-year students owned the slaves who waited on them and made them do crazy things. I had to crawl under the tables and tie shoestrings to the other masters together, it was hilarious when they tried to stand up.

My least favorite class was speech class. One day our teacher got into an argument with a student. Ronnie told him he couldn't be in a play and the teacher got so mad he pulled out a gun and shot him. The class thought it was real and I, along with several girls, started crying. Ronnie got up off the floor. The teacher turned to the class and said now write about what you just saw. We were told to go in the hall if we didn't stop crying, which is where I went. Several of the students were really upset and decided to toilet paper his house, but I wouldn't go. The teacher lived around the corner from me and the next day there was toilet paper streaming from all trees in his front yard.

I felt this passion inside of me to be a nurse. My senior year in high school, I joined Future Nurses of America Club. Then, early in 1965, we had career day and several student nurses from the area hospitals came to talk. So impressed with the student nurse from St. Vincent's Hospital,

I signed up to be a candy striper (teenage volunteer) that day. Then every Saturday morning, I would take the Community Traction bus from Perrysburg on Second and Louisiana bus stop to downtown Toledo. There I exchanged to a bus going to St Vincent's. It was a scary experience for me at first. It was my first time on my own away from Perrysburg.

At the hospital, I worked with the EKG technicians out of the cardiologist, Dr. Applebaum's office. My job was to run all over the hospital and place EKG strips on patient's charts. It was a time when the order of Gray Nuns ran the hospital. The new B and C wings were just opened, and they were tearing down the old section of the hospital, between the two wings. I remember running through the tunnel after being scared at seeing a rat. One of the Gray Nuns wearing a long gray robe with a black cape and black bonnet grabbed me and hugged me, saying she just loved the little volunteers. I was afraid I was in trouble for running.

One day my senior year, Dad came to school to find me and asked if I would help Emma Hubert at her rest home there in Perrysburg after school. Emma fell and broke her leg. It was such a good experience for me. I would set up the dinner trays and take them to the five residents. I would also bathe a patient who was too weak and help her put on her night gown. I took the bus there after school and Dad picked me up after work, around ten pm.

While I was taking my final exam May 25, 1966, they announced over the PA that my baby brother Walter was born. I was embarrassed and excited at the same time. After graduation, St Vincent's Hospital called me and wanted to know if I wanted a job there as an aide. I was so surprised. They said they hired their volunteers first. I had already applied for St. Vincent's School of Nursing and was told I would have to take a speed-reading course before they would accept me. When it was time to sign papers for the nursing school, Mom would not sign the papers. She said I wouldn't stick with it; I would just quit and get married. My dad went for the interview and said my mom was sick and signed for her. I did get a scholarship from Perrysburg High School towards my schooling, but it was only three hundred dollars. I took a job as an aide and was placed in the newborn nursery on night shift. Excited, I thought I could work at night and play during the day but found myself sleeping wherever I went during the day.

Then I went to live with my great aunt Minnie in Point Place. It gave me more freedom and time to study for my reading class and it was close to the Community Traction bus stop. I paid Minnie fifteen dollars every other week on pay day for living there. She ended up spending the money on me half the time. We became the best of friends. I also got to see more of my grandma Miller, her sister. Minnie would pick Grandma and Bill Miller up and drive us to Tiedtke's downtown store to spend the day. She was a crazy driver and always scared me. We would eat in the large restaurant there at Tiedtke's overlooking the Maumee River, which was a real treat. Grandma always had to buy me something.

Minnie had a little chihuahua dog that would bark like crazy when I came in late. Minnie went to bed as soon as it got dark outside. One time, she got up out of bed with a baseball bat and came to the door. I was never out late after that happened. I finished my reading class, got accepted at the nursing school and went to the dorm to live that fall.

It was so much fun living in the dorm, and I became friends with several girls there. One girl, Jan, and I would see who could outdo the other with pranks. She would write on my mirror with lipstick, and I would write on hers with her toothpaste. Then she would place cereal under my sheet in the bed and I would place Vaseline on her toilet seat. Once she placed toilet paper all over my room. It looked like a spider web. The worst was when she put my mattress in the elevator, and we ended up getting detention. Which meant you could not go home for the weekend. The phone was at the end of the hall and there was only one phone for everyone on the floor. We would fight over the phone. It would be nothing to see three or four students in the phone both.

One day Jan said, "Theresa, let's go get a pack of cigarettes from the vending machine."

I said, "Why, we don't smoke."

She said, "Let's try it."

One puff and it felt like I was dying. I coughed and struggled to breathe. I never took another puff of any cigarette.

I ended up failing English Literature at Mary Mann's College, one of several college courses we were required to take. The head of the nursing school told me I could not come back in the fall. I felt terrible. My grandma Miller died, also, that spring of 1967. I had friends who were drafted and in Viet Nam. Another friend enlisted and ended up in Korea. The final blow was my parents got a divorce. It was a terrible time.

I got a full-time position and continued working as an aide in the newborn nursery. My family and friends were supportive and helped me get through the year. Dad bought a used car for me to use. My friend Dana and I took oil painting lessons under William Scott who I felt was a great local artist, who gave lessons in the basement of his house. I started painting in high school as a hobby and enjoyed it. Robin and I continued back with piano lessons, but with Lenore Cocanour this time.

In May1968, I went to Bowling Green LPN school. While in school, I continued to work at St Vincent's Hospital on weekends. After I graduated in May 1969, I bought a new car, a Karmann Ghia. What a fun car to drive around. I continued working at St. Vincent's Hospital, but on the day shift.

In late June, a neighbor asked if I would babysit two little boys for a few days while their mother went to her mother's funeral in New York. They were three and five years old and their mother, who I met once, just dropped them off, no clothes or toys and they stayed for over two weeks. My father went out and bought them clothes and toys. We gave the boys lots of love and attention and they were fun to take care of. On July fourth, my cousin asked if I would go out on a blind date with him and Jan, the nurse friend of mine. It was to see *Herbie the Love Bug* at the Maumee Drive-in so I said I would if I could take the two little boys with me. I could not believe it when he said yes.

After we got to the drive-in, just when the show started, they announced a tornado had been sited going through Maumee. A heavy storm came through, the electricity went out and everything turned pitch black. When we left, it was pouring rain and lightning struck across the area. I screamed and knocked over a glass of Pepsi sitting on the back window. The Pepsi ran down my back and I was thinking the glass broke, so I jumped in Larry's lap. That was how I met my husband.

It was a whirlwind romance with Larry coming over almost every day. Everywhere we went they played *Sweet Caroline* by Neil Diamond that summer. We loved it, and it became our song. On July 20, we were over at Larry's parents' house when the moon landing of Neil Armstrong was on the television. I thought how amazing this was, but was shocked when his father Clay said it was made up, he wasn't really on the moon. I said how can you say that, and he replied no man could ever go to the moon.

I married the love of my life on September 25, 1969, in my friend Jan's church. The Catholic Church would not marry us without Larry getting an annulment, since he was married previously to Ginger and they had a son together. We talked about eloping to Tennessee since my parents were divorced and having a hard time. My grandmother Jones convinced us to have a small chapel wedding, saying I would regret it all my life if I eloped. It wasn't until after she died that I found out her and grandpa eloped.

Clay and Aretta, Betty and George Jones Jr., Larry and Theresa, Joanne Clark, George Jones III 1969

Four months after I was married, I was sick to my stomach

constantly. I finally went to the doctor and found out I was pregnant. Larry and I were so excited and happy, but the next month I had a miscarriage. I was so upset until my mom told me she had miscarriages between all us children. The next month I found myself pregnant again.

Seven years later, I did get married in the Catholic Church when Larry and Ginger's marriage was annulled. By then, we had three children: Wayne Patrick in 1970, Andrew Michael in 1972, and Laura Marie in 1974.

Larry, Theresa, Larry Jr., Andy, Laura and Wayne 1976

When our children were young, I worked part time. Larry worked for the City of Perrysburg and wanted to get a second part-time job to help make ends meet. I told him my father worked two jobs and was one of the reasons my parents divorced. I wanted a life together with him.

They were fun children who really enjoyed life. The first seven years, we moved frequently until we finally bought a little house on Eckel Road. I didn't want to live anywhere but Perrysburg. Larry was incredibly supportive of anything I wanted to do and spent time watching the children so I could pursue my dreams. He had his bowling every week, which he became exceptionally good at. He was in the senior's PBA when he turned fifty and has had twenty-seven 300 games, which included practice so only four were sanctioned by PBA.

Mom married Clarence in 1970 and had Michelle (nicknamed Shelly) in 1971. Summer vacations were especially important to us. Most of the time, we went to Tennessee to visit Larry's grandmother Sarah, who he called Ma Maw. We went on to the Smoky Mountains, every year doing something different. When my mom, Clarence, Michelle and Walter moved to Orlando, Florida, we split the time between Tennessee and Florida.

When Sarah became too old to take care of herself, she lived with her children and finally with us in 1977-1978. The next month after her mother Sarah died, Larry's mother Aretta came home drunk and passed out, smoking a cigarette. She died of smoke inhalation long before the fire started burning the living room on June 9, 1978. Aretta was bipolar and after her divorce from Clay in 1977, she became more depressed, drinking heavily. We were in a state of shock after getting the phone call from the police at 4:00 in the morning. We had to go see the house and I can still smell that awful smell. We made the arrangements for her funeral and she was cremated. We buried her with her mother in Elk Valley, Tennessee. Thanks to the help of family and friends, we made it through those sad days.

Since Larry and I both worked full time, we decided to make one day a week our children's day, doing something special for them. Taking them roller skating, movies, arcades, fishing, hiking, swimming, etc. Most of the time, they decided where we were going. During supper, I would read the Children Bible Stories and we had some interesting conversations.

Dad married Arlene in 1972. I was so surprised. I really didn't know her. She had three grown children and I found her hard to get along with. Then I found out she had a terrible disease, Scleroderma. They ended up moving to San Diego, California for her health. In 1981, we took a three-week vacation and went out to San Diego in a van pulling a camper. The children made it a fun trip. On the way, we went to Memphis and saw Elvis's house. Then through the Painted Desert and spent a day at the Grand Canyon. It took us five days to get to San Diego. Dad took us to Ensenada, Mexico, for the day. Also, we went to the San Diego Zoo, Disneyland, Universal Studios, Knotts Berry Farm, the tar pits, Crystal Cathedral and the Queen Mary in LA. Then on to Las Vegas where we camped behind the Star Dust. Dad flew back to San Diego from there. Arlene said she was too sick to go anywhere with us. What a fun vacation, even though we broke down in Colorado on the way home. The wheel bearing on the camper burned up and delayed us a couple days.

In October of 1976, I heard Billy Graham was coming to the Silver Dome in Pontiac, Michigan. I figured it was a once in a lifetime experience to see the famous evangelist. So, we took all four children. It was a very moving experience. He had a powerful way of speaking. Over forty thousand people were there.

I went on taking classes at night at Owens Technical College and got my Registered Nurse License in 1979. The hospital had a reimbursement program for those who wanted to go back to school. They wanted to go to an all RN hospital. Afterwards, I took an ICU course and began working in the new Neurology Intensive Care unit there at St. Vincent. I really enjoyed this because they rotated you between regular Neuro-floor, stepdown and ICU. We had a great team of nurses who worked together. We became family, going out together and having family parties.

When Minnie became too old to live by herself in 1981, I moved her into my house. I remained close to her over the years. She even flew to my mom's house in Orlando for a while. When she realized it was too much work for me, she asked to be placed in a home. We found a wonderful place for her at the Sacred Heart Home for the Aged. They had great parties there and even mini vacations for their residents. It was at one of the parties I had my first caviar, saw my first wheelchair square dancing, and heard great live bands. She died there in 1989 at the age of ninety-four.

Several of us nurses on my unit decided to go back for our Bachelor in Science of Nursing together, taking one to two subjects at a time. I always enjoyed school; I saw it as a form of entertainment. I took the children to class with me, usually one at a time, which was an experience. I received my BSN in 1987.

My stepson, Larry, married Kelley in 1987 and had four beautiful little girls, Kristen 1988, Brandi 1992, Paige 1995, and Myranda 1998. My daughter, Laura, ended up having two good-looking boys, Austin 1993, Tylor 1997, and one beautiful girl, Chelsea 1994. Now, we were taking trips with our grandchildren. We bought a pop-up camper and had many fun trips with them. My favorite were the ones at Mohican State Park area where we went canoeing, horseback riding and rode to go-carts.

We bought an acre of land in 1989 in the country and built my dream house. I always wanted a house with an open area where the kitchen, living room and dining room was one big area. In our old house, I would be in the kitchen, cooking, while my family and friends were on the other side of a wall, visiting in the living room. I also wanted a basement; we have tornados here and we would go to the inner bathroom when the tornado warning went off and it frightened me. With my brother, George, as our building contractor, our house was built. Dad moved back from San Diego and helped build it. We moved in on Thanksgiving Day 1990.

In 2007, I had an achiness in my left breast, and it would not go away. I went to my family doctor and she ordered a mammogram which was normal. She sent me for a cardiac work-up and all those tests were normal. The cardiologist suggested I have a cardiac cath. I went to St. Vincent's Medical Center where I worked to have the cath. I always read a book to calm my nerves, so I took a western story by Zane Gray. It helped; when I got to the table, I was feeling pretty good. The dye they placed in my catheter caused a warm burning sensation. Then the cardiologist said I had an eighty per cent blockage in my right coronary artery and placed two stents in. It felt like someone slugged me in the jaw. Afterwards, I had more energy, I could climb stairs without getting short of breath and no more achiness in my left breast.

Over the years, I was active in Genealogy, going to conferences, joining Ohio Genealogy Society, Wood County Ohio Genealogy Society and Daughters of the American Revolution. We took vacations, doing research on the family tree and going to ancestral home sites. I wanted to write the information in a book, but to bring the people to life. I didn't want a bunch of facts only. A friend of mine talked me into joining All Writers' Workplace and Workshop to help me with the process. My first book published with a publisher was *Sarah's Story* in 2017.

I worked at St Vincent Mercy Hospital for forty-five years, retiring in 2012 after having a stroke. It started in May of 2012. I had heartburn and dizzy spells. Then June 11, I finally went to my family doctor, and she prescribed Prilosec. I went back to work on June 15, and I became weak and dizzy walking down the hall. By the time I made it to the floor, I was very weak and felt faint. They wheeled me down to ER and admitted me, thinking I was having a heart attack. The next day, during my cardiac stress test, my right side became extremely weak. I was rushed to the MRI and it showed I had left brain stem stroke. On June 19, I was sent by ambulance to the University Hospital in Cleveland at night. Early the next day, I went to surgery for angioplasty. I had immediate improvement on my right side. The weakness gradually left and, with rehab and physical therapy, ninety-nine percent returned. I felt that knowing I was a nurse, everyone went out of their way to give me exceptional care.

It was so hard for me to make up my mind to retire. I really loved being a nurse, but I was too weak now. I decided to volunteer at the hospital after I retired and was placed in the Palliative Care (end of life care) and the Spiritual Care Department. This was so rewarding, a real joy in my life. Most of the time I listened and comforted the patients and family, besides offering prayers and communion.

My son, Andrew, married Maria in March of 2014 in Las Vegas. We planned a trip out to LA to visit my Uncle Frank (my father's brother) who was under the care of hospice. Andy and Marie planned their marriage to follow after our visit to Las Vegas for their wedding. Everything that goes into a wedding was done at MGM Hotel. They had a beautiful little girl, Eiya, later that year.

A Thursday in September of 2015, Larry and I went on the bus pilgrimage with Bishop Thomas to see Pope Francis in Philadelphia. We left early Thursday morning at the recreation center in Maumee, Ohio. The news media were there to send us off. We got to our lovely hotel later that evening. Friday, we met at the breakfast buffet at the hotel and our group was assigned a tour guide, who was truly knowledgeable of the area. We left for a tour of old town Philadelphia and ate lunch at a tavern where John Adams, Ben Franklin and George Washington ate. That evening, we went to the Longwood Gardens; what a beautiful peaceful place.

Saturday, we met at the breakfast buffet, where they passed out special passes needed to get to the area to see Pope Francis. After we got to Philadelphia, our bus parked by Citizen's Bank where a long lines of tour buses were parked. Groups of people were standing everywhere, passing out bottles of water, selling t-shirts, along with all kinds of souvenirs. Long strings of porta potties were everywhere. We took the subway from there, which was very fast moving to Rittenhouse Square downtown. Our tour guide told us to meet back there at 8:30 that night. There were police, TSA agents at the check-in points at the gates and the lines went faster than the airport. Then we walked to Benjamin Franklin Parkway. Huge screens were set up so everyone could see the "Festival of Families." Bands, singers, songs sung by people from all over the world in their native costumes were there. It reminded me of It's a Small World at Disneyworld. Everyone was extremely friendly. Lots of happy well-behaved children were there. Screams came in waves as the pope approached. First, police on bikes, then followed by black vans, then a large truck with lights and cameras. At last, the Pope, standing in his Pope Mobile, waving and smiling to the crowds. The lady behind me said, "Well, I can cross it off my bucket list."

Sunday, Larry, and I were so exhausted we slept in and watched the Pope on TV live from the site at the hotel. It was an amazing experience.

In March of 2020, the hospital told me because of the pandemic with Covid-19, I was not to come back volunteering until it was over. I returned a little over a year later, in April of 2021, after receiving the vaccine. I was happy to finally return, but I had to wear a face mask, a plastic face shield and was told not to go in any room with patients positive for Covid.

Then on June 1, 2020, I had a right partial hip replacement, after falling on my sidewalk trying to pull a stubborn weed. The next day after surgery, I was very weak from the bleeding from the surgery site. The social worker told me I would have to go to a nursing home since I wasn't good enough to go to the Rehab Hospital. This scared me because the nursing home patients were dying from COVID-19. When the physical therapist came in to evaluate me, I pushed myself so hard to walk with the walker across the room and into the hall. I passed to go to Rehab I was so happy. They allowed one visitor at a time there which meant so much to me. The nursing homes were not allowed to have visitors.

Chelsea and Ariyah Smith

Larry and I were at a hobby show on April 18, 2021, when my daughter Laura called, crying, saying, "Mom, where are you? I went to check on Chelsea and found her dead in bed with Ariyah (9 months old) rubbing her arm."

I screamed, "No! No! No!"

Larry turned to me and said, "You're screaming."

I said, crying, "We have to go now," and told him what Laura said.

Larry started shaking and I said," Are you sure you can drive?" He said he could. I called my sister, Robin, who lived close to Laura and told her what happened and asked her to go be with Laura until I could get there. When we arrived there, a police car was in front of her house and EMS were there. I wanted to see Chelsea, but Robin said, "You don't want to see her like this." The EMS were placing her on stretcher and taking her out the front door. I held Laura, her poor body trembling as she cried her heart out. People started coming and congregating at the back door. Laura's sons, Austin and Tylor, were there, crying. Everyone was crying.

That night, right after I just fell asleep, I saw Chelsea standing at my bedside, crying with mascara streaking down her face. She said, "I didn't want to leave my baby. I didn't want to leave my baby."

I said, "Don't worry, Chelsea, we will take good care of Ariyah." I woke up, sitting in my bed crying uncontrollably. It seemed so real to me. I never saw her again.

The next few days were surreal, planning the funeral with Laura. Family coming in from out of town. My brother George and my sister Robin helped by taking over with the wake. I felt I had angels around me, leading me. Laura loved Chelsea's baby so much, she took over custody. Laura babysat Ariyah while Chelsea worked so the baby was already attached to Laura.

My heart was so exposed to emotions the next few weeks, I never felt this much hurt and overwhelming grief before. It was so hard. I cried for two days almost continuously. Larry said, "I understand you're sad, but try not to cry around people, you only make them feel worse." I took his advice which helped me think of others instead of how hurt I felt. I gave it to Jesus. Gradually, I felt better. I still have moments; I think of Chelsea and tears come, but I turn it around and think of the happy moments.

Researching my ancestors has really inspired me. I wondered how they survived the loss of their children and grandchildren. Many lost several at all ages. Their strong religious faith and family community got them through the hard times. I felt we as a family needed to circle the wagons, to get through this.

My ancestors were hard-working, honest people who followed their Christian faith. Whether it was Puritans, Quakers, Mennonites, or Methodists, they had strong convictions with deep faith. They fought for their personal freedoms, especially religious, and went out of their way to help others less fortunate, especially the slaves, through the Underground Railroad to fighting in the civil war.

Genealogy of Larry and Theresa Smith

LARRY LAVERNE. SMITH b. 6 February 1948 Elk Valley, Tennessee m. (1) Ginger Jefferies 1966 (2) THERESA L. JONES 25 September 1969 b. 1 December 1947 Toledo, Ohio

Child of Larry and Ginger:
Laverne Laverne Smith Jr. b. 3 October 1967 m. (1) Kelley Ann
    Ashley 2 July 1987 Toledo, Ohio b. 1969 (2) Carmen Marshall
    5 December 2015 Northwood, Ohio b. 20 July 1979

Child of Larry and Kelley:
1. Kristen Ann Smith b.28 December 1988 Toledo, Ohio
Children of Kristen and Ryan Bowman:
Landon Rosalio Bowman b. 26 November 2013 Defiance, Ohio
Brayden Bowman b. 20 June 2015 Defiance, Ohio
2. Brandi Laraye Smith b. 24 August 1992 Toledo, Ohio
Child of Brandi:
Oliver Bentley Smith b. 12 June 2019 Napoleon, Ohio
3. Kayann Paige Smith b. 8 February 1995 Toledo, Ohio
Children of Paige and Jeremy Barnes:
Aurora Skye Barnes b. 28 April 2018 Napoleon, Ohio
Jaxston Michael Barnes b. 14 May 2020
4. Myranda Scarlet Smith b. 28 July 1998 Toledo, Ohio

Children of Larry and Theresa:
1. Wayne Patrick Smith b. 12 November 1970 Toledo, Ohio m.
    Gail Hammond 2004 Petersburg, Michigan divorced 2010
2. Andrew Michael Smith Skoraro b. 8 March 1972 Toledo Ohio
    m. Maria Lourdes Chua Gudani 29 March 2014 Las Vegas,

Nevada b. 9 June 1975 Manilla, Philippines

Child of Andrew and Maria:

Eiya Raylan Skoraro b. 25 October 2014 Cleburne, Texas

3. Laura Marie Smith b. 20 September 1974 Toledo, Ohio m. Steve Iman 14 March 2013 Toledo, Ohio b. 31 January 1960

Children of Laura and Jason Allen Jones:

Austin Jennings Jones-Smith b. 13 February 1993 Toledo, Ohio

Chelsea Rayne Smith b. 15 August 1994 Toledo, Ohio d. 18 April 2021 Oregon, Ohio

Child of Chelsea and Dillan David Rose:

Ariyah Rayne Smith b. 28 July 2020 Maumee, Ohio

Child of Laura and Garrett Alexander:

Tylor Hayden Alexander-Smith b. 17 November 1997 Toledo, Ohio

Charts

Pedigree Chart for Robert James Shirk

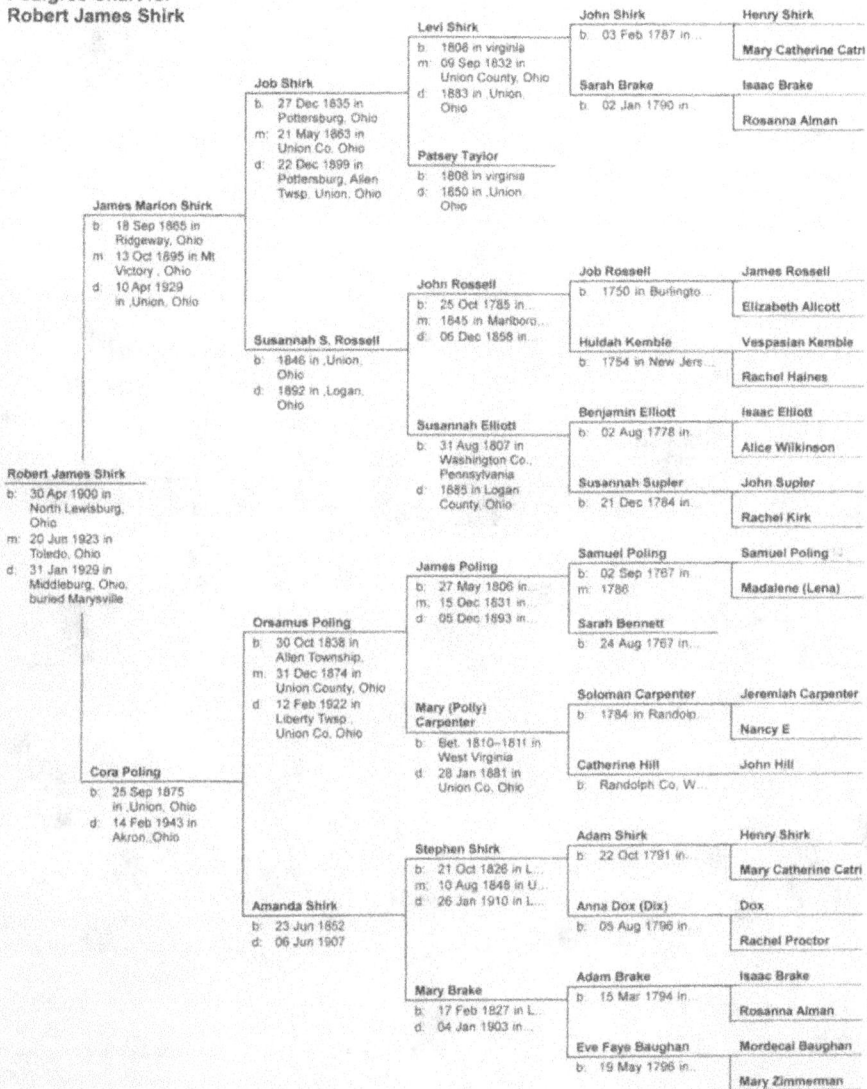

			John Shirk	Henry Shirk
		Levi Shirk	b: 03 Feb 1787 in ...	
		b: 1808 in virginia		Mary Catherine Catri
		m: 09 Sep 1832 in Union County, Ohio	Sarah Brake	Isaac Brake
	Job Shirk	d: 1883 in ,Union, Ohio	b: 02 Jan 1790 in	
	b: 27 Dec 1835 in Pottersburg, Ohio			Rosanna Alman
	m: 21 May 1863 in Union Co. Ohio	Patsey Taylor		
	d: 22 Dec 1899 in Pottersburg, Allen Twsp. Union, Ohio	b: 1808 in virginia		
James Marion Shirk		d: 1850 in ,Union, Ohio		
b: 18 Sep 1865 in Ridgeway, Ohio				
m: 13 Oct 1895 in Mt Victory , Ohio			Job Rossell	James Rossell
d: 10 Apr 1929 in ,Union, Ohio		John Rossell	b: 1750 in Burlingto ...	
		b: 25 Oct 1785 in ...		Elizabeth Allcott
		m: 1845 in Marlboro ...	Huldah Kemble	Vespasian Kemble
	Susannah S. Rossell	d: 06 Dec 1858 in	b: 1754 in New Jers ...	
	b: 1846 in ,Union, Ohio			Rachel Haines
	d: 1892 in ,Logan, Ohio	Susannah Elliott	Benjamin Elliott	Isaac Elliott
		b: 31 Aug 1807 in Washington Co., Pennsylvania	b: 02 Aug 1778 in ...	
				Alice Wilkinson
		d: 1885 in Logan County, Ohio	Susannah Supler	John Supler
Robert James Shirk			b: 21 Dec 1784 in	
b: 30 Apr 1900 in North Lewisburg, Ohio				Rachel Kirk
m: 20 Jun 1923 in Toledo, Ohio			Samuel Poling	Samuel Poling
d: 31 Jan 1929 in Middleburg, Ohio, buried Marysville		James Poling	b: 02 Sep 1767 in	
		b: 27 May 1806 in ...	m: 1786	Madalene (Lena)
		m: 15 Dec 1831 in ...	Sarah Bennett	
	Orsamus Poling	d: 05 Dec 1893 in ...	b: 24 Aug 1767 in ...	
	b: 30 Oct 1838 in Allen Township,			
	m: 31 Dec 1874 in Union County, Ohio	Mary (Polly) Carpenter	Soloman Carpenter	Jeremiah Carpenter
	d: 12 Feb 1922 in Liberty Twsp , Union Co. Ohio	b: Bet. 1810–1811 in West Virginia	b: 1784 in Randolp ...	
				Nancy E
		d: 28 Jan 1881 in Union Co. Ohio	Catherine Hill	John Hill
Cora Poling			b: Randolph Co. W ...	
b: 25 Sep 1875 in ,Union, Ohio				
d: 14 Feb 1943 in Akron, Ohio			Adam Shirk	Henry Shirk
		Stephen Shirk	b: 22 Oct 1791 in.	
		b: 21 Oct 1826 in L...		Mary Catherine Catri
		m: 10 Aug 1848 in U...	Anna Dox (Dix)	Dox
	Amanda Shirk	d: 26 Jan 1910 in L...	b: 05 Aug 1796 in	
	b: 23 Jun 1852			Rachel Proctor
	d: 06 Jun 1907		Adam Brake	Isaac Brake
		Mary Brake	b: 15 Mar 1794 in ...	
		b: 17 Feb 1827 in L...		Rosanna Alman
		d: 04 Jan 1903 in ...	Eve Faye Baughan	Mordecai Baughan
			b: 19 May 1796 in ...	
				Mary Zimmerman

Pedigree Chart for
Isaac Brake

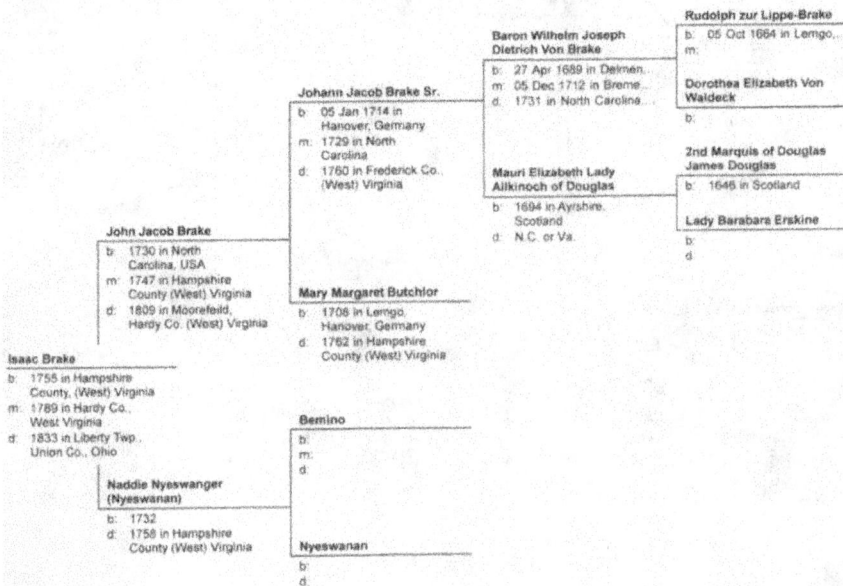

Rudolph zur Lippe-Brake
b: 05 Oct 1664 in Lemgo,...
m:

Baron Wilhelm Joseph Dietrich Von Brake
b: 27 Apr 1689 in Delmen...
m: 05 Dec 1712 in Breme...
d: 1731 in North Carolina...

Dorothea Elizabeth Von Waldeck
b:

Johann Jacob Brake Sr.
b: 05 Jan 1714 in Hanover, Germany
m: 1729 in North Carolina
d: 1760 in Frederick Co. (West) Virginia

2nd Marquis of Douglas James Douglas
b: 1646 in Scotland

Mauri Elizabeth Lady Ailkinoch of Douglas
b: 1694 in Ayrshire, Scotland
d: N.C. or Va.

Lady Barabara Erskine
b:
d:

John Jacob Brake
b: 1730 in North Carolina, USA
m: 1747 in Hampshire County (West) Virginia
d: 1809 in Moorefeild, Hardy Co. (West) Virginia

Mary Margaret Butchlor
b: 1708 in Lemgo, Hanover, Germany
d: 1762 in Hampshire County (West) Virginia

Isaac Brake
b: 1755 in Hampshire County, (West) Virginia
m: 1789 in Hardy Co., West Virginia
d: 1833 in Liberty Twp., Union Co., Ohio

Bernino
b:
m:
d:

Naddie Nyeswanger (Nyeswanan)
b: 1732
d: 1758 in Hampshire County (West) Virginia

Nyeswanan
b:
d:

Major John Rossell
b: 1633 in London,
England
m: 1666 in London,
England
d: 1686 in New York,
New York

Makor John Rossell
b: 1609 in Nottingham, E.
m:

Thomas Rossell
b: 1609 in Newton, Long
Island, New York
m: 1691
d: 1747

Mary Johnson
b: 20 May 1635 in
London, England
d: 1674 in Newton, Long
Island, New York

Renold Johnson
b:
m:

Zachariah Rossell (Roszel)
b: 1700 in Eayrestown,
Northhampton twsp,
Burlington, New Jersey
m: 04 Jun 1725 in
Northhampton,
Burlington, New Jersey
d: 26 Mar 1761 in
Northhampton, Burlington,
Burlington, N.J.

Evis Sherwood
b: 1677 in Northhampton,
Burlington, N.J.
d: 1704

James Rossell
b: 1727 in Northampton,
New Jersey
m: 13 May 1745 in
Northampton, Burlington,
New Jersey
d: 1817 in Somerset,
Pennsylvania

John Hilliard
b: 1678 in
Dorsetshire, England
m: 19 Dec 1689 in
Burlington, New Jersey
d: 05 Jan 1720 in
Burlington, New Jersey

Mary Hilliard
b: 1695 in DewBerry
Hill, Northampton,
Burlington, N.J.
d: Aft. 1761 in
Northampton, Burlington,
Burlington, N.J.

Bernard Devonish
b: 1645 in Northampton,
B., New Jersey
m: 06 Oct 1666
d: 22 Feb 1747 in
Northampton, B., New
Jersey

Martha Devonish
b: 1681 in Northampton,
B., New Jersey
d: 10 Nov 1735 in
Burlington, New Jersey

Martha Beaks
b: 1645 in Burlington
County, New jersey
d: 1698 in Drewberry Hill,
Burlington, New Jersey

Pedigree Chart for
Isaac Elliott

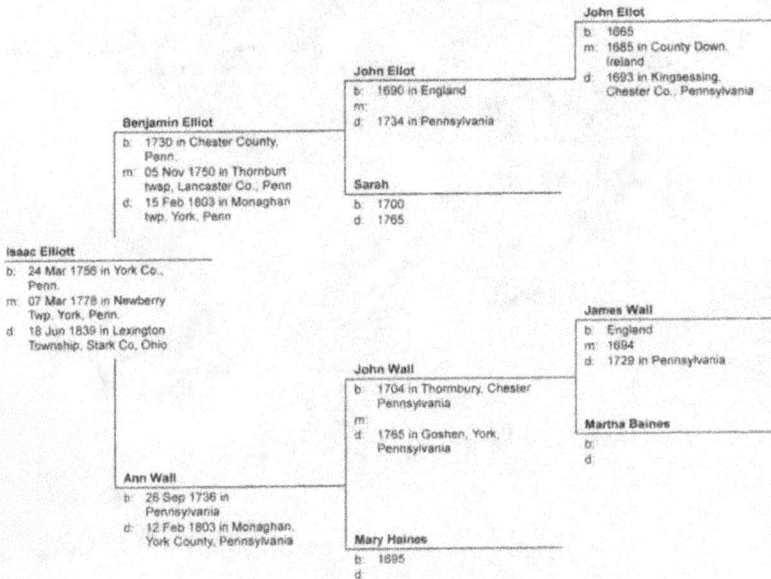

Isaac Elliott
b: 24 Mar 1756 in York Co.,
   Penn.
m: 07 Mar 1778 in Newberry
   Twp. York, Penn.
d: 18 Jun 1839 in Lexington
   Township, Stark Co. Ohio

Benjamin Elliot
b: 1730 in Chester County,
   Penn.
m: 05 Nov 1750 in Thornburt
   twsp, Lancaster Co., Penn
d: 15 Feb 1803 in Monaghan
   twp. York, Penn

Ann Wall
b: 26 Sep 1736 in
   Pennsylvania
d: 12 Feb 1803 in Monaghan,
   York County, Pennsylvania

John Eliot
b: 1690 in England
m:
d: 1734 in Pennsylvania

Sarah
b: 1700
d: 1765

John Wall
b: 1704 in Thormbury, Chester
   Pennsylvania
m:
d: 1765 in Goshen, York,
   Pennsylvania

Mary Haines
b: 1695
d:

John Eliot
b: 1665
m: 1685 in County Down,
   Ireland
d: 1693 in Kingsessing,
   Chester Co., Pennsylvania

James Wall
b: England
m: 1694
d: 1729 in Pennsylvania

Martha Baines
b:
d:

About the Author

Theresa is retired Registered Nurse, BSN, after working at St. Vincent's Mercy Medical Center in Toledo, Ohio for forty-five years. She lives with her husband, Larry, of over fifty-three years in Perrysburg, Ohio. They have four children, eight grandchildren and six great grandchildren.

Theresa has been active in Genealogy for the past fifty plus years. She is active in the Wood County Ohio Genealogical Society and with the Daughters of American Revolution (DAR). She is also active in the Professional Registered Nurses Honor Guard for the Toledo, Ohio area. In her spare time, she loves traveling with her husband and spending time with her family.